Strategies
FOR IMPLEMENTING

Writer's Workshop

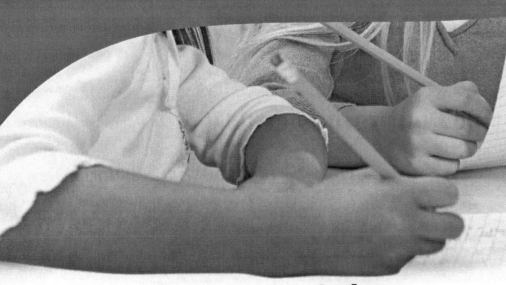

Authors

Richard Gentry, Ph.D.

Jan McNeel, M.A.Ed.

Vickie Wallace-Nesler, M.A.Ed.

Forword

Cathy Collier, M.A.Ed.

Publishing Credits

Corinne Burton, M.A.Ed., *Publisher*; Kimberly Stockton, M.S.Ed, *Vice President of Education*; Conni Medina, M.A.Ed., *Managing Editor*; Sara Johnson, M.S.Ed., *Content Director*; Christine Dugan, M.A.Ed., *Editor*; Kyleena Harper, *Assistant Editor*; Lee Aucoin, *Multimedia Designer*; Kevin Pham, *Production Artist*

Shell Education

5301 Oceanus Drive
Huntington Beach, CA 92649-1030
http://www.tcmpub.com/teachers

ISBN 978-1-4258-1517-2

© 2016 Teacher Created Materials, Inc.
Printed in USA. WOR004

Table of *Contents*

Foreword

I am a natural-born talker. I have always been comfortable with talking to anyone, anytime, anywhere. My mother often began my parent-teacher conferences with, "I already know Cathy talks too much, what else can you tell me about her?" For me, becoming a reader was a natural progression from my passion for talking, considering that reading is, in fact, storytelling. Reading became another way for me to have a conversation— this time with characters in a book. The characters became friends I could laugh, cry, and grow with through the course of the story and after. I soon learned that taking my love of talking and reading and putting it into written words created a whole new adventure. With writing I could talk to lots of people at once, and share my stories and experiences with others. As a teacher, my love of teaching writing is built on talking and reading. If you can talk about something, you can write about it. Giving my students the necessary tools to become writers is important to me, as I want my students to love writing as much as I do.

Classrooms have changed dramatically over the past several decades. Classrooms of the past provided activities and lessons focused on one level, assuming all students were at that same level at the same time. Assessments were rigid, unbending, and focused on a "norm." Teachers were expected to set a single stage for a single performer and require a single outcome.

In the differentiated classrooms of today, teachers are looking for something to help all their students. Teaching students at varying levels within the same classroom is now the reality, and the expectation is to meet our students at their current level and help move them forward. Assessments now mean different things to different students at different times. However, the final goal of creating writers remains steadfast. As a teaching veteran with more than 25 years in the classroom, I am always looking for great ideas, lessons, and strategies to help me propel my students into the world of writing, and I believe that *Strategies for Implementing Writer's Workshop* has done a wonderful job encompassing all of this.

The authors have divided this book into three parts: Time to Teach, Time to Write and Confer, and Time to Share. The sections provide a comprehensive look at each area, providing picture examples, ready-made mini-lessons, forms, anchor charts, and more. The authors take time to set the stage for writing before writing even begins, building routines and establishing norms to create a safe environment for students to craft authentic writing. Just as a student becomes a better soccer or piano player by practicing playing, a student becomes a better writer by practicing writing. Having time to write and talk about writing is an essential part of the process for students. The authors provide a multitude of activities to allow skills to develop and writers to form. In the final section of the book, the authors recognize that every piece of written work is looking for an audience. Sharing writing cannot be underscored; the authors provide a variety of publishing ideas to appeal to different learners. Though assessment is a necessary part of the process, the authors allow teachers and students to make critical decisions about these assessments. Allowing students a hand in the assessment process builds a place of respect and motivation for all learners.

I am excited to recommend this book. Having a single source to help motivate, create, and reward writers is worth its weight in gold.

—Cathy Collier, M.A.Ed.
Reading Specialist
International Literacy Association Board Member

Acknowledgments

We stand on the shoulders of national and world-renowned researchers and teachers of writing. First and foremost, our late friend Donald Graves comes to mind. But there are so many others: Lucy Calkins, Ralph Fletcher, Donald Murry, Vicki Spandel, Ruth Culham, Katie Wood Ray, Carl Anderson, Charles Temple, Jean Gillet, Stephanie Harvey, Debbie Miller, Regie Routman, Steve Graham, Virginia Berninger, Laura Robb, and Connie Hebert to name a few. Thank you for your inspirational work.

We applaud the work of the educators at Northwest Regional Education Laboratory. And thank you to the faculty at Auckland University, teachers, and workshop leaders who were inspirational reaching back many, many years. Thank you for the contributions of the group at Harvard Educational Press, our professional journals, and others who keep us up to date.

Thank you to scores of teachers and districts who invited us into their classrooms and inspired us. We always feel blessed to be in the company of inspirational teachers and children who share their work and imaginations. We continue to learn from you.

Thank you for special contributions to this book from Steve Peha of Teaching That Makes Sense; Susan Sturock of *TheReadingMind;* Dannettte Menaker, an extraordinary teacher at UMS-Wright Preparatory School in Mobile, Alabama; and Bill McIntyre, an educator in Fort Lauderdale, Florida.

We are grateful to teachers who invited us to share this project with their students. Marlinton Middle ELA teachers allowed us to photograph, model, and visit at any time, as did Jan Jonese, Stephanie Burns, and Lisa Burns. Teachers at Nutter Fort Elementary School, New River Elementary, Ansted Elementary, and Meadow Bridge Elementary continue to welcome classroom modeling as we try out new strategies, and give us valuable feedback. Valerie Daniels contributed to this project from her kindergarten classroom in Deltona, Florida as did Christine Richards from her middle grade classroom at Southport Middle School in Port Saint Lucie. Terry Morrison, Technology Specialist at Simpson Elementary, partnered with us engaging students in writing through technology.

The Shell Publishing family is outstanding. Thank you to our wonderful editor, Sara Johnson, who is cheerful and tireless. And thank you to all the family at Shell Publishing for giving us this opportunity to publish with them and making our book outstanding—especially Corinne Burton, Kimberly Stockton, Conni Medina, Christine Dugan, Kyleena Harper, Lee Aucoin, and Kevin Pham.

A special shout out to our families. From Jan to husband, Lanty, forever supportive and by her side. And to her children, Jamey, John, Jackie, Jeffrey and Charlie for giving advice when needed, yet holding back and giving her the space to create. Jan expresses special gratitude to her grandchildren: Tempe, Josh, Jesse, Michael, Calee, and Hayden. Their future and this generation is why we continuously push forward with professional development.

Vickie shouts out to husband Clint and son Luke, and Richard shouts out to Bill Boswell—for standing behind us and offering unfailing support. Love and gratitude for all that you do.

The Three-Legged Stool Model of Writer's Workshop

Strategic teaching is based on planning how to accomplish desired outcomes and then taking action. As a strategic writing teacher, you need great plans of action to achieve your goals. Your most important goal is clear: teach your students how to write.

In this resource, we gathered the best strategies we have seen in our collective 100-plus years of teaching students how to write. These are the strategies that help meet today's standards and that work for us, for our researcher colleagues, and for our hundreds of best-practice-writing teacher friends. The strategies are evidence-based and are compiled in an accessible, easy-to-use format. You can implement them individually, but used together, they make up the successful operating procedures in classrooms where students are becoming writers.

Strategies for Implementing Writer's Workshop is built upon a three-legged stool model for Writer's Workshop. Strategies are included for each of the legs of the stool that Writer's Workshop must stand on: Time to Teach, Time to Write and Confer, and Time to Share. This powerful organizational framework gives you the strategies you need to be successful.

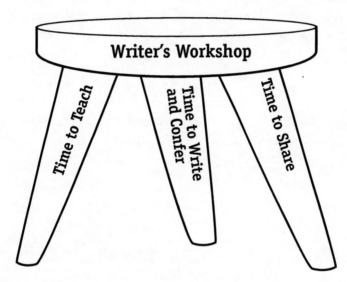

Time to Teach

Chapters 1 through 3 address the leg of "time to teach." When the strategies for effective classroom management and practices from these three chapters are put in place, instructional time can be maximized.

Chapter 1, Strategies for Building a Community of Writers, describes the essential characteristics of the Writer's Workshop community and gives strategies and classroom snapshots for designing and organizing space; establishing routines; managing writing tools and resources; developing learning walls, anchor charts, and writing centers; bringing real-world writing into the classroom; talking writing to writer; and using mentor texts in order to build a foundation for successful writing instruction.

In **Chapter 2**, Motivating Student Writers, strategies for engaging and motivating students during instruction are provided. We show you how to read and write like an author, use the language of motivation, motivate student writers with author celebrations, and build classroom morale.

Chapter 3, Whole-Group Instruction, shows *how* to teach through engaging mini-lessons, routines, structure, partner talk, and movement that launches effective time to teach.

Time to Write and Confer

Chapters 4 and 5 address the leg of "time to write and confer." The strategies in these chapters support effective writing practices and help students develop writing prowess and stamina.

Chapter 4, Independent and Small-Group Instruction, focuses on the effective writing conference by organizing and planning for small-group and individual conferences, creating a conference schedule, providing a conference structure, communicating conference expectations, and preparing a conferring toolkit.

In **Chapter 5**, Strategies for Writing Across the Content Areas, the key aspects of building writing skills and stamina are addressed. Strategies are provided to help students read and write increasingly complex text, to link writing to what they are interested in, and to give them ownership and autonomy by selecting their own writing topics.

Time to Share

Although strategies for time to share are provided throughout the book, the real strength that makes this leg stand on its own is in **Chapter 6**, Strategies for Publishing Student Writing. The final step of publishing and sharing for a meaningful and authentic audience is what provides a purpose for writing and increases student motivation. This chapter explains why to publish, provides principles for publishing, and explores a variety of publishing options. This chapter also provides many fantastic ideas for writing celebrations that we have found to be effective in our work.

Finally, **Chapter 7**, Strategies for Assessment, provides an overview of both formative and summative assessments and shares strategies for setting assessment goals and achieving assessment outcomes. This chapter also includes strategies for gathering evidence of student learning from multiple sources and involving students in self-assessment and setting learning goals. It is the culminating piece that brings Writer's Workshop all together.

Our Goal

The goal of this book is to help you strategically develop student writers through the Writer's Workshop model. After reading this book, you should feel confident in doing the following:

- Building a community of writers
- Motivating student writers
- Maximizing good instruction
- Having students writing every day and in every class
- Having students share writing publicly
- Monitoring writing outcomes through assessment

Don't forget that being strategic is a mindset. It starts with you. The best strategy for becoming the best teacher of writing you can be is your desire to be one. We hope this book will get you started. If you are already a stellar writing teacher, we hope it will help you continue on that path. Don't just be a good writing teacher—be strategic. Be amazing!

—Richard, Jan, and Vickie

Essential Characteristics of a Writer's Workshop Community

A sense of community implies that in the classroom, all aspects of the writing environment will contribute to the comfort of every student. The physical arrangement, use of space, traffic flow, and resources determine the success of any literacy environment. In classrooms with strong classroom communities, student risk-taking is accepted and celebrated by teachers, even as more rigorous standards are implemented. "A classroom that respects what the students bring to it, what they are capable of and interested in, and that welcomes them into an active intellectual community is more likely to achieve rigor" (Beers and Probst 2013, 24).

Moving along the path to an intellectual writing community involves the teacher reducing ownership of the community and distributing that ownership to students. This does not mean relaxing the structure, but rather increasing the structure so that Writer's Workshop can operate without constant teacher oversight. This can be challenging and involves close observation of student behavior in interpersonal interactions, careful note-taking, and a gradual releasing of responsibility with the teacher making adjustments along the way.

The eight essential characteristics below help teachers develop a community of writers where all ideas are valued and where student engagement is rigorous and challenging.

1. **Teach active engagement.** Classrooms are too often places of "tell and practice" (Richart, Church, and Morrison 2011, 9). Writer's Workshop was never designed in that format. Engaging students in conversation generates ideas. Instead of "tell and practice," a more active approach to learning might sound more like "invite and engage!"

2. **Teach active listening.** Respectful listening does not happen without sufficient modeling by the teacher and practice by the students. Active listening in action requires student-peer conversations or conversations between team members to sustain the momentum of the conversation by questioning, elaborating, providing support, and complimenting. Active listening is dependent upon peer conversations that are clear, concise, and positive. Active listening grows out of meaningful engagement in student discussions about writing.

3. **Practice behavior narration.** Behavior narration is a technique that can be used to establish acceptable conduct in the classroom during instruction and work time. Statements of behavior expectations provide students with direction for where to be and what to do. *"Jamal is going directly to his seat without wasting time. I see the students at Table 3 have their writing folders opened and are quietly working together."* Establishing a supportive relationship through positive statements about behavior can greatly reduce classroom disruptions.

4. **Know your learners.** Identifying student interests, strengths, weaknesses, controlled techniques, skills, and strategies is an important part of writing instruction. Documenting information helps target the learning in conferences and small literacy groups. Plans of instruction regarding student writing skills and strategies will likely change. As your skills of observation and documentation of student writing grow, you will truly begin to "know your learners."

5. **Use writing resources in different subjects.** It is difficult to truly teach all of the necessary writing standards unless they are integrated throughout the school day. By getting familiar with different types of writing that are taught at your grade level and selecting mentor texts to match, you can effectively integrate writing across the subject areas. For example, science and social studies resources and techniques can be integrated into the Writer's Workshop block.

6. **Provide immediate feedback.** Feedback should be shared with students quickly. Affirmations and authentic praise throughout the day are also important. For example, *"What a talented young writer you are! I noticed the lead in the beginning of your story sounds just like the author...." "You must be so proud that you figured out how to write that word by yourself. Great work!"*

7. **Share details about the day's writing schedule.** Students should not feel as though they are guessing what is intended for writing time. It is important to be clear, yet systematic and engaging, adjusting instruction as needed. These phrases support students in understanding the expectations for writing: *"Yesterday, we..." "Today, I will show you..." "It will help you..."*

8. **Increase the rigor of read alouds.** Using mentor texts that have rigorous vocabulary is an important way to expand students' word knowledge base. It is also important to consider pre-teaching vocabulary that might confuse students. When reading a word that may not be familiar to students, it can be helpful to stop briefly and give a short, student-friendly definition. The first read aloud of a text is for meaning. In-depth discussion of the writer's craft takes place in a follow-up reading.

A successful writing community should include all of these essential characteristics in a well-organized Writer's Workshop. The strategies presented in this book will help blaze a trail for increased student achievement and motivation, as well as boost your confidence as a writing teacher.

With our eight essential characteristics of a writing community as a foundation for the classroom, it's time to visualize where that community will reside by designing and organizing space.

Designing and Organizing Space

Efficient use of classroom space for writers can look very different depending on the grade level. The important thing to keep in mind is that students need to be able to move easily around the classroom for whole-group mini-lessons; small, guided writing groups; and peer/partner conferences. Space and resources also need to be available for gathering information for research projects.

The following strategies will help support successful classroom design and organization:

- Use space efficiently

- Visualize traffic flow

- Purge nonessential resources

Strategy 1: Use Space Efficiently

Using space efficiently in the classroom does not happen by accident. It takes thoughtful planning and consideration. Creating a classroom map on paper will help give you a clear starting point for using the space efficiently. This reduces the stress of moving and rearranging. It also saves time and increases productivity. Moving furniture around can be done on paper much more easily than actually moving real furniture.

Never underestimate your ability to utilize space efficiently. Window ledges, the floor, and baskets from a local dollar store can become units of storage. Organizing space to improve student achievement requires only an ability to think outside of the box. For example, crates in the whole-group meeting area can be used for teacher or student storage, serve as chairs for pulling students into a mini-lesson, or to add punch and vitality to a meeting area. Add a board with hinges, cover with filling and colored fabric, and you have created added space and a place where students of all ages can come to receive essential literacy information.

 ### Strategy 2: Visualize Traffic Flow

Movement in the classroom should be without distraction and should help to maximize learning. Visualize where and how students move for each activity throughout the school day and prepare the classroom accordingly. Consider space for whole-group instruction, small groups, partner work, and work centers. Students need to be able to move throughout the room as their writing assignments require. There needs to be space made for partners to conference during revision time, and room for modeled writing during small-group work. Students should be able to move effortlessly and feel comfortable in their own space without infringing upon the personal space of others. Teach students how to move from place to place beginning on day 1, and with review and practice at all developmental levels, it will be remembered by learners and will develop strong classroom management.

Managing is a key component of student achievement and promotes writers as independent learners. One simple consideration is the placement of trash or recycling bins. Writing is often messy and requires drafts and more drafts. Placing a small container within each pod of students rather than near the door or teacher's desk eliminates the need for students to constantly get out of their seats to throw paper away. A strategically placed can of pencils with a sign—Pencil Sharpener Closes at 10:15—can also eliminate a disruption or unnecessary movement throughout the day/class period.

 ### Strategy 3: Purge Nonessential Resources

Throw away or donate all the classroom materials that you don't need. Nonessential resources should be boxed up and stored. Students come to the classroom with different levels of structure in their lives, but they all need to see an inviting, organized environment that supports them in their work. By getting rid of nonessential items, necessary writing tools such as paper, scissors, highlighters, sticky notes, and tape become more easily accessible and students can manage their own time without interrupting the teacher or other students.

Figure 1.1 Sample Classroom Design and Organization 1

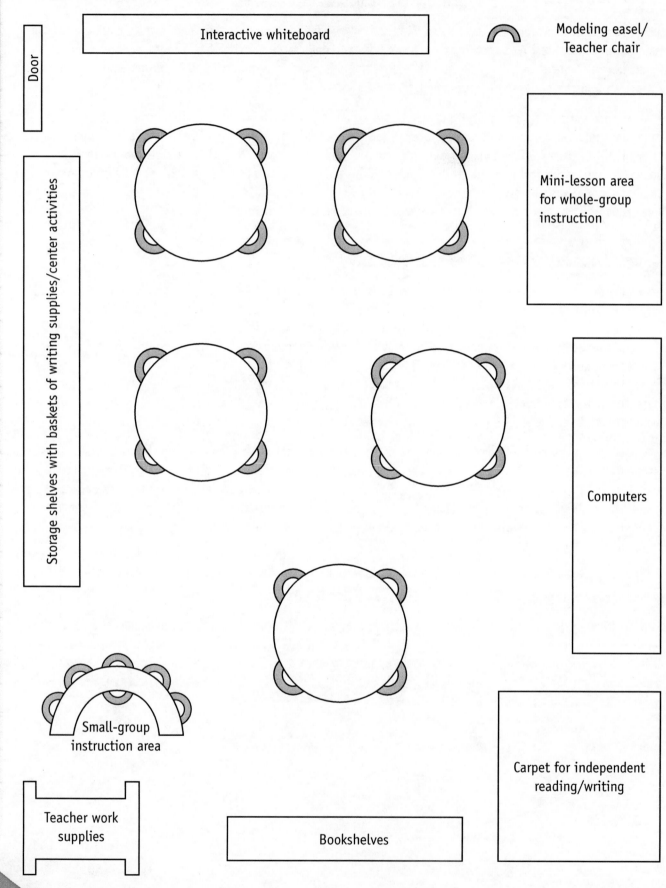

Figure 1.2 Sample Classroom Design and Organization 2

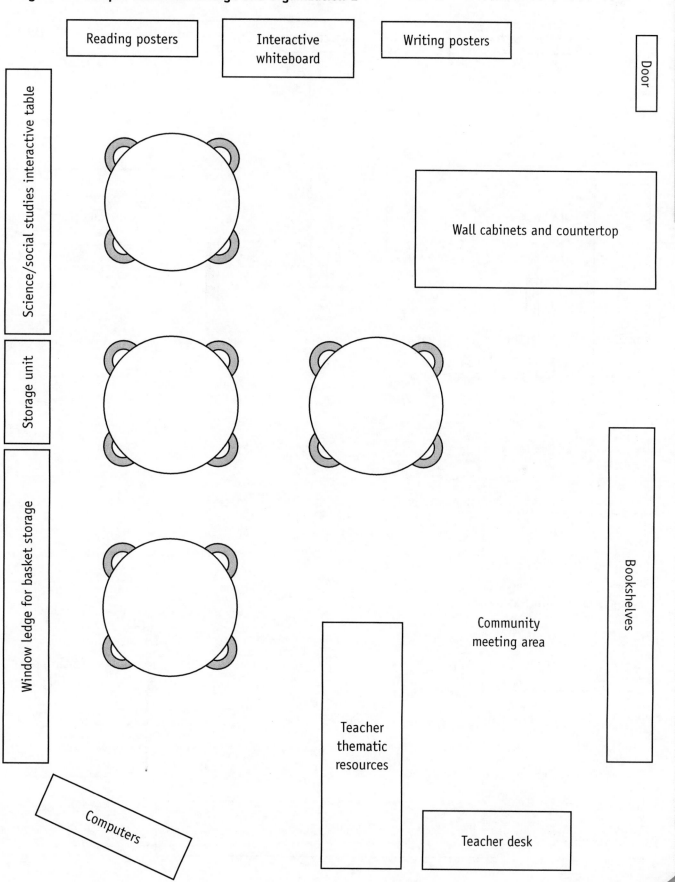

Figure 1.3 Sample Classroom Design and Organization 3

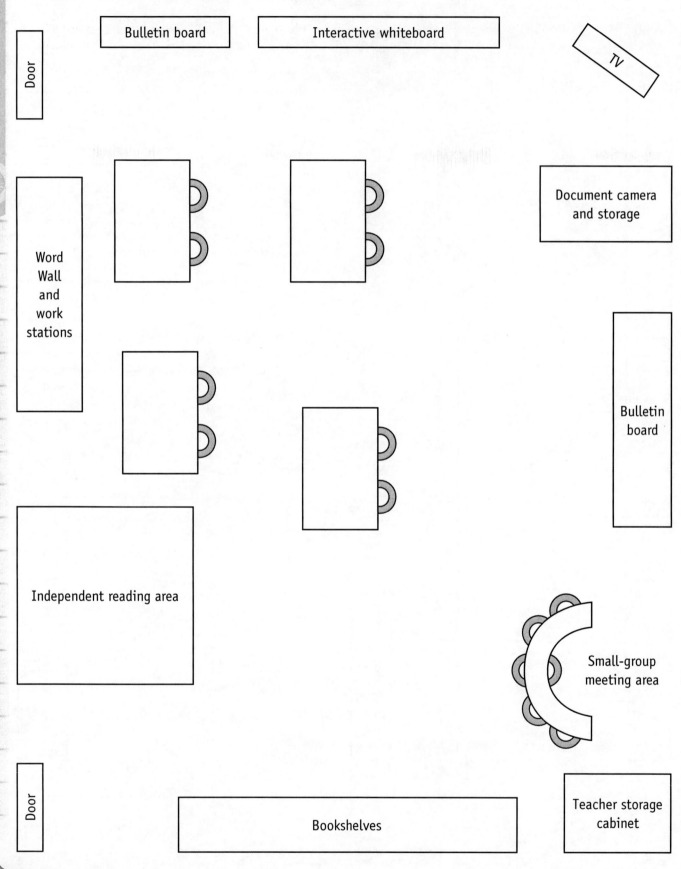

Establishing Routines and Transitions

In our work as consultants over the last 20 years, we have heard comments from student teachers, teachers, principals, and district administrators about the importance of classroom management, routines, and movement.

We know about routines and transitions that have been tried successfully hundreds, if not thousands, of times in classrooms across the globe. However, what we hope you walk away with is something new, something different; perhaps even something that may contribute to your becoming a trailblazer in terms of classroom management. What you see in classroom examples may give rise to an exciting new twist in your own implementation of a community of writers.

The following strategies will help support successful classroom routines and transitions:

- Build a routine chart together
- Integrate movement

 Strategy 1: **Build a Routine Chart Together**

Writing structures and routines are highly respected when students retain ownership. We often invite students to have input into the various routines we use in Writer's Workshop. For example, one routine chart we use focuses on what Writing Workshop looks like, sounds like, and feels like. Keep in mind there are certain expectations that are non-negotiable that you add to the chart. After discussing non-negotiable routines, allow students to create an even higher standard of excellence by adding their own expectations. The sample chart (Figure 1.4) is one routine chart created with students as an anchor chart for how we want our classroom to look, sound, and feel. This routine chart, created with student input, works not only for Writer's Workshop but also for everyday writing in the subject areas at all grade levels. Add your own personal ideas to this list.

Figure 1.4 Sample Routine Chart for Writer's Workshop

Looks Like	Sounds Like	Feels Like
Anchor charts	Beehive/buzz	Productive
Students active	Questions asked and answered	Comfortable
Regulated behavior	Two voices	Exciting
Visuals placed appropriately	Conversation/affirmations	Relaxed
Vocabulary available	"I can" attitude	Confident
Students engaged	Quiet during think time	Organized "chaos"
Organized and colorful	Pauses and action	Purposeful
Individualized and differentiated	Students making decisions	Comfortable sharing thoughts

Time to Teach

 Strategy 2: **Integrate Movement**

The expression "a rolling stone gathers no moss" is a perfect visual when thinking about getting students engaged, on task, and keeping their brains active. If students are moving and chanting, they are less likely to be off task or misbehaving during transition time. Charles Hillman, a neuroscientist specializing in kinesiology, compared brain functions of "high fit" and "low fit" children. He reported that exercisers made greater gains in fitness and on cognitive tests. These results confirm that students who move outperform their peers on self-regulation, working memory, cognitive flexibility, and multitasking (Pappano 2015). If this is the case, why not adjust classroom routines to include simple movements as part of Writer's Workshop?

Movement from one activity to another—from seats to whole-group mini-lesson, from mini-lesson to writing practice time, and from practice time to small-group instruction—should weave in movement activity. Movement can also be added at the beginning of the writing lesson, in the middle when students need a "brain break," or when sending them off to work independently or with partners. Regardless of how you decide to incorporate movement in the day, do it in a way that works for you and your students. If jumping jacks get your students too wild, try something less vigorous such as toe touches. The important part is not how big the movement is, but that it is incorporated strategically throughout the day.

Mini-lesson: Writing a Friendly Letter Grades K–2

1. Tell students that there are five parts of a friendly letter (heading, greeting, body, closing, signature).

2. Touch head with both hands for the first part of a friendly letter, saying "Heading!"

3. Wave at students for the second part of a friendly letter, saying "Greeting!"

4. Sweep with both hands down the body, saying, "Body!"

5. Smack both hands on knees, saying "Closing!"

6. Pretend to write your name in the air, moving from your left to right, (directionality), saying "Signature!"

7. Transition students to seats for their guided/independent writing by chanting/singing, "We're going to write a letter." Repeat three times.

Mini-lesson: Sentence Fluency Grades 3–5

1. Explain to students that an appositive is a noun or noun phrase that adds additional details in sentence writing.

2. Build an anchor chart and model how to add interesting information and variety to sentences. Here is an example to begin the chart: "My dog, Cooper, (appositive) loves to run and chase birds."

3. Show students that the appositive can be removed without changing the meaning, but that it does add details, and needs to be enclosed with commas. Incorporate multiple examples into the chart, using the names of your students.

4. As you model the lesson, weave in an "appositive action" movement by completing a karate chop motion to indicate where the commas enclosing the appositive are to be placed. Say: "We call this 'appositive action karate chop.'"

5. Consider giving students a challenge item such as "Kudzu, a giant plant with enormous leaves, was brought to this country from Japan" and apply "appositive action."

6. Have students transition to the appropriate places in the room for guided and independent writing practice.

Mini-lesson: Writing Conventions Grades 6–8

1. Explain to students that writing multisyllabic words can be a challenge. Yet, with an understanding of the six common syllable rules, using the patterns makes spelling conventions easier.

2. Over several days, build the following chart:

Rule 1: CVC	**Rule 2: CV**	**Rule 3: CVCe**
closed syllable/short vowel con**den**sation	open syllable/long vowel mi**cro**scopic	consonant/vowel/consonant, silent *e* comp**lete**
Rule 4: R-controlled	**Rule 5: Vowel teams**	**Rule 6: Stable/Consonant le**
the vowel sound is changed by the *r* sound **cor**onation	when a syllable has two vowels, the first vowel is usually long. im**peach**ment	the syllable has a consonant that precedes the *le*, usually found on the end of words. sprin**kle**

3. Each day have students search reading material for examples of the six syllable rules and record on sticky notes. They must provide evidence of their reasoning.

4. Have students come to the front of the room each holding a letter card for a multisyllabic word, such as 12 kids holding the letters c-o-n-d-e-n-s-a-t-i-o-n. Have students move to get into syllable-pattern groups and time them to see how long it takes.

5. Have each syllable group do a chant for their syllable. For example, the c-o-n group will choose the syllable rule that applies then clap and chant "c-o-n is CVC Rule 1!" The d-e-n group does the same, respectively. The s-a group will chant, "s-a is CV open syllable, Rule 2!" The t-i-o-n group would recognize that their syllable is different and chant "Exception!"

6. When students are ready to share their writing, have them provide evidence that shows how they used multisyllabic words accurately.

Managing Writing Tools and Resources

Once students begin writing several different pieces, they need a place to store their important work. In grades K–8, we recommend that students use two writing folders/notebooks. Students use writing folders/notebooks to organize the writing they are currently working on and to store support tools like word lists, editing checklists, and personal word walls. They use portfolio folders/notebooks to hold their non-published and published work representative of their growth as writers.

Take a look at the following strategies and examples:

- Creating the writing folder/notebook

- Creating the portfolio folder/notebook

- Designing and organizing a writer's folder/notebook

- Examples of writing folders/notebooks

Strategy 1: Creating the Writing Folder

A writing folder is an excellent tool for storing writing samples. Inserts can be provided, which scaffold student achievement on many different levels. Depending on developmental level, you might want to include the following inserts in the student's writing folder:

Grades K–2	Grades 3–5	Grades 6–8
Alphabet chart	Vowel teams	Writing rubric
Months of the year and days of the week	Vowel digraphs	Chart of the six syllable rules
Family words	Graded high-frequency word list	Transition words for informative, narrative, and opinion writing
Short vowels/long vowels	Checklist for assessments/rubric	Vowel digraphs and diphthongs
Consonant digraphs and consonant blends	Transition words for informative, narrative, and opinion	Self-publishing ideas
High-frequency graded word list	Commonly misspelled words	

Personal preference will guide your decisions on a management system that works for your needs. Here is a suggestion for how to create a writing folder.

1. **Select a durable, two-pocket, three-prong folder for each student.**
   - The left inside pocket is for pieces that students are currently working on. For grades K–2, place a green dot on the pocket. For grades 3–8, write "In Progress" on the pocket.
   - The right inside pocket is for pieces that students have completed or want to save for a later date. For grades K–2, place a red dot on the pocket. For grades 3–8, write "Completed" on the pocket.
   - Provide time for students to personalize the outside of their folders.

2. **Determine where students will store their folders.**
   - Where will your students keep their writing folders? At their desks for easy access during any writing activity? In a writing bin with the rest of the class and used only during writing time? In containers labeled by rows? How will your students retrieve them and put them away in a timely manner?
   - Establish management procedures that are specific and become routine in your classroom. These may be changed from year to year based on the students you have in your classroom. The procedure might be tweaked a bit throughout the year to create smoother transitions.

3. **Use daily mini-lessons to build the writing folder.**
   - As you model and teach students to use writing tools, students add the anchor chart support pages to the middle section of the folder. Plastic sleeves are great to protect these pages, as we expect students to reference them often in their writing.
   - The middle of the folder also includes tools that guide student writing such as word lists, alphabet and vowel charts, editing checklists, graphic organizers, or personal word walls.
   - Have students in grades 3–8 store these support tools in their writer's notebook rather than in the writing folder.

Strategy 2: Create the Writer's Notebook

Designing and Organizing a Writer's Notebook

In grades 3–8, students use a writing folder to store writing pieces and a writer's notebook to practice writing and to hold ideas and resources that guide and support them throughout the writing process. Joanne Hindley sums up the contents of a writer's notebook beautifully in this quote from her book *In the Company of Children*.

A writer's notebook can be many things: a place to make mistakes, to experiment, to record overheard conversations or family stories, to remember an inspiring quotation, to free associate, to ask questions, to record beautiful or unusual language, to jot down the seeds of unborn stories or story beginnings, to tell the truth or to lie, to record memories, to embellish memories, to remember what you've been reading, to record stories you've heard about other people, to remember one word that conjures up an image, to remember things you're surprised by, to observe, to record impressions, or to describe a picture or a person or an image you can't get out of your head. A writer's notebook is a receptacle, a tool to hold on to things. (p. 13)

The writer's notebook "gives you a place to live like a writer" (Fletcher 1996). Fletcher says his writer's notebook is the most important tool he uses as a writer and shares that, "Keeping a writer's notebook is one of the best ways I know of living a writing kind of life" (1996, 4).

We suggest your students' writer's notebooks be:

- **Personalized:** The notebook is a personal reflection of the student and his or her journey through learning the writing process. It should hold photographs, words, and phrases that personify the student.

- **Organized:** We recommend organizing the notebook for easy access to specific writing topics and strategies. This helps students quickly revisit resources taught throughout the year when needed.

- **Cumulative:** The notebook is created over time and gradually builds by continually adding mini-lesson resources, writing examples, and student writing.

1. **Select the type of notebooks you prefer for each student.**
   - Decide what works best for you and your students. Consider durability, cost, and purpose. Some teachers use binders and not folders. Others use composition notebooks or spiral notebooks and use a folder for storing ongoing writing pieces.

2. **Celebrate and decorate the writer's notebook.**
   - Discuss the value and meaning of this important writing tool and how each one will be similar, but different. Emphasize that it holds the ideas, memories, pictures, words, and phrases that are their very own. They are writers!
   - Take time to share notebooks as a class. Lay out all the notebooks with a pen and paper for each and do a gallery walk. Students leave a compliment/comment for students about their notebooks, such as *I like the way you..., Can't wait to learn more about...!*

Time to Teach

3. **Determine where students will store their notebooks.**

- Similar to the writing folder, it is important to establish management procedures that are specific and become routine in your classroom for storing and using the writer's notebooks.

- Keep in mind that the notebooks are a place to gather ideas, thoughts, and inspirations for writing. If they are tucked on a shelf and not accessible to students, it may be a missed opportunity to record genuine writing observations.

4. **Organize the notebook.**

- Decide what will work best for you, your students, and your writing curriculum. We typically have students divide their composition notebooks into sections with 10–15 blank pages with chapter tabs labeled:

  Chapter 1: Table of Contents

  Chapter 2: Management

  Chapter 3: Ideas

  Chapter 4: Organization

  Chapter 5: Voice

  Chapter 6: Sentence Fluency

  Chapter 7: Word Choice

  Chapter 8: Conventions

  Chapter 9: Miscellaneous

5. **Begin adding resources to the writer's notebook.**

- As you teach mini-lessons, students add resources from the lesson to the left side of an open page and practice the writing skill on the right side of the notebook.

Examples of Writer's Notebooks

Using the right organizational plan builds the right environment for writing success. A kindergarten teacher uses the OWL (Organized While Learning) notebook in Figure 1.5 to organize students for writing. The third-grade crates are organized by groups and distributed at the beginning of writing class (Figure 1.6). Three crates represent three Writer's Workshop sessions as this group is departmentalized. Notebooks are slipped into folders so that both writing tools are available at the beginning of class. A middle school teacher embraces the idea of a tabbed notebook as displayed in Figure 1.7.

Figure 1.5 Sample OWL Notebook

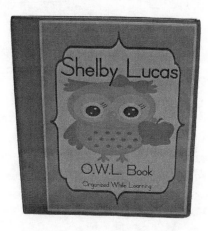

Figure 1.6 Sample Writing Notebook Crates

Figure 1.7 Sample Tabbed Writer's Notebook

Time to Teach

Develop Learning Walls, Anchor Charts, and Writing Centers

Classroom snapshots and sample classroom conversations help show how the following three strategies can be implemented across grade bands:

- Use word walls
- Use anchor charts
- Create a classroom writing center

 Strategy 1: Use Word Walls

Word walls can be organized in all sorts of ways (alphabetically, by subject, for genre study), but they can also include different word categories (high-frequency words, content vocabulary, spelling vocabulary, etc.). If attractive, timely, and appropriately placed using cheers, chants, clapping, and moving, word learning can happen throughout the day and across curriculum.

Word walls can be placed on chart paper and hung across a clothesline if space is limited. High-frequency words for primary students can be alphabetized for ease of word location. Content-area words need to be placed where they are accessible for writing instruction for arguments, position papers, reaction papers, reports, and manuals for vocational education. Math vocabulary connected to instruction can hang from a coat hanger with small clothespins. Word walls need to be creative and provide the necessary support to build word knowledge. Using word walls supports student writers, allowing them to devote more attention to their message and build automaticity for word knowledge.

Word Walls for K–2 Writers

The goal of a word wall in grades K–2 is to target specific vocabulary and high-frequency words needed for easy recall in reading and writing. The area should be colorful and attractive and easily accessible by all students.

Classroom Snapshot: Word Walls
Grades K–2 . . . .

1. Locate an area in the room that will accommodate your targeted word list of high-utility and high-frequency words.

2. Introduce the lesson by explaining that knowing how to write words with ease is necessary for reading and writing projects.

3. Choose three to five words to introduce with scaffolding and support. Use visuals when possible and introduce in context.

4. Say the word. My turn, "I Say _____!" Have students repeat the word. "You Say _____!"

5. Touch to the left of the word and say the word. Tap under and say each letter. Have students clap, snap, or stomp their feet as they chant the letters of the word. Repeat this a few times, as necessary.

6. Use the word in a sentence.

7. In partner pairs, engage the students in a routine. Say the names of the letters and think of a sentence to use the word in context.

8. Display the word.

9. As an option, have students put the words in a vocabulary notebook and make a picture. Or, place students in pairs and have them create a word search.

Word Walls for Grades 3–5 Writers

Word Walls in grades 3–5 can use an alphabet chart with sticky notes that are organized by units of study, domain-specific tier 3 words, or targeted words for writing projects. These walls can be portable and moved from space to space when systems departmentalize. If students have difficulty, then differentiate words by creating a personalized alphabet chart for students to keep in writing folders.

 Classroom Snapshot: Word Walls
Grades 3–5 ·······································

Introduce students to the idea of a portable word wall. The words displayed on the actual word wall will relate to what is being studied in class or a piece of literature/informational text that is being studied.

1. Choose five to seven words to focus on each week, adding a different activity each day.

2. Words for a research project about the study of the brain might include impulsive, creativity, intelligence, chemicals, neurons, microscopic, and spatial.

3. Place a word on a sticky note on the alphabet chart in the proper box.

4. Move to the board and break the word into syllables. Touch to the left of the word: "I say microscopic. You say, microscopic." Slide your hand quickly under the word left to right.

5. Write the word in syllables on the board.
   - *mi* open syllable/long vowel
   - *cro* open syllable/long vowel
   - *scop* closed syllable/short vowel
   - *ic* closed syllable/short vowel

6. Give the meaning of the word.

7. Have students engage in a discussion saying the word in syllables, using fingers to tap out syllables, and using the word in a meaningful sentence

8. Keep the word wall posted in the room for use in reading and writing projects.

9. When finished with theme words, move them to an anchor chart and start a new list.

Aa	Bb	Cc	Dd	Ee	
Ff	Gg	Hh	Ii	Jj	
Kk	Ll	Mm	Nn	Oo	
Pp	Qq	Rr	Ss	Tt	
Uu	Vv	Ww	Xx	Yy	Zz

Word Walls for Grades 6–8 Writers

The goal of word walls in the middle school classroom is to build oral and written words that are high utility and will increase student achievement in all content areas.

Consider creating a calendar of words for your classroom and introduce two new vocabulary words each day. Invite students to go word hunting and bring in challenge words for the class Calendar of Words. The Calendar of Words can match units of study in content areas or special writing projects.

Classroom Snapshot: Word Walls
Grades 6–8

1. Introduce students to the location of the word wall. Talk about why a word wall is important and useful in the classroom.

2. Choose two words from the daily calendar described above (e.g., articulate: express clearly; clarify: explain to make easier).

3. Define each and use in a sentence.

4. Explain how these words can be used in daily life, as well as across other content areas.

5. Have students move into small groups to interact, explain, define, and use words in oral conversation.

6. Add the words to a vocabulary notebook using a picture, a student-friendly definition, and a sentence.

7. Display the words on the word wall and challenge students to use them in their writing as well as in conversations.

Strategy 2: Use Anchor Charts

Anchor charts help keep learning uppermost in the minds of students as the displays are permanent and visible. Students are expected to refer to them in daily instruction. These charts should be created by and with students for the benefit of students. Discussion of strategies charted are reminders to students they can return to gather and use essential information. Anchor charts can be generated in all content areas and displayed for use during the Writer's Workshop schedule.

Classroom Snapshot: Anchor Charts
Grades K–2

Have chart paper and markers ready.

1. Tell students, "Writers, today we will be creating a chart of sentence builders to extend and enrich our sentence muscles."

2. Model this process for students by saying, "I will generate a couple of sentence ideas and we will extend those ideas using rich details."

3. Title the anchor chart Sentence Builders. Then, write the start of generic sentences on the chart, such as the following:

   - I know how to
   - I went to
   - The dog went
   - I wish that
   - My favorite food is

4. Lead students in an interactive discussion about adding details to increase sentence variety. Record students' ideas for completing the sentences onto the anchor chart.

5. Display the chart for the class to see, but make it portable so that it can be moved into an area for guided writing follow-up.

The chart in Figure 1.8 was generated in a second-grade class to add details to sentences.

Figure 1.8 Sample K–2 Anchor Chart

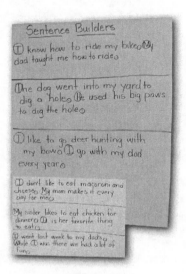

 Classroom Snapshot: **Anchor Charts**
Grades 3–5 . . . .

1. Tell students that as writers they need to choose an idea and tightly organize their thinking around that idea while grouping related ideas together.

2. To model this for students say, "To organize our thinking we can use a visual to remind us of idea grouping. We need an introduction, details that support the main idea, and a concluding statement." Label the anchor chart "A Whopping Good Paragraph." See Figure 1.9.

3. Draw or sketch a hamburger during your explanation to show the three components of an organizational structure. The top bun is the introduction, the meat and ingredients in the middle are the details, and the bottom bun is the conclusion.

4. In small groups, have students plan their thinking for the next writing piece, visualizing a hamburger as sketched on the anchor chart.

5. Pull students back together and refer back to the visual on the anchor chart. Hang it up in the classroom as a visual reminder unless you need to pull it to a small guided-writing area.

Figure 1.9 Sample Grades 3–5 Anchor Chart

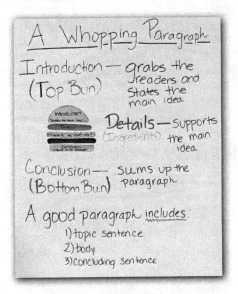

 Classroom Snapshot: **Anchor Charts**
Grades 6–8 ·

1. Introduce students to the lesson by demonstrating the importance of visual cues to support the concepts they are learning. As learners, they will be aware of how to write more challenging words and longer texts.

2. At the top of the chart, write "Dapper Dialogue".

3. Select a text that uses dialogue well and project it for the class to see. Have students reflect and discuss how dialogue aids in meaning and how to read it fluently.

4. Model how dialogue is used to record a character's exact words.

5. List examples of tag words that indicate that quotations are needed: pleaded, screamed, nagged, replied, etc.

6. Place sticky notes of excellent examples on the Dapper Dialogue anchor chart. Place the chart in a visible place to be used throughout instruction.

Figure 1.10 Sample Grades 6–8 Anchor Chart

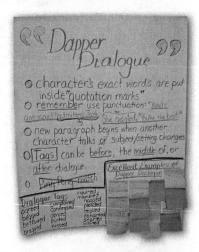

These classroom snapshots model the type of rich language that can be developed through the use of anchor charts.

A Classroom Conversation Grades K–2

The students have gathered in the whole-group meeting area in front of an anchor chart with the words who, what, where, when, and five short sentence stems written on it.

Teacher: We have been adding when and where to our sentences to create a more vivid image. Today we will create rubber band sentences. The longer the sentence, the more you stretch the rubber band. Here is my sentence. "The fish swam." The sentence tells who and what. Who can add a where to build a more interesting sentence?

Student 1: The fish swam in the ocean.

Teacher: Great job!

The teacher writes the suggested "where" to the sentence on the anchor chart.

Teacher: Now who can add a "when" to further stretch the sentence?

Student 2: The fish swam in the ocean in the middle of the night.

Teacher: Wow! Let's use our rubber band and check our sentence for interest and length.

The teacher stretches a rubber band to show how the length of the sentence changed with more detail that was added. Then, the teacher turns to the anchor chart and reads the remaining small sentences: "The kitten slept"; "The tiger roared"; "The boy cried"; "The duck swam."

Teacher: Writers, you will meet with your writing partner and practice adding the "when" and "where" to each sentence.

The students work with their partners adding vivid details to the sentences and the teacher moves about and praises their effort or uses questions to prompt struggling students.

A Classroom Conversation Grades 3–5

Teacher: Writers, yesterday we worked on building excellent sentences using appositives to strengthen and lengthen. Today, we will use a circle chart to create interesting words to replace an overused word that shows a character is speaking.

Teacher models substituting "said" in a page from mentor text *Bedhead*.

Students: That's too many saids.

Teacher: You're right! Now I'll reread and substitute words for said. How did these words make my story more interesting?

Student 1: You didn't have to repeat yourself.

Student 2: It gets annoying and boring!

Teacher: Here are words I pulled from literature.

Teacher writes substitute words for said on a circle chart. Teacher uses familiar material for strategy instruction.

Teacher: You will be working in groups to create more interesting words using some stories we've already read. Turn to a partner and tell them what your group will be doing.

Students energetically talk and the teacher circulates around the room and praises, confirming that students understand what to do next. To differentiate instruction, the teacher gives groups different texts for the group work and uses questions to prompt any struggling students.

A Classroom Conversation Grades 6–8

Students are gathered on crates and carpet in the meeting area with sample narrative texts.

Teacher: Writers, we've been working on narrative writing using the text *The Table Where Rich People Sit* as a model to build from.

The teacher rereads an excerpt from the text and models on an anchor chart how to put exact words from the text in quotation marks.

Teacher: Today, we will check our writing for character talk and remember to enclose exact words using quotation marks. Turn to your partner, find an example of dialogue from the text, and then record it on a sticky note. Please put your thumbs up when you are ready to share.

Student 1: He replied, "Well, tell me some Bubby."

The student places the sticky note on the anchor chart.

Student 2: My family responded, "Here is why we are rich."

The student places the sticky note on the anchor chart. Students continue sharing examples from the text and placing them on the anchor chart.

Teacher: Now it's time to evaluate your own writing and make revisions to include dialogue.

Strategy 3: Create a Classroom Writing Center

The writing center is an area in the room where individuals or small groups of students gather to engage in a writing activity. Sometimes a teacher will be working with a guided writing activity or individual conferring session while a small group conducts peer conferences, revisions, or editing sessions in the writing center. The writing center is not static and can change as the need develops. The location of the center is not fixed and can even be located at a group of student desks with a small writer's toolbox moved onto the table to share.

Classroom Snapshot: Sample Writing Center Grades K–2

The goal of a K–2 writing center is to reinforce and practice strategies and behaviors that strengthen literacy learning. Centers provide multileveled activities where students learn to practice independently and collaboratively. Place the center in a quiet corner, arranged with multiple seating options (four at most) with a bulletin board displaying a variety of writing projects or samples of past student projects.

Writing tools include a variety of premade writing paper, examples of published books, technology available for research and publication, a variety of writing pencils, markers, some form of correction tape, and an alphabetized high-frequency word wall nearby. Add to this list as students make progress and more rigorous expectations can be met. Here is a short checklist for analyzing a primary writing center.

- Is the center organized and inviting?

- Are mentor texts integrated into the center?

- Are all materials neatly labeled for primary writers?

- Are displays of writing at student eye-level?

- Is the center located so that the teacher has a view while conducting other activities?

 ## *Classroom Snapshot:* Sample Writing Center
Grades 3–5

A quality writing center in grades 3–5 is a well-defined area designed for thinking, talking, and practicing life skills for writing success. Attractive, organized, and colorful shelves of books organized by genre should be labeled and accessible for student cross-content writing. Include artifacts from the science and social studies world to get creative writing juices flowing. Helpful sentence stems/frames and transition words and phrases can be placed on a bulletin board adjacent to the writing center, along with rubrics and exemplar writing examples so that students can compare their work to other student examples. Writing should be fun as well as rigorous, so have students come to the writing center to create alternate forms of writing as well, such as rhymes, jingles, and lyrics to familiar tunes to remember content. Here is a short checklist for analyzing your writing center in grades 3–5.

- Are all resources clearly labeled and organized for easy access and return?

- Is student work organized to turn in or stored in center folders/notebooks?

- Is wall space available for displaying student artifacts?

- Is there a variety of writing mentor texts clearly labeled and displayed?

- Is there a high level of choice based on your observations of student writing behaviors?

 ## *Classroom Snapshot:* Sample Writing Center
Grades 6–8

A good writer will apprentice himself/herself to experts in writing agreement. Therefore, a high-quality writing center for middle schoolers should contain thought-provoking, interesting material, including ideas and lists of possible topics. Tubs of biographies, historical novels, and picture books should be provided. Include bulletin board photos of sports figures, national heroes, charity organizations, community leaders, science discoveries, and current events to spark creativity and ideas for writing.

Sentence stems and paper-fold graphic organizers provide support for students who need additional methods of planning. Tools for publishing, such as technology, dictionaries, and generic word walls should also be provided to support the writing process. Here is a short checklist for analyzing your middle-school writing center.

- Are students able to collaborate with partners in the center?

- Have mentor texts been organized according to style of writing or genre?

- Is the center motivating, engaging, and appealing to writers of both genders?

- Is the use of the writing center as routine as daily teeth brushing?

- Have you included attractive charts, photos, and resources that promote writing?

Strategies for Toolkits and Talking Writer-to-Writer

As a writing coach, talking one-on-one with your students is key. There are several tools you can use as a teacher to help discuss writing to students. The strategies that follow focus on:

- Creating a teacher toolkit/tote

- Using conversation cards

- Using mentor texts

 ## Strategy 1: Create a Teacher Toolkit/Tote

Just as a clipboard serves as an important tool for sports coaches during a match or game, teachers ("coaches" of writing) need a small tote to access necessary resources during instruction. The tote needs to be small enough to carry as you move from table to table to confer individually or in small groups, or move to a designated area for guided writing. The importance of the toolkit rests on the understanding that availability of writing resources is necessary for conferencing, pacing, and efficient use of writing time. The concept of the toolkit/tote and how to use it always stays the same, but depending on the grade level, thematic unit of study, and time of year the resources included may change. Totes/toolkits may include the following:

- mentor text(s) recently used (for modeling)

- exemplar writing samples by grade level in all genres

- student writing samples (poetry, reports, recipes, directions, manuals—depending on instruction)

- rubrics for narrative, informational, opinion/argument, and research writing matched to appropriate assessments

- teacher conferring notebook for formative assessment (see Chapter 7)

- handheld thesaurus and dictionary

- teacher personal notebook/writing folder with personal texts (for modeling)

- editing checklist

- sticky notes for instructional strategy for students to "have a go." (Do not write on student papers. They are the owners of their work. Any notes should be placed on a sticky note for practice or changes based on your teacher talk.)

- scissors, tape, glue, and correction tape to support revisions/editing

- small container of extra pencils

- magnetic chips to move into letter-sound boxes (Elkonin boxes)

- magnetic wand to quickly pick up chips so that time is not wasted

- small whiteboard and markers to practice word work, to use letter-sound boxes and show sound/symbol, to practice high-frequency words, to break words into syllable components, or to reinforce six syllable rules: 1—open syllable (end in vowel–*ta ble*), 2—closed syllable (vowel closed in by consonants–*riv er*), 3—r-controlled (*farm*), 4—vowel teams (*ea, ee, ai, brain*), 5—consonant le (*responsi ble*), 6—vowel/consonant silent *e* (*com plete*).

Strategy 2: Use Conversation Cards

Have you ever observed a coach fully engaged throughout a football game, pacing the sideline, tapping a player on the shoulder for a job well done? Have you noticed the talk, the pointers as the game is progressing, the clipboard with play possibilities or changes when change is needed? Great coaches do not just start to make changes when the score is 45–0, and winning is out of reach. Neither do writing coaches, and if you teach writing, YOU ARE A WRITING COACH!

The secret to talking writer-to-writer is to build an internal control and a self-extending system so that the writer becomes the problem solver. The process of a self-extending system will carry over into all content areas and into a student's life skills, as well.

The sample conversation cards in Figure 1.11 provide teacher support when moving around having a conversation with a student or pulling a small group of struggling writers to the side.

Figure 1.11 Sample Conversation Cards

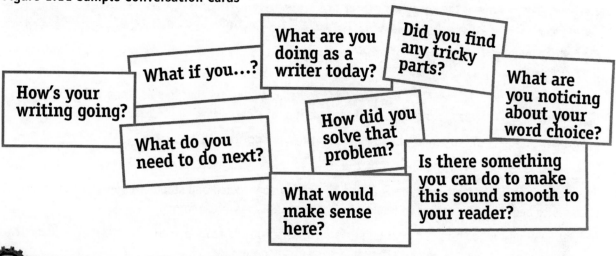

 Strategy 3: Use Mentor Texts

Read alouds, both literary and informational, should be incorporated into daily literacy time and further studied to analyze the author's writing craft. Students tend to imitate literature in which they have a vested interest. For example, middle school students interested in Gary Paulsen literature tend to write about nature, survival, and the wilderness. Take students outside their immediate comfort zone by using literature that stretches and builds their background knowledge.

Mentor texts help motivate writers and provide a model for them to emulate. Students can craft solid narrative, informational, and opinion writing if they have a pattern to explore. A text can be used as a mentor text for a variety of different reasons. For example, text structure, language choice, hooks, endings, imagery, or dialogue can all be great topics for mini-lessons using a mentor text as a guide.

The following is a short list of great literature to use as mentor texts. Study the craft, make notes on anchor charts, decide who is telling the story (point of view), and how the story is crafted. Even in the early years, dig deep into texts.

Mentor Texts for Grades K–2

- *I Like Myself!* by Karen Beaumont: This text is great for rhyming words and repetitive sentence structure. It also is a good guide for writing personal narratives/poetry.

- *Wallace's Lists* by Barbara Bottner and Gerald Kruglik: This text is a wonderful model to help students begin making lists of interesting topics about which they would like to write.

- *Apples* by Gail Gibbons: This text is fantastic for examining how images and diagrams contribute to overall understanding of the topic/concept.

- *Harold and the Purple Crayon* by Crockett Johnson: This text is great to get students thinking about the tools that writers use.

- *I Wanna Iguana* by Karen Kaufman Orloff: This text is helpful to model opinion/argument writing.

- *Knuffle Bunny* by Mo Williems: This text can be used to illustrate how to write with speech bubbles.

Lesson Idea: Using a Mentor Text Grades K–2

1. Remind students that writers often get their ideas from stories in books. Say, "We can study an author and use their craft as a model for our stories."

2. Read the mentor text, *I Just Forgot* by Mercer Mayer. Remind students that in this story, Little Critter forgets to do many of his daily responsibilities, such as brushing his teeth, making his bed, and forgetting his lunch.

3. As a class, create an anchor chart about things that may be difficult to remember.

4. Model how to take a few of the ideas from the chart to create your own story.

5. Provide each student with a small book (a few sheets of paper folded and stapled together). Then instruct students to begin writing their own books about things that they often forget.

6. Circulate around the room to see whether students understood the story pattern. Are students engaged? Do you notice writing stamina? Prompt struggling students as necessary.

7. Once writing is complete, have students share their book writings with a writing partner, then in groups of four.

Mentor Texts for Grades 3–5

- *The Grouchy Ladybug* by Eric Carle: This is a funny book that can be used as a model for how to incorporate dialogue.

- *Hope Is a Ferris Wheel* by Robin Herrera: This text provides a good model for exploring metaphors.

- *It's Disgusting and We Ate It! True Food Facts from Around the World and Throughout History* by James Solheim: This text is great to examine a variety of text features, such as captions and sidebars.

- *Brave Irene* by William Steig: This text is full of strong verbs.

- *The Great Fuzz Frenzy* by Janet Stevens: This is a superb book for teaching students to use onomatopoeia.

- *Owl Moon* by Jane Yolen: This book is rich with details and visual descriptions.

Lesson Idea: Using a Mentor Text Grades 3–5

1. Display the text *Everybody Needs a Rock* by Byrd Baylor. Remind students of the format and basic structure, written in column layout. Discuss and chart anything noticed as you skim through the book.

2. Read aloud the simple 10-rule text on how to find a rock. Tell students to pay particular attention to the introduction and the conclusion so that they can imitate the style.

3. Discuss the setting of the book (the Southwest) and how the author's rules pertain to that type of climate and geography.

4. Reread the introduction aloud. As a class, brainstorm ways to imitate the author's style while making the story more relevant to today's students. For example, "I'm sorry for kids with tricycles, bicycles, horses, goldfish..." changes to: "I'm sorry for kids who only have movies, tablets, and cell phones."

5. Fold a sheet of paper in half and model the column format with text flowing down both sides. Write your Rule 1 and Rule 2 for how to find a rock in your geographic region (see below for an example).

   - **Rule 1:** Go somewhere very quiet where you can hear the birds singing and the water gurgling across the rocks in a stream.

   - **Rule 2:** When you're looking for your rock, don't let anyone interrupt your search. Choose a rock from a mountain where the forest thins out as you climb to higher elevations.

6. Divide students into groups of four. Have them begin to brainstorm rules for finding a rock in their own geographic location. Allow several minutes of talk time and then bring them back to whole group.

7. Remind students the sky is the limit. Encourage students to be creative and think of locations around the school or their home where they may go to find a rock. Provide them with the tools and send them off to write their 10 Rules for Finding a Rock.

Mentor Texts for Grades 6–8

- *Doll Bones* by Holly Black: This paranormal-mystery text is great for setting and character development.

- *Enormous Smallness: A Story of E. E. Cummings* by Matthew Burgess: This book provides a beautiful example of mood and tone.

- *The Music of the Dolphins* by Karen Hesse: This text uses typical grammar, usage, and mechanics rules to convey style, tone, and emphasis.

- *Middle School Is Worse than Meatloaf* by Jennifer L. Holm: This text shows a great example of a personal narrative, especially for middle school students.

- *The Year Down Yonder* by Richard Peck: This text presents a variety of high-quality sequence and transition words.

Time to Teach

Lesson Idea: Using a Mentor Text Grades 6–8

1. Remind students of the targeted vocabulary word wall for domain-specific words needed for success. Explain the importance of increasing vocabulary exposure.

2. Read aloud *The Boy Who Loved Words* by Roni Schotter and build an ABC chart of interesting words from the text. When reading aloud, give a brief, student-friendly meaning of difficult words: e.g., periphery (surrounding space), swarthy (dusky color), clamor (loud complaint or demand).

3. In small triads, have students remember as many words as they can from the active read aloud. Pull back together as a whole group and add their thinking to the word chart.

4. Make a paper fold of four squares. Show students how to write a word in each square, sketch a picture to illustrate, and use the word in a sentence. When completed students should have a word, picture and sentence in each of the four squares with a new and unusual word to build word knowledge.

5. Collect all examples, copy, make a cover, and staple together a book for each student. Books will be stored in a writer's folder for future writing projects. Consider having students bring in a four-square paper fold with four challenging words they found in their independent reading. Compare the class lists and have students choose five words for everyone to learn.

In summary, mentor texts are indispensable when embedded in Writer's Workshop. Students are required to search for author craft, communicate their understanding of text structures, and increase literacy skills in the process. Students will thrive in an environment that celebrates the work of a variety of authors. Studying mentor texts also opens the door for exposure to many sources of information. Embrace, enjoy, and energize your classroom using mentor texts to strengthen writing stamina, hone the writing craft, and increase student achievement.

Motivating Student Writers

The late Donald Graves, who founded the Process Writing Laboratory at the University of New Hampshire in 1976, led a worldwide revolution in teaching writing. In doing so, he discovered three keys to motivate writers: choice, ownership, and audience (Graves 1983; Gentry 2013). Figure 2.1 shows how these three motivators dovetail perfectly with three scientifically based keys to motivation: autonomy, mastery, and purpose (Gentry and Peha 2013).

Figure 2.1 Motivation for Writing (Gentry and Peha 2013)

Donald Graves	Daniel Pink
Choice of topic	Autonomy (to be self-directed)
Ownership over the process	Mastery (the urge to get better)
Writing for a real audience	Purpose (personal satisfaction)

1. **Choice of topic** is related to autonomy. Pink (2009) says autonomy is our desire to be self-directed, which leads to engagement. The strategies in this chapter give writers a choice in writing that fits the need to be self-directed.

2. **Ownership** is akin to Pink's "mastery," because ownership often leads to mastery. In scores of presentations to teachers, Graves famously repeated this mantra: "Kids want to write!" They want to *own* the ability to write and the ability to read back what they have written. The strategies in this chapter engage writers so that in writing they begin to master the fundamentals and feel successful. This motivation to write through ownership creates an urge to get better (Pink 2009).

3. **Writing for a real audience** provides purpose. Writers engaged in the purpose have a motive when they help you make a grocery list, send a "Thank You" note to someone, or write an opinion piece for an actual classroom newspaper. Each of the strategies in this chapter provides opportunities for students to write for a real audience and increase the writer's autonomy, sense of mastery, and sense of purpose.

These three intrinsic motivators are like the butter, sugar, and flour that go into a cake. You can't build a community of writers in your classroom without these important ingredients. In our experience, *motivation is what makes a successful writing program.*

In addition to these intrinsic motivators, teachers must create a motivational classroom environment for writers. In this chapter, we show you how to implement strategies that invite the writers in your classroom to "tune in." The actions and words of the adult in the room help determine enthusiastic learning. The famed psychologist Haim Ginott (1972) is frequently quoted, "I've come to the frightening conclusion that I am the decisive element in the classroom. It's my daily mood that makes the weather. As a teacher, I possess a tremendous power to make a child's life miserable or joyous. I can be a tool of torture or an instrument of inspiration. I can humiliate or humor, hurt or heal. In all situations, it is my response that decides whether a crisis will be escalated or de-escalated and a child humanized or de-humanized" (15–16). This quote serves as a reminder that you—and your efforts to motivate—can help determine whether your students will become writers, readers, and life-long learners.

Time to Teach

To understand the importance of motivation for young writers, let's focus on three key questions:

1. What does research say that shows a strong correlation between student engagement and achievement?

2. Why is it important for teachers to consider motivation when planning writing instruction?

3. Why do teachers need to motivate students to enhance engagement?

Students can perform "at the top of their game" if appropriately motivated by their teachers. Open the door to opportunity. Specifically, students persist toward reaching academic goals and writing targets if the teacher has created a community where all writing is valued and celebrated. Six key techniques keep the temperament even in the classroom, keep students moving in the direction of their writing target, and improve engagement and motivation (Rockwell 1995, Ito 1996):

1. **Interest Boosting:** When needed, change the tempo of the lesson. Increase or decrease the pace, depending on student need. Observe your audience to decide if your students have connected. The eyes tell the story! Additional movement or discussion may be needed.

2. **Antiseptic Bouncing:** If you notice students who are interrupting or beginning inappropriate behavior, first quickly redirect. You may have introduced a lesson that is too easy or too difficult. On the rare occasion that that does not work, it may be necessary to temporarily remove a student from the classroom in a non-punitive way. This is known as antiseptic bouncing.

3. **Routinized Support:** Predictability within the writing community increases attention and focus, thereby increasing achievement.

4. **Interject Humor:** Humor relaxes and a giggle or "belly laugh" can immediately change an environment. Humor invites achievement!

5. **Rearrange and Change Around:** If you're finding the lesson falling flat, change the structure. You may simply need to change things up a bit to refocus attention.

6. **Propinquity:** This means moving close by. If you interrupt potential behaviors before they happen, you're less likely to intercede and instruction can move forward. When planning writing instruction, keep these six techniques in mind and you will be rewarded with students engaged in high-quality writing opportunities."

Use the Language of Motivation

"Language is one of the most powerful tools available to teachers. It permeates every aspect of teaching and learning" (Denton 2015, 1).

Just as internalizing story patterns provide a gateway into competent story writing, the language of a caring teacher provides a gateway into student literacy acquisition. "Caring relationships with teachers helps students build resilience. By fostering these relationships, we learn about students' interests and goals, which are fuel for motivation" (Ferlazzo 2012).

Here are four tips for using the language of motivation successfully:

1. **Give affirmations for a job well done.** Positive verbal responses result in better intellectual and literacy gains at all socioeconomic status and age levels. "Positive messages are essential to motivation. Subtle shifts in teacher language infuse positive messages throughout our interactions." (Ferlazzo 2012, 1). Build a safe, supportive classroom environment based on trust, with a sprinkling of humor. Spotlighting a specific strategy provides an opportunity to teach, honor, and affirm a job that is well done.

- Wow, your opening sounds just like the author _____.

- I appreciate how you've pulled evidence from all of your sources to support your point of view. This makes your writing very strong.

- Look at how you've concluded your piece! You're sounding just like the author _____.

2. **Invite students to collaborate.** Collaboration with partners or in small groups during all phases of the writing process improves writing by building language acquisition, increasing word power, improving sentence construction, and reorganizing for clearer meaning and flow. Throughout your writing program, provide opportunities for students to work together to share their writing.

- Writers, meet with a partner to discuss _____.

- Take turns sharing in your group about why you chose to end your story in such a way.

- Writers, make a group of four and share at least two details you've included that support your position.

3. **Affirm positive behavior in Writer's Workshop with motivating language such as praise.** Students build trust when they have a vested interest in the learning environment. Organize the classroom with the support and input of students. Begin with your vision and your expectations, then allow students to contribute their ideas regarding what constitutes positive behavior and motivating language.

- You are really showing respect! Listen to how this class is supporting the efforts of everyone.

- Wow! Listen to that intellectual aggressiveness! You're practicing just like a basketball star.

- What an excellent example! Your work ethic needs to be honored.

4. **Accept approximations and provide positive, timely feedback.** It is important to keep in mind that student writers are not yet able to write and communicate as adult authors do. Show appreciation, enthusiasm, and excitement for their approximations.

- You are working very hard! Look at how you almost spelled that challenging word correctly! Here's what that word looks like. Let's try it again.

- That's an amazing piece of writing! You added many specific details. Great work!

- Wow! You did that all by yourself. Good thinking!

The following strategy can also assist you with using motivational language.

 ## *Strategy 1:* Use Positive Language

"Our words and tone of voice play a critical role in establishing the nature of our relationship with students and also can influence students' relationships with each other." (Denton 2015, 6)

Walking the halls of any school building gives an insight into the nature of interactions, from administration to teacher, student to student, and student to teacher. The culture of the school plays an important role in whether students feel respected and supported in their learning, and school systems should promote motivation that results in long-term success and productivity at every level from custodial to administration.

Positive language can and should be used in all areas of Writer's Workshop. During the writing phase as students are working, it is important to circulate around the room to motivate and encourage them to keep writing even if they are struggling a bit. During this time, praise can be divided into three categories: specific compliments; ideas for taking it to the next level; and try it now, then I'll be back.

Time to Teach

Specific Compliments

- I really liked how you _____. As a reader, I could _____.

- The way you described _____ was so cool/awesome/interesting/haunting! I could see it happening in my mind!

- What a fantastic way to _____. I like that you chose to _____.

- I appreciate you taking the time to _____ (use the rubric/check yours against a mentor text/ etc). It is really going to help move your writing forward/elevate your writing.

- I noticed how you _____. Great work!

- You made your story sound just like _____. Well done!

- What praise did you receive from your partner? Very nice work!

- I can tell that your peer conferencing time was useful. You're definitely on the right track!

- Extraordinary use of the mentor text to _____. Great work!

- You should be proud! I can tell that _____.

- Returning to the mentor text to get an idea for _____ was an excellent idea.

- You were so open-minded and receptive of your group suggestions! I can tell it took your writing to the next level.

Ideas for Taking It to the Next Level

- You might try _____.

- You know what you might do to amp up the level of your writing? Try to add _____ (suspense/ excitement/drama/dialogue/etc.).

- How about trying _____ (technique)?

- Have you considered adding/trying_____? I think it might help move your writing in the direction you'd like to go.

- How do you think it might sound? (Have student say the idea out loud/rehearse to the teacher before writing it.)

- I noticed that you _____. That's a great use of our anchor chart for support.

- Look at our anchor chart to remind yourself _____. I think that might take your writing to the next level/elevate your writing.

- Have you thought about asking a peer for feedback? Listening to someone else's ideas might help take your writing to the next level.

Try It Now, Then I'll Be Back

- Go ahead and try that right now. How might that sound? (Ask the student to say it out loud first.) I'll be back to see how it goes.

- Go ahead and try that right now. If you decide it's not right later on, that's okay, but let's at least try it. (Get the student started before you leave.)

- Give it a shot, and see how it sounds.

- You never know, that strategy might be cool to try in a few different places. Once you've written it, show it to your partner and see if he/she agrees that it works.

- Use the information in the anchor chart to help you _____. I will be back in a few minutes to see how it went.

Motivate Student Writers with Author Celebrations

Most writing should not remain private. Its purpose is to share, to explain, to persuade, to illuminate, to call attention, to entertain, to make the reader think and feel and see. Writing is a way of joining and contributing to the human community. (Murray 2005, 164)

If we adhere to the teachings of Donald Murray (1982), Pulitzer Prize-winning author for editorial writing, we understand that as writers, we are constantly rehearsing in our heads ideas, phrases, and thoughts. Eventually we will move our thoughts onto paper and draft again and again through the revision and editing process. Some of our writing will make it into the "public arena."

Writing teachers develop their own guidelines for presentation or publication. Classrooms often hold an author's tea, inviting family and friends to listen, view, and celebrate student writing samples. For this purpose a kindergarten student might sort through his or her writing folder or writing journal and pull out a favorite piece that would be edited with teacher support for sharing and display. A third-grade student might sort through his or her writer's notebook to find a story mountain graphic organizer to explain one way to organize narrative writing at a parent/families curriculum night function. Sixth graders may entertain an audience on a Back to School night by delivering a rousing rap on capitalization, which they wrote as a class.

Here are a few of the many events that teachers use to help celebrate student writing. These celebrations are important because they provide a real audience and an authentic purpose for writing. Celebrations bring joy to the life of the writer and capture the spirit of Writer's Workshop through the eyes of the audience. Depending on the developmental level of your group, add ideas to the following list and encourage other classes to join you in author celebrations. Make these events grade-level or schoolwide and bring all stakeholders, care givers, and families into the school community. This can build bridges of success in profound ways.

Author's Luncheon/Tea

Family and friends are invited to a luncheon to celebrate student writing. Students share their writing aloud, either with the whole group or to their own families or friends. Providing snacks makes the gathering feel like a true celebration! Make sure to invite a few staff members to work with students who do not have a family member or friend attending. Consider using themes for the luncheon/tea, such as a celebration of students' stories written in the style of Eric Carle; a biography project where students come to school dressed as their book's topic and read their work; an interview presentation where students share how they gathered information for a school newspaper edition.

Writing Campout

Students set up tents in the gym, bring sleeping bags, and spend the night writing by flashlight. Each group of five students has a chaperone to monitor writing and the adult chaperone should be writing, too. Every 20–30 minutes, students come out of their tents to play games and share writing work. Schedule this in a safe, fun way, adding in brisk activity at the end of each chunk of writing time. Lights go out at a designated time, with a rocking chair and author sharing before bedtime. End the campout with breakfast, honoring group accomplishments and writing success. This can be modified to occur during the day if an overnight stay is not permissible at your school.

Rack Up the Mileage Competition

…William Faulkner, Ernest Hemingway, Graham Greene, and many other writers counted words and kept a written record (Murray 2005, 25)

Here, students are awarded mileage points based on the number words, sentences, or paragraphs they write. This activity is not about high quality but about increasing the quantity of writing. Connect this to social studies by having students calculate how many miles, in what direction, and where they might travel based on their earned mileage points. This project would provide motivation and competition for intermediate and middle school, but may be a challenge for early writers.

Beach Party

A beach party is set aside as a day for students to celebrate writing achievements. This can be done after themed-writing units of study or even after state assessments. Other possibilities for the celebration include when students have written a story or informational piece with a beach setting or theme. For example, after the study of *Hello Ocean*, a mentor text using rhyme that students used as a model for their own pieces.

Students bring in rubber rafts, inner tubes, beach blankets, and beach chairs. The event includes beach party snacks and opportunities for students to share their writing.

Read to a Fuzzy Friend

For primary students, sharing their writing with classmates can be intimidating. Holding a stuffed animal gives reassurance to very young students who may feel "stage fright." Reading to the fuzzy friend also adds variety to sharing time at the end of Writer's Workshop and gives teachers the opportunity to highlight recent mini-lessons through the share.

Invite a student to the Author Chair. Holding the fuzzy friend, the student shares writing with their classmates. Selection of students for sharing may be to help build writer confidence or be based on a particular goal for a mini-lesson the teacher wishes to highlight. The audience participates by providing feedback to the student who reads their story holding a stuffed animal in their arms. Limit sharing time and the number of students who share to make the experience feel important to the students who share.

Election Party

Get ready for election time! Have students vote for a favorite writing text. Have a primary and a general election. Who wins the election? Maybe the winner can decide on the next writing assignment or help teach a new skill.

Spotlight on Writing

Fill the hallways with student writing displays and have an open house. Students lead their families and friends to their important texts. No one is left out and everyone has writing displayed.

Hats Off to Writing!

Celebrate student writers with a family night called, "Hats Off to Writers!" On hat day, staff and students are given the option of wearing hats to school and the day moves into an after-school event. Families are invited to a celebration where student writing has been displayed. Students are invited to share their pieces. This celebration is a fantastic way to culminate a writing unit of study, a focus on a particular author, or recognize excellent learning.

Techno-Talk

Use an Internet-based tool to provide students with pen pals in another country so that students can share their writing pieces back and forth. This provides an authentic purpose and audience for their writing as well as an opportunity to practice word-processing skills by transcribing their writing into digital form. This opportunity can be broadened to include specific writing pieces that describe culture, transitions, and family, allowing students to make multicultural connections with their pen pals.

Hundred Day Celebration

Brainstorm 100 reasons to write. Each student makes a sign to place in the hallway that indicates a reason why students need to write. Students can collaborate in teams to create the sign. The end result is 100 reasons that writing is important for people of all ages.

Build Classroom Morale

Teachers have a great deal of control over the classroom environment. Ordinary encouragement presented in a meaningful way can teach students that the classroom community accepts all voices and invites multiple perspectives. Encouraging words can provide constructive feedback for writers who may need guidance and support before moving forward with an assignment. Alfie Kohn has shared seven ways that schools can stifle the love of reading in students, along with four principles that teachers can live by to help restore high morale and regard for literacy (Strauss 2014). We have adapted these principles to show how schools do the same with writing, and how teachers can reverse those trends to re-establish a love of writing through the following strategies:

- Provide students with writing choices

- Encourage collaboration and feedback

- Provide unusual twists on familiar writing activities

- Use realia

Time to Teach

Strategy 1: Provide Students with Writing Choices

Many classroom teachers use writing prompts to begin and encourage writing. In some ways, it is the path of least resistance that requires little effort. However, using the same prompt for everyone is a one-size-fits-all approach to writing instruction. According to Calkins, Hartman, and White (2005), the secret lies in differentiated materials. When we use a one-size fits-all approach, we stifle the creativity of student learners. Student choice, based on personal experiences, is key.

Instead of simply prompting, offer choice. Students should be filling a writing space with ideas from their own lives that are excellent topics for narratives and opinions. Teachers can also keep lists of topic ideas for when students get "stuck."

Here are some ways to provide choice for students during the writing phase of Writer's Workshop:

Ponder Pockets

A Ponder Pocket is a place for students to keep ideas they may want to write about all in one place. It can be created from a sheet of paper made to look like a pocket, a paper bag, or a sheet protector labeled *Ponder Pocket*. Students drop in photos, clip art, lists of ideas, etc. into their Ponder Pockets. Children's literature can even be used to inspire ideas for the Ponder Pocket. Ideas are tested and tried, eliminated, used, or kept on the back burner for future writing projects.

Alphabet Books

Use an alphabet book such as *Chicka Chicka Boom Boom* by John Archambault and Bill Martin as a mentor text to encourage the creation of student-made alphabet books. Students can make alphabet books on themes such as beginning sounds or content-area topics such as weather, space, or people. Students can choose their letter and materials for the content.

Biographies

Biographies provide a lot of opportunity for student choice and interest to be considered. Students can write about people from history, science, literature, current culture, or beloved people in their community. Biographies are a great way to search out people in communities and celebrate local citizens to keep communities alive through the eyes of young people!

My Favorite Treasured Memories

Scrapbooks, photos, music, movies, art, sketches, and trinkets make up memories of our lives. Those memories become seeds for ideas for writers that grow and bloom. Listing and writing about treasured memories helps students see value in collecting and storing images as good personal topics for writing. Extend this idea by teaming up with *Wilfrid Gordon McDonald Partridge* by Mem Fox as he gathers a list of items for Miss Nancy, a patient in an elderly care facility, to stimulate her memory. Fox's book helps students make the idea of treasured memories more concrete and gives them a model for turning a treasured memory into a more elaborate story. Treasured memories make great writing topics.

Class Newspaper

Students generate ideas for contributing to a class newspaper. In small groups, they decide whether they would like to write for the sports section, editorial section, social pages, the front page, or even the comics. Publishing a class newspaper builds collaboration and group writing skills, while also developing student choice in the content and writing approach.

Mentor Text

When provided with a variety of mentor texts, student writers build choice in how they will approach their writing project. Using an idea from literature, nonfiction, historical, or science fiction books builds the sense that good writers should always be reading good books.

 Strategy 2: **Encourage Collaboration and Feedback**

In the real world, problems are solved when adults of varying ability and interests work together to engage in collaboration and feedback. The same scenario can work in the classroom. We find that intentionally grouping students with different dialects, abilities, interests, and personalities can strengthen the writing experience. Remind groups that all opinions must be valued, respected, and acknowledged. Collaborative groups may convene after the modeling lesson, during the writing process, or at the end of the writing session to share ideas or accomplishments and provide feedback.

Collaboration during Writer's Workshop can be structured and designed by the teacher with student input. It includes both teacher-to-student collaboration and student-to-student collaboration, as well as feedback. Focused feedback or "talk time" should be built into the lesson immediately after the teaching component. When students are generating ideas for choice or revisions, they need ample opportunities to talk with others before, during, and after writing.

 Classroom Snapshot: **Collaboration and Feedback**
Grades K–2 ·

Immediate Oral Feedback:

A young student beginning a journey into the writer's world needs both teacher and student collaboration. It's helpful for the teacher to listen in to student "talk time" and provide specific language about what they're doing well. For example, after the mini-lesson, before sending the class off to write, students pair up and collaborate about a possible writing topic.

The teacher listens and responds, "Great work, writers! I love how you're setting a perfect example of how to think of story ideas!"

Guided Small-Group Instruction:

Students listen in as the teacher further refines points from a mini-lesson on punctuation. Partners in the group discuss their use of punctuation in their current pieces.

After students provide feedback to each other, the teacher consults with each partner pair, giving additional feedback regarding their punctuation choices.

Quick and to the Point:

In a mid-workshop teaching point, a teacher may interrupt student writing to say: "One, two, three, eyes on me. I would like to spotlight Randy for his amazing onomatopoeia examples."

Share out a couple and respond, "You are a hard-working group of writers. Back to work!" (Randy received feedback and so did his classmates.)

Classroom Snapshot: Collaboration and Feedback
Grades 3–5 . . . .

What to Do Next:

Intermediate writers love playing with words. After an interactive read aloud on word choice using *Max's Words* or another favorite book designed to increase a writer's vocabulary, send students off in small groups to cut and paste interesting words. Use newspapers, magazines, or whatever is available.

Move around each group and listen to peer conversation. Encourage students to provide feedback to each other using questioning strategies: Why did you choose that word? What makes that word interesting? How will we use that word in our writing?

Find the Writer's Voice in a Piece that is Noteworthy:

In groups of four, students read aloud a piece of their writing where they have tried to show their uniqueness and personality. They ask the members of the group, "Does my fingerprint show through in this piece? Can you feel my emotions? Can you see my personal touch?"

Have each group share their favorite piece illustrating voice. Honor this with a quick note. "Wow! This sounds like a real storyteller (or professional writer)!"

Group Feedback:

Have a student volunteer a piece that is being developed involving an important character. Say, "I've noticed we need to include more details to create a visual for our reader." Invite groups to make a chart of specific details about the main character in the story. Remind students to create details that clearly represent the visual character.

As a group, share details and select those to be added to the writing piece. Discuss what makes each selection the most visual representation of the character.

Classroom Snapshot: Collaboration and Feedback
Grades 6–8 . . . .

Peer Think-Share and Edit Later:

Engage students in notetaking on a triad sheet (sheet divided into three parts) during lecture, reading, and discussion, of a three-part unit such as the three ancient civilizations of South America. Create time for peer thinking and sharing. Editing comes later.

Choose Thesis and Begin Writing:

Using their notes, have students choose a thesis and begin writing, choosing their own specific topic and organization. For example, they might compare and contrast religion, art, social structure, type of writing, or cities related to the three ancient civilizations. Encourage students to share their topics and provide feedback with questions such as "What makes that topic interesting?" "How are the civilizations alike and different in the area you chose?

Trade and Share:

Have students trade papers and share, focusing on questions or statements such as "What's most interesting about this piece?" "Here's an example of really good writing!" "This makes me want to know more about _____." Ask students to share part of pieces that have a "Wow!" factor. (When I read this part I said, "Wow!")

Group Feedback:

Invite student volunteers who found the assignment interesting, fun, and personally meaningful to share with the whole class. Have a group discussion about how to enhance writing by choosing topics that are personally meaningful, by sharing, and by getting feedback.

 Strategy 3: Provide Unusual Twists on Familiar Writing Activities

Dare to be different! To keep students interested in what is happening in the classroom during writing time, create activities that surprise them with something unusual. Try some of the following ideas to bring writing enthusiasm back into the classroom with something unique and different:

- Wrap a finished writing product as a gift and present it to someone special. Family members appreciate gifts from the heart that are made with the hands. A writing project is the perfect gift: a poem, a story, an editorial, or a newspaper report. An alternative is to take the gifts to a local nursing care facility and ask the staff to connect you with patients who need extra attention.

- Use fabric or wallpaper and bind a story into a published book. Some schools have their own publishing room manned by parents. Or, create your own publishing nook in the classroom with discarded wallpaper books, craft paper, scissors, glue, and cardboard—the tools necessary for publishing. If no money exists to get books professionally bound, pound the pavement to wallpaper stores and ask them to donate expired wallpaper samples to your classroom.

- Create a writer's group and exchange ideas with other writers. Organize a small group of interested students to join a writer's group for sharing ideas. Intermediate and middle school writers would need a teacher sponsor if the group were to be held outside of normal school hours, but the possibilities are endless. Schools already devote time to literature projects. Take additional steps to form a local writing project opportunity.

- Take published writing samples to another location in the community—a local senior citizen facility, a kid-friendly café, or a nearby church or business. Work with students to create a display, and then have a field trip to visit the students' work. Displays can be arranged in local libraries, coffee shops, or malls. Small businesses are often open to writing sample presentations and local banks often love showing off reading, writing, or artistic work of the students in their community, as well.

- Teach students how to make written documents look aged. This is a unique way to complete writing projects and give the appearance of a historical document. To do this, use parchment paper, calligraphy writing or typing to give the appearance of an old document, tear around the outside edges, and singe with some type of heat. (The singeing part should only be done by an adult.)

 ## Strategy 4: Use Realia

One important way to motivate students during writing is to begin a writing lesson or activity with an interesting opening, or teacher tool, that uses real objects to pique student interest. Using a visual draws the writer into the lesson, generates interest, and preserves the momentum as students move into independent writing time. The realia part of the lesson should take no longer than three to five minutes because the longer session should be focused on student writing time. Following, we offer a few simple strategies using familiar items around the house to spark creativity.

Treasure Chest

A treasure chest builds anticipation and motivation. A beautifully decorated old shoebox will serve the purpose of a treasure chest. Teachers should not feel the need to make an investment for an actual chest/trunk, as any kind of box will serve the intended purpose.

The purpose of the treasure chest is to hide a specific piece(s) of realia that sparks ideas for writing. Use treasure chest objects to ask the question, "What do you think we might want to write about today?"

The following are examples of realia to use in the treasure chest to support writing from any genre:

- photos of people (famous or familiar)
- plastic insects or other interesting creatures
- plastic animals
- small toys
- primary source documents or photos
- an old shoe (where might this shoe have traveled?)
- a newspaper article about a current event

- seashells
- fossils
- postcards
- interesting or strange photos
- coins (domestic or international)
- interesting rocks or geodes

A Gift Bag

Writers need to build the understanding that we've all been given the gift to achieve our potential. It is a gift that can be improved, developed, and polished. Using a gift bag assists students as they explore ideas to generate stories from their own life. Items in the gift bag can be changed and expanded. Simple memorabilia from your life can be the start of a great story. Students can be encouraged to build their own gift bags and use them to write their own personal stories.

You may choose to build an anchor chart as a visual reminder or say the following to students: "Writers, today is a special day. I'm sharing some of the special gifts that I've received that remind me of stories/experiences in my life. Those experiences have special meaning and I can celebrate them through my writing." Pull each item from the bag and give a brief explanation as to why this might be an excellent idea for writing. The following are examples of realia to use in the gift bag to support the writing of personal narratives or other genres of writing:

- a video game
- a small car
- a favorite doll
- a special ring or piece of jewelry
- a photo of a favorite place
- a set of trading cards

- a picture of your favorite athlete
- a gift from a special friend
- a family heirloom
- a playbill or event program
- a vacation souvenir

Doctor's Bag

Students are fascinated by a doctor's bag. As toddlers, they begin to understand doctors and nurses and their roles in our lives. Walk into any toy store and find a selection geared to the medical field. As students get older, they often have more background and experience—some good and maybe some not so good—with doctors and medical facilities. The bag represents a tool that provides an opening for a discussion of roles and responsibilities of familiar community helpers. It also invites discussion of health and fitness, which are all topics that can make for great narrative or information writing pieces, among others.

Some potential realia for inside the doctor's bag include:

- healthy and/or unhealthy snacks/foods
- doctor's tools
- eyeglasses
- sunscreen
- bandages
- gauze

- sling or wrist brace
- false teeth
- medicine bottle
- hearing aids
- antiseptic

A Sports Bag

Students will likely be sitting on the floor in wild anticipation as you slowly pull items from your sports bag that you intend to use for motivation. A sports bag is accessible, and many students may use one to haul their equipment to and from school and home. As early as preschool, students may play T-ball, soccer, or basketball, or be involved with dance, music, gymnastics, horseback riding, etc. The following are suggestions for realia to include in a sports bag and can be used to support mini-lessons on personal narrative, explanatory writing (rules of games), and even sequencing (how to play):

- sports balls
- trading cards
- hockey stick
- athletic shoes
- ballet shoes

- skateboard
- ski/snowboard gear
- gymnastics grips
- bow and arrow

- softball glove
- swim cap
- ice skates
- board games

As you can see from the above examples, when you begin a lesson with interesting and engaging realia, building morale is an easy goal to attain. Creating your plethora of ideas will generate a whole host of ideas from students. Using objects to model passion and enthusiasm for the world around them will make a difference for students who might struggle to develop their own ideas.

Peter Johnson defines the "leading edge" as the place at which a student reaches a bit beyond what he or she already knows or can do (Johnson 2004, 13). The role of a writing coach is to move students to their "leading edge" behavior by starting lessons with simple, familiar items that allow students to dig into their own lives and experiences and then translate those ideas onto the page.

Conclusion

In our work, we have found that gender choices for writing topics parallel the results of research studies on gender choices and motivation for reading (Coles and Hall 2002). For example, in our experience boys seem more motivated by reading and writing about "gross things," science, science fiction, technical manuals, graphic and visual manuals, thrillers, sports biographies, and comics. This is just one example of how student interests can't be ignored. To instill a love of literacy learning and motivate writers, we must build a classroom that supports all learners and become an advocate for adjusting choices. Students will be engaged if they're writing about something of importance to them. Teach the motivated! Support and develop the unmotivated! As you build your "three-legged stool" for successful implementation of Writer's Workshop, remember that the legs need to be attached. By securing your legs to a solid foundation of motivation and choice, you will be setting the example of appropriateness and building an incredible connection to your students.

Whole-Group Instruction

Components of Effective Whole-Group Writing Instruction

Writer's Workshop includes three foundational components: instructing, writing/conferring, and sharing. Each component plays a valuable role in the teaching process and creates a predictable nature to writing instruction. Although the focus of instruction, topics, and genres of writing may change, students are empowered by knowing they will receive explicit modeling, opportunities for discussions, time to practice writing skills, and time for sharing every day. Students who are comfortable in a predictable environment can be more focused on learning and more productive.

With the ever-increasing academic diversity in today's classroom, whole-group, small-group, and individual writing instruction provides students with learning opportunities tailored to meet their individual needs. Each of the Writer's Workshop components lends itself to one or more of these groupings.

Figure 3.1 Components of Writer's Workshop

Component	Grouping Practice(s)	Instruction/Action	Suggested Time*
Instructing	Whole Group	Explicit Instructing Modeling Demonstrating Discussing	5–15 Minutes
Writing and Conferring	Small Group Partners Individual	Explicit Instructing Demonstrating Conferring Writing/Illustrating	15–30 Minutes
Sharing	Whole Group Small Group Partners	Reflecting Supporting Critiquing Celebrating	5–15 Minutes

*These times should reflect time of year, grade level, developmental of writing levels of students, and mini-lesson.

Whole-group instruction is perhaps the most traditional form of teaching. When used properly, it can be both efficient and effective during Writer's Workshop to share the same skills and subject matter with the entire class. Whole-group instruction includes the following benefits:

- All students are exposed to the same curriculum.

- Students gain a sense of belonging and feel part of the classroom community.

- Students do not have to worry about being labeled based on readiness level.

- Students benefit from learning from each other and hearing others' opinions and understandings.

In this chapter, you will find five strategies for effective whole-group instruction that serve as the umbrella over small-group instruction and individual or group conferring as well:

- Design SMART whole-group instruction (including sample lessons for grades K–8)

- Write and talk like a writer

- Engage students in whole-group instruction through talking

- Engage students in whole-group instruction through movement (including sample lessons for grades K–8)

- Be a writer!

Strategy 1: Design SMART Whole-Group Instruction

The relationship between whole-group instruction and the "Instructing" component of Writer's Workshop lies in the writing mini-lesson. Although "mini" in length, the content is carefully selected to capture and inform students at the time, but also "contain opportunities for deeper and longer thought over time" (Angelillo 2008, 40). Typically a short, explicit lesson (5–15 min.) that focuses on a specific writing skill or author's craft, the mini-lesson serves like super glue that holds writing instruction together. Without this explicit teaching, the writing time looks more like journaling—free writing with little direction from the teacher through the writing process. It is through whole-group mini-lessons that teachers raise a concern, explore an issue, model a technique, reinforce a writing strategy, and provide opportunities for "writerly conversations" with their students (Calkins 1994, 193).

Make the most of whole-group instruction by teaching SMART: **S**park curiosity and interest, **M**odel writing skills and strategies, **A**ctively engage students, w**R**ite to become better writers, and **T**alk writer to writer.

- **Spark the curiosity and interest of students by making connections and by clearly stating what students will learn.** Connections are related to ongoing student work and may be presented through a piece of literature, a newspaper article, a manipulative, a sample of student writing, or a previously taught mini-lesson/series of lessons. Be explicit when stating the mini-lesson focus. Tell students what they will learn, not just what they will do. For example, instead of saying, "Today we will find interesting language in books by author Jane Yolen "try saying, "Today, I will teach you how author Jane Yolen uses alliteration to add imagery to her writing."

- **Model writing skills and strategies to provide students with a repertoire of tools they can draw upon to improve their writing.** Most often modeling is presented in the form of a demonstration where the teacher thinks aloud during a step-by-step process. Modeling is not just talking about how something is done and/or showing students a sample of a finished product. It is teacher talk about the mental process that occurs during the writing that specifically identifies the important details, the skills, or strategies that students need. Here is an example for thinking aloud during the revision process. "As we read this story about my school day together, I'm thinking I have left out a few details about what happened. I know one way to add details to my story is to ask questions. First, I will read this sentence (*teacher reads sentence aloud*), then I can ask *when*—When did I go to the library? It was after lunch, so I can add an insertion mark, a caret, and add the words, 'after lunch.' Next, I will ask the question, *where?*, etc. This may seem rudimentary. However, all writers, regardless of age, need to hear a writer's thought process and develop an understanding of how and why certain choices are made. Besides demonstration, modeling may take the form of an inquiry lesson or guided practice.

- **Actively engage students to not only hold their interest and keep them on task, but also to create opportunities to discuss, practice, process, and retain writing information.** Engaging students might be as simple as quick choral responses; partner responses like Turn and Talk or Think-Pair-Share; physical responses like Thumbs Up, Thumbs Down or response cards; or allowing students to try out a new technique in their writing immediately after a quick demonstration. Consider the ancient Chinese proverb, "Tell me, I forget. Show me, I remember. Involve me, I understand." Active engagement can lead students to deeper thinking, problem solving, and the confidence to complete a writing task. For example, read a simple sentence aloud and ask students to turn to a partner or group of four to come up with details that would make the sentence more complex and engaging.

- **wRite to become better writers.** There is no argument that to improve our skills as a runner, a cook, a driver, etc., we must devote time for consistent practice. We commit to that time because we give value to the new endeavor. The same holds true with developing writers. Providing a consistent time for writing practice strengthens students' writing "muscles" and stamina as they develop an awareness of the value writing has in their everyday lives. Each time we write for and with our students, we too are becoming better writers and teachers of writing. As we share the process of working through a writing draft—writing, rereading, ruminating, revising, editing—students develop an awareness of the struggle and commitment involved in the writing process. It is through you that they recognize the value of writing practice and how determination and perseverance produces progress as writers.

- **Talk writer to writer.** It is important to use the language of writing when thinking aloud, talking about, and working on written pieces alongside your students. It is the vocabulary—words like draft, revise, audience, ideas, voice, alliteration—that creates a classroom of students who begin to see themselves and their classmates as authors of important work. Building a community of writers is valuable in the continued writing development of students. Donald Graves states, "It is a learner's perception of who they are and what they can do that has the greatest effect on what they learn" (Allen 2009, 31). Teachers talk writer to writer in the mini-lesson:

  - **before modeling:** making connections, sparking ideas, and creating curiosity

  - **during modeling:** using the writing vocabulary during explicit instruction of writing concepts and engaging students in their own writer-to-writer conversations

  - **after modeling:** to restate the mini-lesson focus and encourage students to apply their new learning into their current writing or add it to their writing toolbox to use in the future.

In addition to teaching SMART, the framework of the mini-lesson is as important as the predictability and consistency of the instruction. Over time, we have developed a lesson framework that supports SMART instruction:

- Think About Writing

- Teach

- Engage

- Apply

- Write/Confer

- Spotlight Strategy

- Share

Time to Teach

Think About Writing

"Writers, we have been working on..."

The mini-lesson begins with an introduction that connects the lesson topic to a previously taught mini-lesson, to authors as mentors, and/or to literacy instruction. This part of the lesson might include revisiting anchor charts, sharing snippets of mentor texts, using realia to pique student interest, or examining a piece of informational text to identify text structure. It reminds students that writing is not an isolated subject, but interrelates in their literacy world, as well as in the overall curriculum.

Teach

"Today writers, I will show you how to...". or "Today writers, we will work together to...."

The intention of the mini-lesson is clearly stated at the beginning of this portion of the lesson. It is here that the step-by-step focus skill or strategy we want our students to attempt in their writing is demonstrated. Teachers can use their own writing, show how an author developed the teaching point, or consider using a student's work for the demonstration. Demonstrations serve as an instrumental part of scaffolding student writers as they develop their understanding of the writing process.

Engage

Scaffolding for writers continues in this part of the lesson by providing a time for short, focused practice of the strategy they might apply in their work. Asking students to "Turn and Talk" or "Stand up, Partner Up," quickly allows opportunities for practice. Often this involves an "oral rehearsal" in which students form a partnership to discuss and practice the skill, while the teacher listens in, providing praise and supportive suggestions.

Apply

"Writers, always think about how important it is to...."

This is the final phase of the actual mini-lesson, before students move off to begin their important writing work. The intent here is to echo the mini-lesson concept across the lesson. The key instructional focus is, again, explicitly stated and writers are encouraged to practice the strategy/skill in their current writing or add it to their writing goals list to be used in future writing. When done well, students are motivated, enthusiastic, and focused on attempting new ideas in their writing.

Write/Confer

This should be the longest period of time during Writer's Workshop, but sadly often is shortened by lengthy mini-lessons. Writers become better writers by writing, practicing the strategies, skills, and craft of writing. Teachers are responsible for providing that valuable time, as well as scaffolding writers through guiding and conferring during this writing time. Writing conferences can take the form of one-to-one, small group, table conferences, etc. The specific format is less important than just taking the time to talk writer to writer in conversations that will help students become better writers. (Additional information on conferences may be found in Chapter 4.)

Spotlight Strategy

"Spotlighting" is a quick opportunity to give affirmation for correctly demonstrating a writing skill or specific tasks. During the writing and conferring phase, students are asked for their attention: "Writers, may I have your eyes and attention?" A quick comment is given that both recognizes and validates the selected writer's work, such as: "Writers, listen to the way Miguel used alliteration in this sentence to give detail and catch the reader's attention. Exceptional writing work!" Students recognize Miguel for his work and then move back into their writing practice, while the teacher continues with writing conferences. Once routines are established, this takes little effort, yet provides a positive example of good writing and encourages other students to risk trying new strategies and crafts in their own writing.

Share

Sharing is an essential element of Writer's Workshop that is also the most frequently omitted due to lack of time. Why do we write? We write to communicate, to explain, to question. We also write so that someone will hear our voice and read our message. Providing opportunities to share gives students credibility and recognition as writers. Take the time to share!

The following are potential mini-lesson topics arranged by grade range. This is not an exhaustive list, but is something to get you started.

Sample Mini-Lesson Topics Grades K–2

Management

- Developing routines of Writer's Workshop
- Using the writing folder
- Talking with partners

Print Concepts (K–1)

- Distinguishing between letters, words, and sentences
- Using spaces in writing
- Knowing where to begin writing, moving left to right, return sweep

Ideas

- Finding a topic in YOU
- Using books/pictures to generate topics
- Sticking to the topic

Organization

- Using telling, sketching, and writing to organize writing
- Using who, what, when, where, why, and how questions to develop writing
- Creating a beginning, middle, and end

Voice

- Matching voice to character and/or event
- Adding interjections to dialogue

Sentence Fluency

- Building sentences with a naming part (subject) and an action part (predicate)
- Using simple and compound sentences
- Using linking words to show time order

Word Choice

- Using adjectives to "show"
- Using action words
- Adding details with prepositional phrases

Conventions

- Using capitals letters for "I" and proper names
- Adding punctuation (period, question mark, explanation point, quotation marks)
- Editing for spelling of high-frequency words, color words, number words, etc.

Sample Mini-Lesson Topics Grades 3–5

Management

- Using a writer's notebook
- Writing like a writer: five-step writing process/traits of quality writing
- Developing procedures for teacher and peer conferring

Ideas

- Generating writing topics based on people, places, things, and you
- Narrowing the topic
- Zooming in to find details

Organization

- Developing powerful paragraphs
- Writing narratives such as poems and stories
- Writing opinion compositions
- Writing expository compositions
- Including beginning hooks

Voice

- Expressing mood through details
- Writing to an audience

Sentence Fluency

- Creating varied sentence lengths using questions
- Varying sentence beginnings
- Using compound/complex sentences
- Using different sentence types: declarative, interrogative, imperative, and exclamatory

Word Choice

- Adding temporal words and phrases to signal event order
- Using specific vocabulary
- Using similes, metaphors, and idioms

Conventions

- Using resources to support writing
- Editing for capitalization, grammar, punctuation, and spelling
- Using commas correctly

Sample Mini-Lesson Topics Grades 6–8

Management

- Responsibilities during Writer's Workshop
- Developing routines for sharing writing

Ideas

- Developing a Top 10 topics list
- Using mentor texts to develop ideas
- Using questioning to narrow the topic

Organization

- Organizing writing through text structure
- Creating poetry through form (e.g., diamante, haiku, limerick, free verse)
- Developing a newspaper article

Voice

- Sharing character feelings and traits in writing
- Using R.A.F.T. (Role/Audience/Format/Topic)

Time to Teach

Sentence Fluency

- Using a variety of sentence structures to expand and imbed details (compound subjects/verbs, prepositional phrases, semicolons)
- Building complex sentences with independent/dependent clauses
- Using simple, compound, complex, and compound-complex sentence structures

Word Choice

- Using figures of speech in writing (metaphors, personification, similes, hyperboles, alliteration)
- Creating topic-specific vocabulary using word webs
- Understanding denotation and connotation of words

Conventions

- Using commas, dashes, and parentheses for emphasis and clarity in writing
- Writing with subjective, objective, and possessive pronouns
- Editing with editing marks

Sample Lessons

The following sample lessons are examples of implementing SMART whole-group instruction. A template is also provided for you to use to create your own mini-lessons.

- Sentence Trees
- Let's Write a S.T.O.R.Y.!
- I Know My Audience
- Varying Sentence Types
- Types of Conflict Themes in Literature
- Comparing Historical Documents

Mini-Lesson Template

Standard

Materials

-
-
-
-
-

Mentor Texts

-
-
-
-
-
-

Procedures

Think About Writing

Teach

Engage

Apply

Spotlight Strategy

Write/Conference

Share

Sentence Trees
(Grades K–2)

Procedures

Think About Writing

1. Explain to students that writers understand how to use words to create sentences with two basic parts: a subject (the naming part) and a predicate (the action part).

Teach

2. Tell students, "Today writers, we will use a tool to help us write sentences about our topic with two parts: the subject and the predicate."

3. Select a topic for your example. Use the Sentence Trees Examples to model and guide your thinking. Consider the age and writing developmental level of your students. The tree can be extended to include adjectives, prepositional phrases, adverbs, etc.

Engage

4. After modeling, think of another topic and have students turn and talk with a partner about possible responses to complete sentence boxes. (This provides a scaffolded practice for students before they move off to work on their own writing piece.)

Apply

5. Tell students, "Writers, always think about how important it is to create sentences with two parts: a subject (the naming part) and a predicate (the action part)." Tell students to look at their writing piece for today. Ask them to check their sentences to make sure each includes both a subject and a predicate.

Sentence Trees *(cont.)*

Write/Conference

6. Provide time for students to complete their own sentence boxes. Check for understanding and move among students to confer and support. If early in the year, consider stopping in on several students for a brief "chat" or consider table conferences. Make note of student performance in a conference log.

Spotlight Strategy

7. Spotlight a student for diligent work and interesting sentences. For example, "Amazing work is happening at Table 4. Antonio has completed his sentence boxes and is already moving on to writing his sentences into a small book. I'm amazed at all your hard work."

Share

8. Provide two to three minutes for students to share their sentence boxes with a partner. Then, select a few students to share with the whole group.

Note: In future lessons, you might model how to move the sentence tree words into written texts (e.g., sentences or paragraphs) or discuss use of pronouns, such as it, he, she, etc., to vary sentence beginnings.

Sentence Trees Examples

Simple Sentence

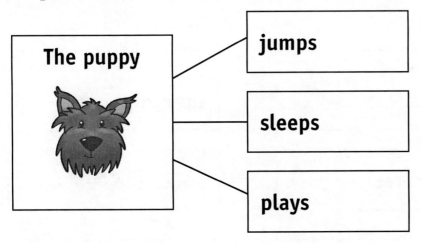

| jumps |
| sleeps |
| plays |

Adding Prepositional Phrases

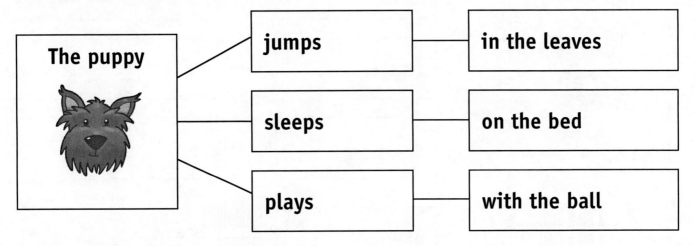

jumps	in the leaves
sleeps	on the bed
plays	with the ball

Adding Adjectives/Describing Words

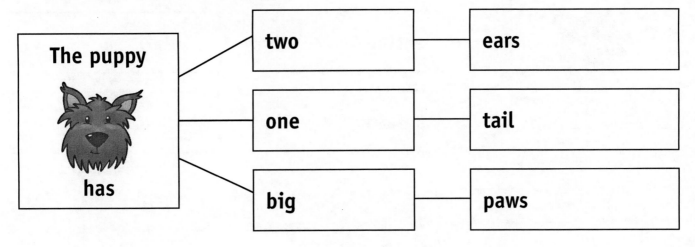

two	ears
one	tail
big	paws

Sentence Trees Examples *(cont.)*

Generating More Text

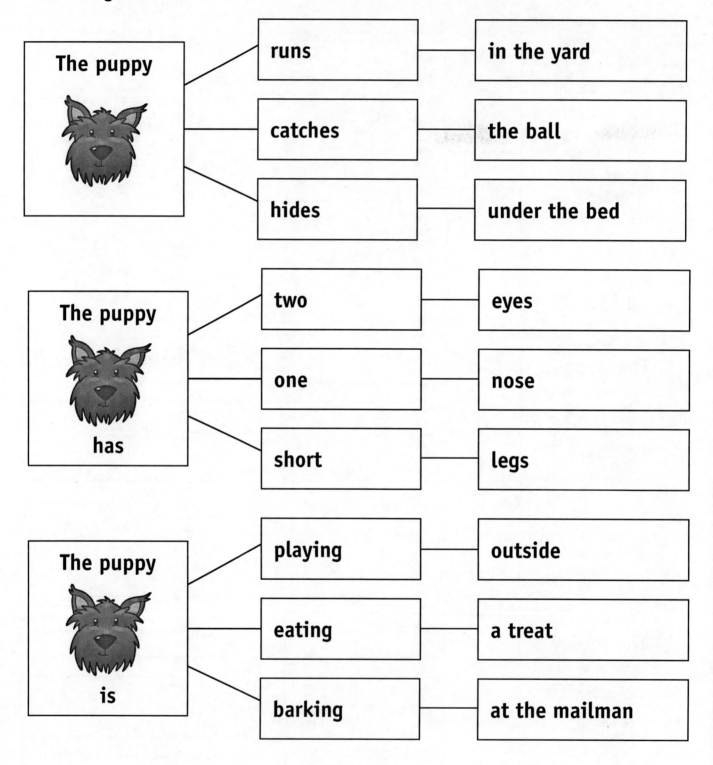

The puppy

runs	in the yard
catches	the ball
hides	under the bed

The puppy ... has

two	eyes
one	nose
short	legs

The puppy ... is

playing	outside
eating	a treat
barking	at the mailman

Let's Write a S.T.O.R.Y.!
(Grades K–2)

Standard

Write narratives in which they recount an event or short sequence of events, include details to describe actions, thoughts, and feelings, use temporal words to signal event order, and provide a sense of closure.

Materials

- *S.T.O.R.Y. Graphic Organizer* (page 67)

Mentor Texts

- Any favorite narrative text

Procedures

Think About Writing

1. Explain to students that writers sometimes use a tool to help them organize their thinking. This helps them stay on track and focused on their story.

Teach

2. Tell students, "Today writers, we will use a tool to help us organize a small moment story."

3. Write the acronym S.T.O.R.Y. on a chart, or display the *S.T.O.R.Y. Graphic Organizer* for students to view.

4. Explain to students that today our small moment story will focus on something that happened to them that maybe did not work out as planned.

5. Use a personal example to complete the S.T.O.R.Y. organizer. For younger writers, you may also choose to sketch and label. Be sure to think aloud throughout the process.

Engage

6. Ask students to turn and talk with a partner about their small moment story. Remind them to use the acronym S.T.O.R.Y. when sharing their ideas with their partner.

Apply

7. Tell students, "Writers, always think about how important it is to organize your thinking before you begin your writing. Select one of your small moment stories or begin a new story focus on our new S.T.O.R.Y. tool to help guide your thinking and writing.

Note: You may have your students move this writing into a writing format, or save it in their folder to extend and publish at a later date.

Let's Write a S.T.O.R.Y.! *(cont.)*

Write/Conference

8. Distribute copies of the *S.T.O.R.Y. Graphic Organizer* to students. Provide time for them to complete their organizers.

9. Check for understanding and move among students to confer and support. Take time to observe and note students readily attempting the task. Those students demonstrating difficulty may be pulled into a small-group conference to provide additional support. Record observations in a conference log.

Spotlight Strategy

10. Choose one or two students from the class that are successfully working on their *S.T.O.R.Y. Graphic Organizer* and spotlight their work. Remember to recognize different developmental levels of writing. Some students may be illustrating, while others are writing lists.

Share

11. Because students orally shared their stories with their writing partner earlier in the lesson, assign or have students find a new partner to share their writing with today. Remind them to use the organizer to retell each part of the story.

Name _____

Date _____

S.T.O.R.Y. Graphic Organizer

S Setting	T Talking Characters	O Opening and Oops!	R Resolve	Y Yes! Problem Solved!
Where and when does the story take place?	Who is in the story?	How does this story begin and what happens?	What steps do your characters take to solve the problem?	How does everything turn out?

I Know My Audience
(Grades 3–5)

Standard

Write routinely over extended time frames for a range of audiences.

Materials

• *I Know My Audience* (page 70)

Mentor Texts

• Any text that models voice

Procedures

Think About Writing

1. Remind students that once we have determined a specific topic, it is important to determine the audience for our writing. We want to consider who will be reading the writing or who we want to inform or persuade with our writing.

Teach

2. Tell students "Today we will learn to use a resource to help us determine the voice we need to use for our writing audience. Knowing our writing audience helps us decide what content to include and how to organize our ideas."

3. Along with students, brainstorm a list of people they might consider as their audience (e.g., principal, parents, classmates, young children, president of a company, relative, senator, congressman, best friend, military personnel, or celebrity).

4. Discuss the type of "voice" that might be used with some of the examples listed and how they might differ. Consider which might be more formal/informal? Personal/impersonal?

5. Select a topic and model how to use the *I Know My Audience* resource sheet to determine the voice, format, and type of content to include in the writing.

Engage

6. Provide students with sample topics (e.g., donations for a community food pantry or healthier lunch choices) and distribute a copy of *I Know My Audience* to each student.

7. Using the *I Know My Audience* resource sheet, have students work in a group to determine the writing options for their audience.

I Know My Audience *(cont.)*

Apply

8. "Writers, always think about how important it is to be aware of your intended audience and the purpose of your writing." Remind students to use their resource sheet as they develop their writing pieces and ask themselves, "Who am I writing to today?"

Write/Conference

9. Provide time for students to write their stories. Check for understanding and move among students to confer and support. Take time to observe and note students readily attempting the task. Those students demonstrating difficulty may be pulled into a small-group conference to provide additional support. Record observations in a conference log.

Spotlight Strategy

10. As you observe and confer with students, be mindful of a few students who are writing to their audience. Select one of those students to spotlight. For example, "Writers, may I have your eyes and attention? Sophia and I were talking about her writing. I could tell right away she was writing about something she cares a lot about: cooking. I also knew her audience right away: students and kids her age. She was using words and content appropriate for them. Nicely done."

Share

11. Have students share a portion of their writing with their partners. Challenge partners to determine the audience of the writing. Remind students to use the *I Know My Audience* resource. Have students share a portion of their writing with their partners. Challenge partners to determine the audience of the writing. Remind students to use the *I Know My Audience* resource sheet as a reference.

I Know My Audience

Who is the audience?

- young child/children?
- classmates?
- parents?
- principal?
- celebrity
- males/females?
- senator/congressman?
- mayor?
- CEO?
- PTA?

Why is my audience reading my writing?

- to be informed?
- to be convinced?
- to be entertained?

What is the background of my audience?

- How knowledgeable is my audience about the topic? Novice? Advanced?
- Should I use "jargon" or acronyms in my writing?
- Will my audience understand technical terms?
- What do I have in common with my audience?
- What does my audience need to know, and why do they need to know it?
- What do I want my audience to do, think, or feel?

What format is best for my audience?

- personal narrative?
- persuasive essay?
- informational report?
- brochure?
- newspaper/magazine article?
- newsletter?
- letter?
- email?
- memo?
- poem?
- editorial?
- brochure?

Varying Sentence Types
(Grades 3–5)

Standard

Write narratives to develop real or imagined experiences or events using effective techniques.

Materials

- chart paper
- paragraph/text to model revisions

Mentor Texts

- Any text that uses interrogative sentences

Procedures

Think About Writing

1. Remind students that authors use different sentence types to add variety to their writing. Many sentences we write are declarative. To add some real interest to our writing, we can add an occasional interrogative sentence—a question.

2. You may wish to share a passage or two from a mentor text to further clarify.

Teach

3. Tell students "Today we will discuss ways we might add interrogative sentences to add interest to our writing."

4. Draw an outline of a large question mark on a chart (to be displayed for student resource).

5. With students, brainstorm a list of words that might begin an interrogative sentence (e.g., who, what, where, when, was, did, will, does, should, would, could, why, is, which, have, whose).

6. Use a sample paragraph/text and model revision by adding an interrogative sentence that adds interest to the writing. Discuss how interrogative sentences might demonstrate a character's thinking in fiction writing (Should I wait for Jose to return or go back home?), but prompt curiosity in nonfiction writing (Why do Dachshund puppies have such large front paws?).

Engage

7. Have students practice changing declarative sentences into questions. Provide students with a sample sentence and have them turn and talk to share possible responses.

8. Remind students to use the question words from the chart to help create their responses.

Varying Sentence Types *(cont.)*

Apply

9. "Writers, always think about how important it is to use different types of sentences in your writing to create variety and interest." Tell writers to look at their current writing and notice the types of sentences. Challenge students to explore their writing for one or two places they might revise by adding an interrogative sentence.

Write/Conference

10. Provide time for students to write. From observations during student engagement activities, select students who may need additional support. Guide students to reread their writing and locate a place to revise with an interrogative sentence.

Spotlight Strategy

11. Move about the room between conferences and spotlight students who have successfully added an interrogative sentence to their writing. Be mindful that the revision must have a purpose, not just to add a question at any point in the text. This should only take a minute or two of time.

Share

12. Have students meet in whole-group sharing today. Ask for volunteers to share a section of their writing that used the mini-lesson strategy. To extend this activity, maybe even to the next day, have students meet in pairs. They should work together to reread their writing and find a place an additional interrogative sentence (or two) may add interest to their writing.

Types of Conflict Themes in Literature
(Grades 6–8)

Standard

Use narrative techniques, such as dialogue, to develop experiences, events, and/or characters

Materials

- *Conflict Themes for Famous Literature and Film* (page 75)

Mentor Texts

- any selected text from *Conflict Themes for Famous Literature and Film*

Procedures

Think About Writing

1. Introduce students to five conflict themes in literature:
   - Man vs. Self
   - Man vs. Man/Society
   - Man vs. Nature
   - Man vs. Supernatural
   - Man vs. Technology

2. Introduce students to the *Conflict Themes for Famous Literature and Film* chart that shows examples of these types of conflict in literature and film. Distribute a copy of this chart to students to insert in their writer's notebook.

   Note: This chart may be adapted to match students' experiences, classroom libraries, local curriculum, etc.

Teach

3. Tell students, "Today we will use ideas from themes of conflict to create a cartoon with simple illustrations and captions from a piece of literature or film that shows a theme of conflict. First, let's make sure we understand each conflict category."

4. Have students brainstorm from the list above and work in triads to choose one example of a type of conflict. Then, have students work together to explain how the example fits the theme. Use *Frankenstein* as an example of Man vs. Technology.

Engage

5. Have students turn and talk with their triad group to discuss the possible best choice for a short cartoon they want to create based on the literature, film, or TV examples they selected. Remind students to use the chart to help create their responses. They may add their own literature, film, or TV selection to the chart.

Types of Conflict Themes
in Literature *(cont.)*

Apply

6. Say, "Writers, always think about how important it is to plan before beginning to write." Have students begin to sketch out a simple storyboard with three to seven cartoon boxes to describe their conflict.

   • What was the problem?

   • Who or what is in conflict?

   • What action took place first, then, next, and last?

   • How was the conflict resolved?

Write/Conference

7. Send triads off to complete their storyboard and begin drawing and writing their cartoon.

Spotlight

8. Share examples from triads whose work may be good examples for the other students or examples of different types of conflict.

Share

9. Have each triad briefly report and receive constructive feedback on their progress.

Conflict Themes for Famous Literature and Film

Man versus Self

Hamlet by William Shakespeare

Sam, Bangs, and Moonshine by Evaline Ness

Chrysanthemum by Kevin Henkes

Man versus Man/Society

The Cask of Amontillado by Edgar Allan Poe

The Giver by Lois Lowry

The Wizard of Oz starring Judy Garland

The Adventures of Tom Sawyer by Mark Twain

Charlotte's Web by E. B. White

Man versus Nature

The Odyssey by Homer

The Great Fire by Jim Murphy

The Old Man and the Sea by Ernest Hemingway

Robinson Crusoe by Daniel Defoe

Man versus Supernatural

A Christmas Carol by Charles Dickens

The Odyssey by Homer

Man versus Technology

Frankenstein by Mary Shelley (or a movie/literary adaptation)

The Terminator starring Arnold Schwarzenegger

The Matrix starring Keanu Reeves

Comparing Historical Documents
(Grades 6-8)

Standard

Organize ideas, concepts, and information, using strategies such as comparison/contrast, including formatting, graphics, and multimedia when useful to aiding comprehension

Materials

- any two historical documents
- books, articles, and other resources to provide historical background and information about the selected historical documents

Mentor Texts

- any texts to model compare and contrast text structure

Procedures

Think About Writing

1. Explain to students that this lesson will help prepare them for writing a piece comparing and contrasting primary historical documents.

2. Having previously introduced students to two documents being studied in relation to a period of history, reread all or a selection of those documents aloud.

3. Display the information below for students. It shows four key elements to consider when analyzing primary source documents.

   - point of view (What point of view is being communicated?)

   - purpose (Why was the document created?)

   - audience (Who was the document created for?)

   - historical context (When, where, and how was the document used?)

Teach

4. Tell students, "This week (or over the next few weeks) we will compare and contrast two historical documents (from your unit of study)."

5. Have students study and take notes on each document separately. Dig deeply into one document before digging deeply into the other, or divide students into two document groups having each group choose a document.

6. Say, "I will show you how to dig deeper into both historical documents by using four organizing questions to structure an in-depth investigation."

Engage

7. Solicit input from students regarding each of the questions (from step 3). After reading each question, have students turn and talk in groups of four to discuss possible responses and/or available resources for digging deeper.

Comparing Historical Documents *(cont.)*

Apply

8. Say, "Writers, always think about how important it is to dig more deeply into a historical document before writing a compare and contrast opinion piece. Decide what resources you can use to investigate the questions more thoroughly. Divide a sheet or sheets of paper into four sections and take notes based on your discussion of each of the four investigatory digging-deeper questions. Cite your resources."

Write/Conference

9. Send groups off to dig more deeply using the available resources. Give them the option to work in groups of four or independently. When students are ready, have them do a summary of their notes and report what new information they learned about the document.

Spotlight

10. Choose several examples of new information about the document that is being studied and what source the student used. Remind students to list their sources.

Share

11. Share summary reports of new information that was learned and where the students found the new information. Plan a follow-up mini-lesson for modeling proper formats for listing sources of reference citations.

Chapter 3

Strategy 2: Write and Talk Like a Writer

Writing can be challenging and even frustrating for writers of any age. By providing a process and a language that becomes increasingly familiar during instructional time and in conversations with peers, students, and even parents, we become more confident in the teaching of writing and our students become capable, accomplished writers.

Teach the Five-Step Writing Process

Often when faced with a writing assignment, many adults as well as students see the writing as a huge task and become overwhelmed. To support our writers, we share the steps of the writing process used by most authors, breaking the assignment into more manageable pieces. The writing then becomes less frustrating and more productive as the writer completes each step:

1. Prewriting

2. Drafting

3. Revising

4. Editing

5. Publishing

Figure 3.2 The Five-Step Writing Process

Prewriting **Planning It!**	Prewriting is the preliminary work used to explore a topic and develop a plan before the actual writing of the draft. Sharing a variety of techniques with students allows them to develop an understanding of which technique best suits their thinking and writing styles. Prewriting might include the following: • brainstorming • note taking • outlining • free writing • interviewing • storyboarding • clustering • questioning
Drafting **Writing It!**	Drafting refers to the process of writing the ideas into a logical sequence while considering your audience and purpose for writing. Encourage students to refer back to a prewriting plan, but also recognize while drafting that the prewriting plan may need to be adjusted to include new thinking. This early writing is sometimes called the "rough" draft because the main goal is to write, not develop a perfect paper.

Time to Teach

Revising **Messing It Up!**	To revise means to reconsider or "rework" your writing, often more than once. Writers look critically at their writing to ensure they have: • focused ideas and supportive details/evidence • logical organization and transitions • clear purpose and audience • appropriate voice • precise vocabulary • fluid and rhythmic flow of sentences

Editing **Fixing It!**	Editing involves checking the writing for accuracy and typically includes reviewing grammar, spelling, punctuation, and capitalization. During editing, writers may also look at paragraphing, citations, and document formatting of the writing. Most writers edit as they write, and sometimes write as they edit. It is a process that continues throughout the writing process that fixes up all the little errors, including dotting the "i's" and crossing the "t's."

Publishing **Sharing It!**	Writers write to be read, to communicate. Publishing is preparing a visually appealing final manuscript for someone to read, even if the reader is yourself, a teacher, a parent, or perhaps for a display, contest, or newsletter. During publishing, writers consider neatness, handwriting, word-processing skills, illustrations, text features, etc. It is through publishing that students begin to truly value the writing process and see themselves growing from a "writer" into an "author."

The following are resources to use with students to support their understanding of the writing process. Students can use these as checklists when self-evaluating their work.

The Writing Process

Prewrite

☐ I can listen and talk to others to get ideas.

☐ I can draw and label a picture.

☐ I can make a list or web to plan my ideas.

Draft

☐ I can use my list or web to guide my thinking.

☐ I can write my ideas in order.

Revise

☐ I can add describing words and verbs.

☐ I can take out ideas not about my topic.

☐ I can reread and check the order of my writing.

Edit

☐ I can use correct grammar.

☐ I can check my punctuation.

☐ I can check my spelling.

Publish

☐ I can write neatly so my work is easy to read.

☐ I can add a title page and drawings.

☐ I can share my writing with others.

The Writing Process

Prewriting: Brainstorming and Organizing Your Topic

☐ What do you want to write about? What do you want to say?

☐ Discuss ideas with a classmate to brainstorm and narrow your topic.

☐ Consider audience and the format for your writing project.

☐ Organize your thinking. Try creating a timeline, outline, list, web, illustration, or graphic organizer.

Drafting: Writing Your Thoughts on Paper

☐ Write your ideas down to create a rough draft.

☐ Expand your ideas using sentences and paragraphs based on the information you gathered during prewriting.

☐ Write on every other line to leave room for revision and editing.

☐ Write now and circle hard words. Fix spelling and punctuation later.

Revising: Taking a Second Look

☐ Add "show me" descriptive words and details to your writing.

☐ Replace or remove worn-out, boring, and repetitive words.

☐ Move sentences and paragraphs to refine the order and clarify meaning.

☐ Reread and refine the beginning and ending.

Editing: Reviewing and Correcting

☐ Check for capitals at the beginning of a sentence, the word "I," and proper nouns.

☐ Check for correct grammar. Does it sound right?

☐ Check for periods and other punctuation.

☐ Check and correct your spelling.

Publishing: Adding Final Touches

☐ Decide how you will publish your writing and create a neat, polished copy.

☐ Create a title page.

☐ Add illustrations and visuals to your writing.

☐ Share your writing with others.

The Writing Process

Prewrite Getting Ready for Writing

- [ ] Determine the purpose and audience of your writing.
- [ ] Select and narrow your topic.
- [ ] Gather ideas and research.
- [ ] Use tools to organize your ideas

Draft Composing the First Copy

- [ ] Just focus on writing.
- [ ] Use notes and research from prewriting.
- [ ] Organize ideas and connect using transitions.
- [ ] Don't worry about mistakes. Edit later.

Revise Making Changes

- [ ] Add details and extend ideas.
- [ ] Remove ideas that are off topic.
- [ ] Move phrases and sentences to add variety.
- [ ] Substitute words that add interest, description, and variety.

Edit Correcting and Polishing

- [ ] Check spelling.
- [ ] Reread for grammatical mistakes.
- [ ] Search and correct capitalization.
- [ ] Polish all punctuation.
- [ ] Check three = you + partner + peer

Publish Presenting the Final Copy

- [ ] Choose a publishing format.
- [ ] Write or use technology to create published copy.
- [ ] Add a title page, illustrations, and visuals.
- [ ] Publish and share with an audience.

Introduce the Traits of Quality Writing

Just as we teach specific content vocabulary in mathematics so students understand what words like *product, sum,* and *addend* mean, we must also teach the language of quality writing. Sharing a common vocabulary for thinking and talking about writing creates an understanding of the qualities most readers and writers consider important in good writing. These traits give us the means to talk, reflect, and work like writers. In *Seeing with New Eyes* (2005), Bellamy shares seven writing traits most commonly recognized as the language of successful writers: ideas, organization, voice, word choice, sentence fluency, conventions, and presentation.

Figure 3.3 The Traits of Quality Writing

Ideas	Organization
Main Content and Details of the Writing	**Structure of the Writing**
• Identifying the topic • Narrowing the topic • Staying focused on the topic • Elaborating on the topic by choosing interesting, important, and informative details	• Developing the text structure; a logical and effective sequence • Hooking with a lead • Connecting with transitions • Applying varied pacing • Crafting an effective ending
Voice	**Word Choice**
Personality and Emotion of the Writing	**Specific and Purposeful Language**
• Being YOU on the page • Expressing sincere feeling • Communicating the purpose • Connecting with the reader • Sharing enthusiasm, point of view, and attitude about a topic	• Selecting specific verbs to "show" action • Choosing precise words • Using descriptive words • Selecting memorable words and phrases; figurative language • Avoiding word repetition
Sentence Fluency	**Conventions**
Rhythm and Flow of the Writing	**Mechanics of the Writing**
• Developing correct and complete sentences • Varying beginnings, lengths, structures, and types • Creating smooth natural cadence • Using creative phrasing to enhance rhythmic flow	• Using capitalization correctly • Using correct grammar • Punctuating correctly and to enhance meaning • Spelling correctly

Presentation

Appearance of the Writing

• Using appropriate handwriting or fonts

• Formatting appropriately for genre

• Adding text features that enhance meaning

The method by which the traits are introduced is not as important as the process. Methods might include anchor charts, songs, posters, or even picture books. The process of presenting the traits one at a time through brief mini-lessons helps students develop an understanding of the meaning, value, and role each trait plays in the writing. Once the traits have been introduced, they become the foundation of writing instruction. The trait language is used to connect each new skill to a trait. For example, "Today, we will be working on sentence fluency as we focus on different ways to begin our sentences."

Anchor Charts, Songs, and Posters

The purpose of an anchor chart is to "anchor" our thinking and that of our students about an essential topic. When students are part of the process, they refer to, talk about, and use the content for guidance. Develop an anchor chart for each of the traits, noting the definition, giving examples, and adding skills and strategies throughout the year. Notice how the content of charts 1, 2, and 3 below grow as students' writing develops.

Figure 3.4 Ideas Anchor Chart (Beginning of the Year)

Ideas

We write about the people, places, and things we love!

We share our ideas with a partner.
We sketch and label our ideas.

Figure 3.5 Ideas Anchor Chart (Mid-Year)

Ideas

We write about the people, places, and things we love!
We write about stories we read.
We write about our feelings.

We share our ideas with a partner.
We sketch and label our ideas.
We can narrow the topic.
We can add details.

Figure 3.6 Ideas Anchor Chart (End of the Year)

Ideas

We write about the people, places, and things we love!

We write about stories we read.

We write about our feelings.

We write to share our experiences.

We write to share our learning.

We write to give our opinion.

We share our ideas with a partner.

We sketch and label our ideas.

We can narrow the topic.

We can "zoom in" to add details.

We can write to "show, not tell" with details.

We bring our stories to life! (add dialogue; characters that move, walk, and talk)

Songs about the traits of writing can be found with a simple Internet search. We find singing and chanting helps students recall the foundational information of each trait. One of our examples follows:

Ideas Song

(Sung to the tune of *Row, Row, Row Your Boat*)

People, places, things you know,

Memories you hold dear.

Make a list to write about

Great ideas appear!

When introducing the traits of quality writing, we turn to our "trait team" posters, including:

- Ida Idea Creator
- Val and Van Voice
- Owen Organization Conductor
- Simon Sentence Builder
- Wally Word Choice Detective
- Callie Super Conventions Checker

Figure 3.7 is a sample poster of Wally Word Choice Detective, designed for grades 3–5. See Appendix D for a complete set of these posters.

Figure 3.7 Sample Traits Team Poster (Grades 3–5)

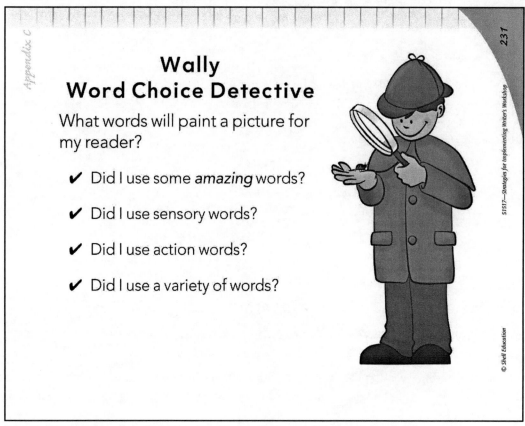

Printed with permission from Shell Education (Gentry, McNeel, and Wallace-Nesler 2012)

Picture Books

A favorite method of introducing the traits of quality writing to students is through the use of picture books. The short, engaging text works well for mini-lesson instruction and captures the attention of writers of any age. By sharing picture books that exemplify one or more traits, students become familiar with trait characteristics and how to include those skills in their own writing. A few of our favorite picture books include:

Ideas

- *Chrysanthemum* by Kevin Henkes
- *Fireflies!* by Julie Brinckloe
- *Grandfather's Journey* by Allen Say

Organization

- *Scaredy Squirrel* by Melanie Watt
- *Roller Coaster* by Marla Frazee
- *Smoky Night* by Eve Bunting

Voice

- *The Recess Queen* by Alexis O'Neill
- *Diary of a Worm/Spider* by Doreen Cronin
- *The Harmonica* by Tony Johnston

Sentence Fluency

- *Bedhead* by Margie Palatini
- *Owl Moon* by Jane Yolen
- *The Wall* by Eve Bunting

Word Choice

- *The Snowy Day* by Ezra Jack Keats
- *Chicken Sunday* by Patricia Polacco
- *Fox* by Margaret Wild

Conventions

- *Punctuation Takes a Vacation* by Robin Pulver
- *Click, Clack, Moo: Cows That Type* by Doreen Cronin
- *Twenty-Odd Ducks* by Lynne Truss

The complex task of writing becomes more manageable as both teachers and students develop an understanding of how the writing process and the traits of quality writing work in partnership. For example, during prewriting we are brainstorming, developing ideas, and thinking through the organizational structure best suited for our audience. Drafting makes way for developing those ideas through good word choice, focusing on the text structure and purpose of the writing. Revision gives us opportunities to add details that develop ideas, reorganize through adding and deleting text, create pace and mood by varying sentences, and refine our writing voice.

While revising refines our writing in a way that "sounds" good, the process of editing provides the opportunity to make the writing "look" good through focusing on the trait of conventions. Finally, when we move writing into the process of publishing, our focus moves to the trait of presentation where we polish the final piece for our audience.

Should we teach the writing process? Yes! Should we teach the traits of quality writing? Yes! But most importantly, we must show our students how the traits of quality writing serve as the focus to successfully completing the writing process.

Figure 3.8 The Partnership: Writing Process and Writing Traits

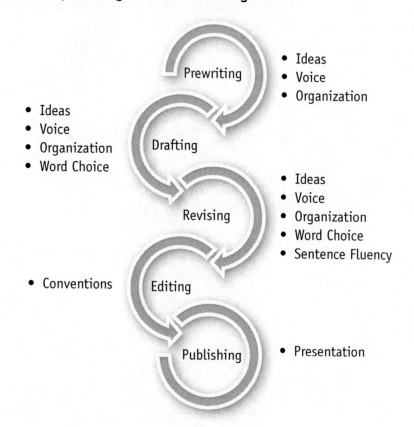

Time to Teach

Use Mentor Texts as a Model

A quick and efficient method for raising the bar for student writing is to expose students to a variety of internal story patterns and elements of writer's craft in children's literature. Seeing these examples in real text helps to stimulate and motivate young writers in an engaging way. Teachers can use picture books and read alouds with different story patterns to motivate writers. We have found that familiarity with various story structures and patterns enhances students' willingness to take risks, stretch themselves, and have fun being creative with writing. Students gain familiarity with specific text structures, enrich their vocabularies, and stretch themselves as writers using authors of children's literature as models to guide them (Cochrane 1984).

Just as predictable books make it easier for beginning readers to read, we found that introducing predictable story patterns through children's literature makes it easy and fun for kids to have success utilizing these models to create more elaborate stories or songs and verses that reflect emotion and writing fluency.

In *Reading, Writing and Caring* (1984), Orin Cochrane built on work by Bill Martin Jr. and Peggy Brogan to describe eight basic predictable story patterns authors use when writing stories. While some of the patterns are a bit simplistic for grades 6–8, using them during whole-group instruction builds confidence, motivation, engagement, and evokes creativity.

In the list below, each pattern is explained, and a list of mentor texts that demonstrate the pattern is provided. Choose one or more of the mentor texts to read aloud to students during whole-group instruction and discuss how the author uses the pattern to develop the story. After sharing the mentor text, try some of the following options:

- Brainstorm, with students, topics they could write about to follow the same pattern.
- Complete a whole-class writing practice using the text pattern. Have students give you ideas and write together on a piece of chart paper.
- Let students write in pairs to develop a particular text pattern. Model it first and then ask students to work together to practice.

Pattern #1: Repetition

In this text pattern, a word, phrase or sentence is repeated. Repetition is a useful reading skill for emergent readers and can also help older readers who need a more ambitious push in their writing. Repetitive patterns can motivate and inspire writers because they are easy to mimic based on a mentor text.

Most repetitive pattern literature, such as the samples provided, are low level for middle school but we have had great success using repetitive pattern literature with intermediate students who struggle with writing. We've had students who proclaim, "This is fun. Maybe I'll be a children's author when I grow up!"

Examples of Repetitive Patterns Literature

Grades K–2

- *A Great Attitude* by Sandi Hill
- *My Name is Alice* by Jane E. Bayer
- *Daddy, Daddy, Be There* by Candy Dawson Boyd
- *Does a Kangaroo Have a Mother, Too?* By Eric Carle
- *Fortunately* by Remy Charlip
- *My Five Senses* by Aliki
- *The Very Busy Spider* by Eric Carle
- *Whose Shoes?* by Stephen Swinburne

Grades 3–5

- *Daddy, Daddy, Be There* by Candy Dawson Boyd
- *Fortunately* by Remy Charlip
- *Imagine A Day* by Sarah L. Thomson
- *Mama, Do You Love Me?* By Barbara M. Joosse
- *Old Robert and the Sea-Silly Cats* by Barbara M. Joosse

Grades 6–8

- *Old Robert and the Sea-Silly Cats* by Barbara Joosse
- *Somewhere Today* by Bert Kitchen
- *The Grouchy Lady Bug* by Eric Carle

Pattern #2: Cumulative

Authors create this pattern by writing a word or phrase and then continually adding on a new word, phrase, or sentence to the text. The word, phrase, or sentence can be repeated, adding additional information. The pattern is a bit more complicated, yet musical, delightful to read, and a way to teach a different story structure. Writers can use specific words and phrases to move the pattern along.

Most cumulative pattern literature, such as the samples provided, are low level for middle school but we have had great success using cumulative pattern literature with intermediate students who struggle with writing. We have also had gifted writers who show amazing creativity emulating cumulative pattern literature.

Examples of Cumulative Literature

Grades K–2

- *A Giraffe and a Half* by Shel Silverstein
- *"Not Now!" Said the Cow* by Joanne Oppenheim
- *The Napping House* by Audrey Wood
- *The House that Jack Built* by Rodney Peppé
- *The Cake That Mack Ate* by Rose Robart
- *The Old Woman and Her Pig: An Appalachian Folktale* by Margaret Read Macdonald

Grades 3–5

- *Bringing the Rain to Kapiti Plain* by Verna Aardema
- *There Was an Old Lady Who Swallowed a Fly!* by Lucille Colandro
- *Over the Steamy Swamp* by Paul Geraghty
- *The Great Big Enormous Turnip* by Aleksei Tolstoi

Grades 6–8

- *The House that Jack Built* by Rodney Peppé
- *The Judge* by Harve Zemach

Pattern #3: Interlocking

An interlocking pattern is sometimes referred to as a chain story. Each event in the story links back to the one on the previous event. Often the ending links back to the beginning as if you're starting the story again. This pattern connects the events. Primary-age students are quite adept at interpreting this pattern and can use it for creating their own books. Older students enjoy writing playful creative stories based on the model. Using this pattern raises the quality of narrative writing, increases stamina, and provides a sense of accomplishment.

Examples of Interlocking Literature

Grades K–2

- *Each Peach Pear Plum* by Allan Ahlberg and Janet Ahlberg
- *Brown Bear, Brown Bear, What Do You See?* by Bill Martin Jr.
- *If You Give a Mouse A Cookie* by Laura Numeroff
- *Jump, Frog, Jump!* By Robert Kalan

Grades 3–5

- *A Dark, Dark Tale* by Ruth Brown
- *Five Chinese Brothers* by Claire Bishop
- *The Day Jimmy's Boa Ate the Wash* by Trinka Hakes Noble

Pattern #4: Familiar Cultural/Everyday Sequence

This pattern uses common everyday occurrences of culture and life events that many students can identify or relate to in their own lives. This kind of story pattern helps students to see themselves reflected in a story and easily make personal connections that can then be used in their own writing. Themes from a student's environment, such as having a terrible day (*Today Was a Terrible Day*), living with an elderly grandparent (*Grandpa's Teeth*), or even sitting outside on the sidewalk observing the traffic (*Nothing Ever Happens on 90th Street*) provide excellent experiences for writing. In addition, common sequences such as days of the week, months of the year, or an alphabet book offer opportunities to explore writing ideas.

Examples of Cultural/Everyday Sequence

Grades K–2

- *What Can You Do with a Paleta?* By Carmen Tafolla
- *Diary of a Worm* by Doreen Cronin
- *Dalia's Wondrous Hair* by Laura Lacamara
- *The Hello, Goodbye Window* by Norton Juster
- *Golden Domes and Silver Lanterns: A Muslim Book of Colors* by Hena Khan
- *Those Shoes* by Maribeth Boelts

Grades 3–5

- *All the Places to Love* by Patricia MacLachlan
- *Bedhead* by Margie Palantini
- *Lailah's Lunchbox: A Ramadan Story* by Reem Faruqi
- *First Day in Grapes* by L. King Pérez
- *Gettin' Through Thursday* by Melrose Cooper
- *Esperanza Rising* by Pam Muñoz Ryan

Grades 6–8

- *Brown Girl Dreaming* by Jacqueline Woodson
- *Testing Miss Malarkey* by Judy Finchler
- *That Book Woman* by Heather Henson
- *One Crazy Summer* by Rita Williams-Garcia
- *I Am Malala* (Young Readers Edition) by Malala Yousafzai
- *In Real Life* by Cory Doctorow and Jen Wang

Time to Teach

Pattern #5: Rhythm-Rhyme

This pattern includes either rhyming words or follows a story that is based on a particular rhythm. Some of these patterns will be familiar to students, and that kind of familiarity with a text may encourage students to consider using the pattern in their own writing.

Examples of Rhythm-Rhyme

Grades K–2

- *A My Name is Alice* by Jane E. Bayer
- *Silly Sally* by Audrey Wood
- *Counting Crows* by Kathi Appelt
- *There's a Wocket in my Pocket!* by Dr. Seuss
- *Hello Ocean* by Pam Muñoz Ryan

Grades 3–5

- *Where the Sidewalk Ends* by Shel Silverstein
- *Enormous Smallness: A Story of E. E. Cummings* by Matthew Burgess
- *Forest Has a Song* by Amy Ludwig VanDerwater

Grades 6–8

- *Bartholomew Biddle and the Very Big Wind* by Gary Ross
- *Old Henry* by Joan W. Blos
- *The Lorax* by Dr. Seuss

Pattern #6: Chronological Sequence

This pattern follows a time sequence that is often used in the real world. Real-world examples of writing in chronological sequence include documenting changes over time in a science experiment, taking notes or responding about a sequence of events, and reporting a historical account. Chronological sequence can move the story across a day, across a week, or across the seasons.

Examples of Chronological Sequence Literature

Grades K–2

- *Cookie's Week* by Cindy Ward
- *Nana Upstairs, Nana Downstairs* by Tomie dePaola
- *The Seasons of Arnold's Apple Tree* by Gail Gibbons
- *The Very Hungry Caterpillar* by Eric Carle

Grades 3–5

- *Alexander and the Terrible, Horrible, No Good, Very Bad Day* by Judith Viorst
- *Caterpillar and the Polliwog* by Jack Kent
- *The Sun's Day* by Mordicai Gerstein
- *The Grouchy Ladybug* by Eric Carle

Grades 6–8

- *Holes* by Louis Sachar
- *10 True Tales: World War II Heroes/Vietnam War Heroes* by Allan Zullo
- *The Great Fire* by Jim Murphy

Strategy 3: Engage Students in Whole-Group Instruction through Talking

Effective whole-group instruction looks much different than a lone teacher simply standing before seated students who may be yawning, on the wrong page, staring off into space, or even reading another text. Today's students thrive in a fast paced, interactive, visual and digital world and learn best when learning is active (Gentry, McNeel, and Wallace-Nesler 2014). "When students are actively engaged, they focus on what is being taught and better process new information" (Lorain 2015). Their learning is enhanced in whole-group mini-lessons that engage students in talking, moving, listening, and viewing.

Just as teachers talk with students as writer to writer, it is also important that students are given opportunities to talk during a mini-lesson. According to a study conducted by Ruhl, Hughes, and Schloss (1987), when teachers provided quick pauses for student interaction about content, they learned more and performed at a higher level. It is through these brief conversations that students become familiar with the language of writing and the skills/strategies of writing. The more that students practice using the vocabulary from any content area, including writing, the easier it becomes a part of their everyday vocabulary. Students learn from each other as they turn to partners and then articulate the content just taught to them. Breaking the content down and explaining it in a language that others can relate to helps clarify student understanding; this understanding is not just for their partners but also for the students themselves (Weimer 2012).

Partner talk is an effective tool in whole-class instruction to promote student engagement when strategically planned and routines are established. It gives teachers and students a means to demonstrate how we think, process, and extend our understanding and ideas. Create opportunities for successful partner talk by considering these suggestions to guide your planning.

- Plan for strategic pauses in instruction.
- Plan questions to increase understanding.
- Develop a protocol for speaking and listening.
- Pair students strategically to promote conversations.
- Provide adequate time to think, talk, and share.
- Share thoughts and responses with the group.
- Provide scaffolding to clarify meaning and support responses.

Time to Teach

 Classroom Snapshot: **Strategies for Partner Talk—Turn and Talk Grades K–2** . . . .

The Teacher:
- Poses the question or directive
- Provides thinking time
- Gives the cue to turn and talk
- Listens and observes
- Sample directives:
    - Turn and tell your partner...
    - Tell your partner two things learned...
    - Turn to your neighbor and repeat...

The Students:
- Turn and look at their partner
- Take turns sharing and listening
- Talk softly with their partner
- Are prepared to share thoughts

 Classroom Snapshot: **Strategies for Partner Talk—Talking Stems Grades 3–5** . . . .

The Teacher: Poses the questions, provides thinking time, gives talking stem

Sample Talking Stems

- Another example of a ____ is...
- I learned that ...
- Four types of sentences are...
- This will help me to...
- My character/setting in my story is...
- My topic is...
- Three adjectives that describe my character are...
- An important detail I am adding to my writing today is...

 Classroom Snapshot: **Strategies for Partner Talk— Stop, Think, Paraphrase, and Jot (STPJ) Grades 6–8** . . . .

S: Stop and listen to the question.

T: Think about the answer to the question.

P: Paraphrase your response with your partner.

J: Jot down specific thoughts with your partner to share with the group and to add to your writing notebook/journal.

Strategy 4: Engage Students in Whole-Group Instruction through Movement

Learning is hard work! In order to learn well, students need to move. Even with intense academic demands, a classroom daily schedule must also provide our students with quick, fun movement breaks to relax and stimulate the physical and mental muscles involved in the hard work of learning. During whole-group instruction, if teachers fail to keep students engaged, students may zone out or find something else of interest to occupy their mind. This can result in a loss of valuable learning time. Research has shown the brain's cerebellum, used for most learning, is also the part of the brain that is highly active during movement activities (Erlauer 2003; Jensen 2005). Thus, with frequent breaks of movement, academic achievement increases (Jensen 2000b). This connection between brain activity and movement can be an effective cognitive strategy to (1) strengthen learning, (2) improve memory and retrieval, and (3) enhance learner motivation and morale (Jensen 2005).

Through careful planning and execution, movement activities linked to instruction can maximize learning for all students. Based on the work of Meyers and Jones (1993), students retain about 70 percent of information taught in the first 10 minutes of an instructional sequence, but only 20 percent in the last 10 minutes when they are not actively engaged in learning. The frequency of movement should be in relationship to the average age of the students in a classroom. For example, the average second grader is seven years old; therefore instruction should include some form of movement about every seven minutes (Jensen 2000a). This movement need not be disruptive to the instructional flow; rather it is movement that is controlled and purposeful.

Physical movement stimulates the mind and body, and increases the flow of oxygen to the brain (Marzano 2007). Therefore, students become more alert even just by standing due to the increase in blood and oxygen flow to the brain (Tate 2004).

Integrating movement during direct instruction isn't a break from learning. It is an opportunity for learning. These movement activities may be used with slight modifications across grade levels.

Partner Talk

It can be difficult for some students to sit, listen, and remain focused on instruction. Adding purposeful movement during instruction allows those students a means to release a bit of energy. The simple movement of turning to talk to a partner stimulates the brain and refocuses attention (Tate 2004).

Turn and Talk, Yes!

In this strategy, when the teacher says, "Turn and talk," the students respond, "Yes!" This quick student response signals and prepares the brain for the discussion that follows.

Stand and Share/State, All Right!

Similar to Turn and Talk, Yes!, in this activity students stand to discuss ideas (Stand and Share) or restate the instructional focus (Stand and State). When the teacher says, "Stand and share/state," students respond with "All Right!" then stand and move right into conversations with their partners.

From Head to Toe

When students are more engaged in their learning through the use of kinesthetic movement, they tend to retain more information (Tate 2004). By using hand and body motions to clarify and convey meaning, students create mental representations of abstract concepts.

Hand Signals

Hand signals like Thumbs Up/Thumbs Down, or showing one finger for yes/two fingers for no allow the teacher to check for understanding during whole-group instruction.

The Wave Response

In this strategy, students answer a question with a one-word response. They quickly stand and give their response one after another, similar to " the wave" at a sporting event. An example question might be to name an adjective that could describe an animal.

The Body Knows

Using simple gestures or sign language gives students a kinesthetic motion to connect to content.

Here are a few examples:

Compare: To show similarities—clasp hands together

Contrast: To show differences—tap fists together and pull apart

Connection: To show how concepts link together—make circle with left thumb and pointer finger then link with right thumb and pointer finger

Fact: Something that is true—fist to palm of other hand

Opinion: To show a personal view or belief about a concept—point to temple

For a sample writing mini-lesson using body movements, see *Movin' to Edit* (grades K–2) on page 101.

Move It, Move It

Sometimes we just need a spark! A little movement can create a quick brain break from intense thinking or simply help to put a little pep in our step. Adding movement into instruction can improve student concentration, attention, and performance (Tate 2004).

Response Cards

Response cards might be as simple as green/red squares that represent yes/no, punctuation cards, index cards, dry erase boards, etc., that students can raise and lower to respond to a question presented by the teacher.

Carousel Activity

In this strategy, the teacher places charts with labels/questions around the room and assigns students to groups. Each group is assigned a different color marker in order to distinguish group responses on the charts. Each group moves to one of the charts to respond to the question for a specified time. When the time expires, the teacher signals with a chime, music, bell, etc. to move to the next chart. All groups rotate in the same direction, thus resembling the movement of a carousel. After the rotation, each group shares one of the charts with the class.

For a sample writing mini-lesson using the carousel activity, see *Be a Word Wizard Notebook Entry* (grades 3–5) on page 104.

I Spy

This strategy is used as a "brain break" or transition to get the blood flowing and break up the learning a bit. It is a call-and-response strategy as well as a strategy for following directions.

Teacher: "I spy!"

Students: (Stop and freeze) "What do you spy?"

Teacher: (Give movement directions) "I spy children jogging in place." Or, "I spy rock stars playing air guitar!" Or, "I spy children shooting basketballs."

Students: Continue until teacher gives another directive starting with "I spy!" etc.

Teacher: (To end activity) "I spy students hard at work." (signaling a return to learning)

Crisscross Change

Here, the teacher gives students a sequence of movements that involve moving across bodies from left to right or right to left. For example:

"Touch your left-hand pointer finger to your nose, and your right hand to your ear." Or, "Bring your right elbow to your left knee."

When the teacher says, "Change!" students reverse. It starts slowly then gradually becomes a faster movement or a different movement.

Just Dance

An occasional song and dance is always a terrific energizer. Keep a song and/or video playlist close by to just have fun, refocus, and refresh!

Clap, Snap, Pat, and Chant

Use your imagination and creativity, add rhythm and rhyme as "memory hooks" to teach the language, process, and literary terms of writing. For example, have students begin a "Stomp-Stomp-Clap" or "Pat-Pat-Clap" rhythm. Then, add a call and response rhyme like:

Action words/Action words

They're called verbs/They're called verbs

Action words are things we do/Action words are things we do

Read and write, laugh and chew/Read and write, laugh and chew

Sing and dance are just a few/Sing and dance are just a few

Action words/Action words

They're called verbs/They're called verbs

Action words are things we do/Action words are things we do

I can name one, how about you!

The rhythm continues as students call out additional action verbs.

For a sample writing mini-lesson using chants, see *Boot Camp Caps Chant Notebook Entry* (grades 6–8) on page 107.

Give It and Get It

In this strategy, the teacher gives students a prompt (e.g., "Create a list of people you want to write about"). After students complete their list, the teacher signals and students walk around the room talking with one another to gather additional ideas they might add to their lists. To do this, students meet in pairs. One student gives an idea and the other student "gets" the idea and writes it down. Then, the roles reverse. Students walk around the room exchanging ideas in this way until the teacher calls time.

Sample Lessons

The following sample lessons are examples of implementing whole-group instruction through movement.

- Movin to Edit
- Be a Word Wizard
- Boot Camp Caps Chant

Movin' to Edit
(Grades K–2)

Note: Revisit this lesson to practice additional conventions for editing, such as use of commas and quotation marks.

Think About Writing

1. Explain to students that authors develop interesting sentences in their writing. Authors know that readers must use strategies to understand when one sentence ends and another begins. Good writers know to begin their sentences with a capital letter and end their thoughts with an ending punctuation mark.

2. Review a mentor text if desired, and emphasize how the author uses punctuation to clarify and add energy to his or her writing.

Teach

3. Tell students, "Today I will show you a fun way to remember how sentences begin and end."

4. Write the following sentences on sentence strips:

   - *my name is Vickie*
   - *how old are you*
   - *i am six years old*
   - *my friend is sam*
   - *we like to hike and look for snakes*
   - *eeek*

5. Place the strips in a pocket chart and read the sentences without stopping. Discuss the difficulty of understanding the message of the words.

Standards

- Uses strategies to edit and publish written work

- Uses conventions of capitalization in written compositions

Materials

- *Movin' to Edit* (page 101)

- Sentence strips

- Markers

- Sticky notes

Mentor Texts

- *Are You My Mother?* by P. D. Eastman

- *No, David!* by David Shannon

- *The Relatives Came* by Cynthia Rylant

(Gentry, McNeel, and Wallace-Nesler 2012b)

© *Shell Education*

Movin' to Edit *(cont.)*

6. Tell students that sometimes we forget to begin a sentence with a capital letter and end it with punctuation. Model using your body as you say the first sentence to help students remember conventions.

   • Stand tall with hands together over head and say the first word in the sentence. *(My)* Tell students this represents a capital letter.

   • Continue saying the rest of the sentence. *(name is Vickie)*

   • Signify the period at the end of the sentence by grinding your right foot into the ground. *(.)*

7. Add sticky notes to the sentence strips to correct them.

8. Continue modeling the remainder of the sentences using body movements to represent conventions. See *Movin' to Edit* (page 101) for body movements that correspond to each convention.

Engage

9. Have students engage in *Heads-up, Stand-up, Partner-up* and work with partners to practice using the body motions to show their understanding of capitals and ending punctuation. Have students practice using the sentence strips. Allow approximately two minutes for student practice. Rove, engage, and support students. Gather students back together and highlight and compliment partners using appropriate behaviors and demonstrating lesson focus.

Apply

10. Remind students they should capitalize the first word in a sentence and finish with ending punctuation to let the reader know when one sentence is finished and another is beginning. Remind students to always check this in their writing.

Write/Conference

11. Provide time for students to write. Observe students to check for understanding. Initiate individual or small-group conferences. Take notes in your conferring notebook.

Spotlight Strategy

12. Spotlight great editors. For example, "Amee did what good writers do! She capitalized the first word of every sentence and has included punctuation at the end of each."

Share

13. Have students meet with partners to share how they included capitals and punctuation in their writing.

Movin' to Edit

Capital: Stand tall with hands together over head

Period: Right foot grinds into floor

Question: Shrug shoulders with hands up

Exclamation: Right arm straight up and down, then punch with left arm

Comma: Right hand karate chop (gently)

Quotation Mark: Bend elbows, slant left and wiggle hands, slant right and wiggle hands

Be a Word Wizard
(Grades 3–5)

Note: There is clear evidence that vocabulary is associated with socioeconomic status. Children can acquire and retain two or three words a day. Do this lesson often with a variety of vocabulary strategies. Use this carousel activity for synonyms and antonyms.

Think About Writing

1. Explain to students that authors use just the right words to paint pictures for the reader. Tell students that since they are authors too, they need to be constantly on the lookout for words that can be used in their writing.

2. Review mentor texts, if desired, and emphasize the word choices the author makes.

Teach

3. Tell students, "Today I will show you how to begin a collection of various words that can be stored in your writer's notebook and called upon when searching for just the right image as you write." Explain that writers are word wizards as they work to conjure up images in the readers' minds.

4. Create a table with four boxes on chart paper. Label the boxes as shown below:

Words or phrases that show happy	Words or phrases that show sad
Words or phrases that show sounds (onomatopoeia)	Words or phrases that show action

5. Gather words that fit in each category. Provide a few examples from the notebook entry to get students started. Continue to build the chart by looking for examples in literature that you will read over the coming weeks.

(Gentry, McNeel, and Wallace-Nesler 2012e)

Be a Word Wizard *(cont.)*

Engage

6. Write the caption from each box on a separate sheet of chart paper and post the charts around the room. Divide students into groups and assign each group a different chart. Provide approximately four minutes for students to add their ideas to the chart. Rotate the groups and have students add words to the new chart. Continue rotating the students until each group has worked on all the charts. Display the charts in the room for students to reference as they write.

Apply

7. Encourage students to increase their word knowledge by collecting and studying words. Provide students with the *Be a Word Wizard Notebook Entry* (page 104) to add to their writer's notebook. Have students write words from the chart activity in their notebook, then proceed to their writing folders.

Write/Conference

8. Provide time for students to write, if time allows. No conferring today. You will need to monitor student groups as they work on adding their ideas to the charts. Notice collaboration, cooperation, and work ethic and make notes in your conferring notebook.

Spotlight Strategy

9. Spotlight groups that have created interesting lists. For example, "This group has successfully collected a whole list of words that paint pictures. I want to add a few of those words to my writer's notebook. Smart work today, writers."

Share

10. Have several students share out to the whole group. Allow students to write down ideas in their writer's notebook that they want to remember.

Be a Word Wizard Notebook Entry

Be a Word Wizard

Authors write memorable stories by *creating images* that capture the reader's attention.

Be a word wizard and conjure up words that paint a picture!

Words or phrases that show happy	Words or phrases that show sad
giggle	whined
joyous	gloomy
tickled pink	blue
Words or phrases that show sounds (onomatopoeia)	**Words or phrases that show action**
bang	swirling
slurp	racing
click-clack	wobbling

Your Turn:

Add words in your notebook that you can stir into your writing. Create additional boxes for word groups, such as *sensory words*, *colorful words*, and *character trait words*.

Boot Camp Caps Chant
(Grades 6–8)

Note: Using chants, raps, and music helps bring engagement, motivation, and joy to classroom learning.

Think About Writing

1. Remind students that certain rules of capitalization must be followed. Knowing which words require capital letters makes writing look clean and polished.

2. Review mentor texts, if desired, and emphasize the use of proper capitalization.

Teach

3. Tell students that they will learn a chant today. Explain that a chant is a song with repeated phrases. Tell them you will be the leader and they will repeat everything you say. Share the real-world example of a boot camp chant in which military personnel repeat the phrases from a person of authority.

4. Ask students to listen for the rules of capitalization in the chant. Think aloud about why an author would want to use capital letters correctly when writing.

Engage

5. Use the chant on the *Boot Camp Caps Chant Notebook Entry* (page 107) and ask students to repeat each line back. Then, use chart paper to make a list of rules and examples from the chant.

Capitalization Rules	Examples
First word in a sentence and all proper nouns	**L**ast week, **J**oey and **I** made an apple pie.
Days of the week and months of the year	Every **T**uesday in **J**une I play basketball.
Names of cities, states, and countries	I live in **S**an **A**ntonio, **T**exas.
Important words in titles	*The **A**dventures of **T**om **S**awyer.*
Places and holidays	On **M**emorial **D**ay, we are going to **D**isney **W**orld.

(Gentry, McNeel, and Wallace-Nesler 2012g)

Boot Camp Caps Chant *(cont.)*

Apply

6. Provide students with the *Boot Camp Caps Chant Notebook Entry* to add to their writer's notebook. Have students work on the *Your Turn* section before proceeding to their writing folders. Have them follow the rules of capitalization in their own writing.

Write/Conference

7. Work with a small group and focus on one or two rules only. Find the skills that are easily confused or forgotten and focus on those skills.

Spotlight Strategy

8. Find and spotlight one or two students who correctly edited for capitalization.

Share

9. Ask students to share their writing in pairs and go over their changes. Encourage students to discuss, reflect, and question the use of capital letters.

Boot Camp Caps Chant
Notebook Entry

Boot Camp Caps Chant

(Repeat each line.)

I don't know but I've been told.

Sixth grade writers are really bold.

We know the rules of the capital game.

That's why writing will bring us fame.

The beginning of a sentence and the pronoun "I,"

ALWAYS need a capital, don't deny!

Days of the week and months of the year,

Names and titles need capitals, dear!

Capitalize names of special places,

Cities and states need upper cases.

We're gonna do our very best,

To capitalize words on every test!

C. A. P. I. T. A. L.

These capital rules will serve us well!

Your Turn:

Use the capitalization rules to make any necessary corrections in your writer's notebook. Then, edit for capitalization in your writing folder.

Time to Teach

Strategy 5: Be a Writer!

Many teachers across the country feel overwhelmed and unprepared to teach writing in their classrooms. Many students who study education take full semester classes solely dedicated to teaching one subject like reading, mathematics, science, social studies, physical education, music, etc. However, courses on teaching writing are few and usually the only writing instruction comes from the essays in other classes.

Becoming a writer along with your students is a great way to develop your writing skills and gain a real understanding of the process of writing. As teachers model their own writing with students, they open up their own thinking and share an important thought process. Students gain an understanding of the writing process as teachers think aloud to select a topic, organize and plan content, make revisions, and edit. Being a writer in the classroom is *showing* students how to write, which is considerably more powerful, more significant, and more memorable than just telling them what to do. During an *Instructor Magazine* interview (2015), Donald Graves was asked, "If you had to choose one thing teachers should do when teaching writing, what would it be?" His response, "Write yourself. Invite children to do something you're already doing. If you're not doing it, 'Hey,' the kids say, 'I can't wait to grow up and not have to write, like you...' You can't ask someone to sing a duet with you until you know the tune yourself."

Being a writer in your classroom...

- **makes the thought process visible.** Modeling writing embeds explicit strategy instruction to scaffold student learning.

- **provides insight and evaluation to writing assignments.** Until you experience writing to a prompt like "Being a Snowflake," you may not be aware of how difficult it is to connect to the topic.

- **demystifies writing as a process that comes relatively easy for authors and teachers.** Many students think teachers and authors just sit down and write and do not recognize the true fact that writing is messy and hard for most people.

- **builds empathy and compassion for students.** We need to remember that writing can be a struggle for students and we need to provide time, support, and encouragement.

- **includes you as a part of the learning community of writers.** As you think aloud through the writing process and share personal stories, opinions, and interests in your writing, students begin to see you as a partner in learning.

- **builds on what we know about writing, developing our writing instructional skills and strategies.** The writing we do brings us closer to becoming experts on teaching writing.

- **presents a positive role model.** We send a valuable message to the writers in our classroom: We value writing and find it useful in our teaching and our everyday lives!

Conclusion

In the past, whole-group writing instruction often focused on a *product*. Teachers assigned a topic, required rigid outlines, imposed structures such as a five-paragraph essay, counted off for errors, and graded everything the student wrote. The teacher was often the only one reading students' papers.

The strategies in this chapter highlight the switch from product to *process*, which changes the role of the teacher. As a process-oriented teacher these strategies help you build student writers through the instructing, writing/conferring, and sharing cycle. Remember that your whole-group teaching is not simply a set of writing skills to be taught—it is a craft to be learned. So, like the artist or potter who learned in studios or workshops, the craft of writing will be taught in a workshop where the student learns to write under the tutorship and guidance of a writing teacher who even in whole-group instruction is the master craftsman modeling and practicing the craft alongside the student.

Independent and Small-Group Instruction

The Effective Writing Conference

Writing and conferring make up the second component of writing instruction. Once the whole-group mini-lesson is taught, students go off to work on their own writing. This writing is most frequently student directed, but at times it can be teacher directed as students practice a specific writing skill or strategy discussed in the earlier mini-lesson before moving into their individual work. This is the students' opportunity to practice and to do the work of writers.

Teachers often hear that in order for students to become better readers, they need more time to just read. Is it also true that to become better writers, our students need more time to just write? Well, yes and no. The need to provide time for our students to write in order to get better at writing is obvious. The time to practice writing is most effective if that time is preceded by explicit writing instruction and partnered with guided writing. Frequently after direct teacher modeling, students may not independently apply strategies and skills into their writing. It is through individual and small-group conferences that teachers can provide the specific instruction students need to develop and understand the complex structures of written language (Graves 1983, Graham et al. 2012).

Individual and small-group conferences serve as the underpinning of writing instruction. Many teachers use these conversations about writing to provide the following:

- positive reinforcement of good writing habits

- opportunities for differentiation through focused, targeted instruction

- immediate and explicit feedback

- an understanding of student capabilities and needs

- opportunities that improve student self-esteem

- useful information to plan future whole group mini-lessons

- a record of progress to use during parent/teacher conferences

- meaningful connections between teacher and student

"Writing conferences are most successful when they occur as a conversation between two writers just 'talking about writing.' It is a time to value students as writers, to differentiate instruction, to teach or reinforce new strategies, and to gather information for forming instructional decisions" (Gentry, McNeel, and Wallace-Nesler 2014, 42). As teachers guide, model, and engage students in "writerly" conversations, they encourage students to recognize their accomplishments, determine skills and strategies to attempt in their writing, and realize their potential as writers.

Three conference formats that can be used in the classroom are chats, table conferences, and skill conferences. Each is distinctive in its structure and purpose.

Chats take place before, between, or after conferences. They are called chats because, like conferences, they involve conversations about writing, but are much shorter. Typically, chats take place as the teacher moves about the whole group and checks in with students to give them a quick nudge to get started, to answer a question, or to remind them about a specific goal or strategy they are focusing on in their writing.

The **table conference** is usually held to reinforce a mini-lesson, focus strategy, or to revisit a previously taught mini-lesson. For example, if teachers are working on including transition words in the text in the whole group mini-lesson, they should meet with table groups throughout the week to reinforce that concept.

Skill conferences involve carefully selecting students with similar strengths or deficits for conferring. These conferences often take on the form of "mini" mini-lessons, as they provide additional support for learning writing strategies as well as how to actually implement those skills in their writing. Students may be pulled to a small guided-writing table or to a corner of the group meeting area. Carl Anderson (2000) explains that these conferences may take on one of four different roles:

- rehearsal conferences: assist students in thinking of ideas and gathering information for writing
- drafting conferences: help students develop the main idea and content, as well as determine the structure and genre of the writing
- revision conferences: focus on rethinking the text by adding, deleting, moving, and substituting text
- editing conferences: help students analyze the mechanics, spelling, and grammar of their writing.

The following strategies help support individual and small-group conferring:

- Organize and plan for individual and small-group conferences.
- Create a conference schedule.
- Follow a conference structure.
- Communicate conference expectations.
- Prepare a toolkit for conferring.
- Notice and note student accomplishments and needs.

In this chapter, you will find five strategies for independent and small-group instruction:

- Organize and plan for individual and small-group conferences
- Create a conference schedule
- Follow a conference structure
- Communicate conference expectations
- Prepare a conferring toolkit

 ## Strategy 1: Organize and Plan for Individual and Small-Group Conferences

When beginning to implement individual and small-group conferences in a Writer's Workshop, teachers often find the task to be daunting. In *The Conferring Handbook* (2003, VIII) Lucy Calkins affirms, "Conferring is hard!" The more conferences you hold with your students, the more confident you will become with the process. Start small, focusing on a few students daily and discussing specific, targeted strategies. Take your time, developing an awareness of the structure and purpose of conferring. Keep it simple, while gradually refining your instruction.

Consider the following questions as you organize and plan for individual and small-group conferences.

What is the purpose of a writing conference?

The main goal of any writing conference is to teach the student a strategy, craft, or skill that not only improves the student's current writing, but also can be applied to future writing. According to Donald Graves (1994), the "purpose of the writing conference is to help children teach you about what they know so that you can help them more effectively with their writing" (59).

When do you meet with students for conferences?

Conferences can actually take place anytime students are writing. If you give an assignment during social studies or science, assign research or prompted writing. All are opportunities for conversations about the process and strategies of writing. Within a Writer's Workshop structure, conferences typically follow the whole-group mini-lesson while students are working independently on their writing. Establish that students are on task, conduct a few follow-up conferences, then move into conferring one-on-one and/or with a small group.

How often do you meet with students?

Make every effort to meet with all students either individually or in a small group once a week. The frequency of the conference often decreases as the developmental level of the writer and complexity of the conversations increases. Meeting with four to five students a day is a realistic goal, but while becoming familiar with the whole process of conferring, begin with a goal of meeting with two students daily and gradually increase that number. In order to ensure time is available for conferring, routines and expectations for independent writing must be established to limit interruptions during conferences.

How long should a conference last?

Individual conferences may last five to seven minutes. Small-group conferences may be longer, about 10–15 minutes, based on the number of students in the group and the skill, strategy, or element of writer's craft being explored. Often the developmental level of the writer determines the length of a conference. For example, kindergarten and first grade writing conferences typically do not require as much time as conferring with an eighth grade writer. Keep in mind these times may be longer initially, but grow shorter as you become more confident in your conferring skills and as students get used to the process. You might set a timer, not to indicate that time is up and disrupt the flow of conferring conversations, but so you can monitor and modify your own teaching practice. These times are suggested to ensure that conferences are held with students as often as possible. The time can be shorter or longer and will be determined as you are sitting side by side or with a group of writers. It is okay to move on when a student quickly grasps a concept or to linger during a teachable moment. You may not give every student equal time, but strive to provide each with the time they need.

Where do you meet for writing conferences?

Conferring can take place at a designated "conference table," at students' desks, or sitting together at a carpet area. The location is really not as important as creating a space where you and the student(s) are listening and talking together about what good writers do. Think of it as a conversation between writers, not just between teacher and student.

How do you decide with whom to meet? One-on-one or small group?

Meeting with students individually once a week or once every two weeks allows time to address individual needs and to foster the relationship between teacher and student. All students benefit from conferences as teachers use this valuable time to personalize and scaffold instruction to meet the writer's needs. Once students develop an understanding of the writing process, they may need to request a conference to move forward with their writing. Be flexible enough to include these students in your conference schedule.

Through observations, conference conversations, and reading student writing, groups of students with similar deficits, strengths, or behaviors often form. If specific writing goals or strategies are expected, groups may be created to reteach. Convenience and efficiency may also play a part in developing groups based on table groups and/or student teams in order to meet with more students per week.

How do I know what to teach during the conference?

No doubt a main topic of conversation centers around what good writers do, like working through the writing process, developing the traits of quality writing and imitating the writing of other authors. Move into the conference with some strategy or technique in mind, particularly when working with small groups. During one-on-one conferences, search for an area of need by asking questions, listening to the writer, and reading the student's writing. Remember this is a conversation and you should value the act of listening. The conversation becomes more meaningful and productive when the student is given the opportunity to define the purpose and direction of the conference." The direction of the conference emerges out of the research. That is, it should not feel like the teacher checks in with the child, and then teachers what he or she had in mind to teach in the first place...or that the teacher checks in, then arbitrarily pulls something out of the sky to teach" (Calkins, Hartman, and White 2005, 58).

Whether working with an individual student or a small group, focus instruction on one, maybe two, targeted teaching points. Of course as you work with students, you may notice a number of teaching points that need attention. Consider what you have taught in previous mini-lessons and conferences, the writer's developmental level, and your observations. Then ask yourself, "What is the one strategy I can teach this writer at this moment that connects to this piece of writing and nudges him or her toward independence?" By staying focused on one teaching point, you can likely avoid any feelings of frustration or being overwhelmed.

 ## *Strategy 2:* Create a Conference Schedule

When beginning to implement writing conferences in your schedule, start simply. Plan to meet with one or two students. Gradually move into a structured schedule that allows for more frequent meetings with your writers. Teachers often ask, "Which is better, individual or small-group conferences?" They are both valuable to students' writing development. You must consider what is relevant for you and your students' needs, the time you have for conferring, and what works best for your teaching style.

Experiment, modify, and be flexible as you try different schedule makeups. Keep in mind your conferences are lengthier in the beginning, but will decrease in time as you become proficient and your students become familiar with the procedures and routines. Eventually, you will discover what works best for both you and your students. Next year, you may need to again adjust the structure to meet the needs of your new students.

Figure 4.1 shares sample schedules that include individual and small-group conferences as part of a Writer's Workshop format. Typically, the writing and conferring portion lasts between 20–30 minutes, sometimes longer depending on the total time allocated for Writer's Workshop. It is divided so the writing/conference time equals or exceeds the time for the mini-lesson and sharing. However, the times are merely approximations as the amount of time for conferring with developing writers is dependent on a number of factors, including:

- **The writer:** When thinking about scheduling conference time, we must consider the writer and adjust the time to meet the needs of each individual student. A five-minute conference for one student may need to be an eight to 10 minute conference for another. More proficient writers may require less instruction and scaffolding during a conference than other students. Another consideration is a student's thinking process, as some need additional time to gain an understanding of the content. The actual act of writing serves as a factor in time management. Some students are quicker at actually putting text on paper, while others seem to struggle letter by letter. The writer's age and attention span are also important
to consider.

- **The context of the conference:** The type of conference and the topic also affect time management. Whether generating ideas, practicing skills, demonstrating, or sharing examples, each may require different amounts of time. For example, generating a list of interesting people to write about may take less time than sharing examples of figurative language from a mentor text and guiding students through finding ways to add similes to their own writing.

- **Your conferring skills:** It takes time to refine your conferring skills and become efficient with time management. Just as you allow students time to develop as writers, give yourself permission to take time to develop as a teacher of writing. Work on improving your skills on individual conferences, and then add in skill and/or table conferences or vice versa. Then, set goals to refine each area and work toward becoming more effective, efficient, and organized. It is a process that takes time and persistence. A Confucius saying comes to mind here: "It does not matter how slow you go so long as you do not stop." The teaching and learning that takes place during conferences as teachers and students share, discuss, and explore writing is dependent on you and your commitment to developing your own conferring skills.

Figure 4.1 Sample Conference Schedules

Sample 1:	Monday	Tuesday	Wednesday	Thursday	Friday
5 Minutes	Chats				
5 Minutes	Individual (Dayvon)	Individual (Cherri)	Individual (Marcus)	Individual (Sammy)	Individual (Dominique)
10–15 Minutes Small group Table 1		Small group Table 2	Small group Table 3	Small group Table 4	Small group Table 5

Sample 2:	Monday	Tuesday	Wednesday	Thursday	Friday
5 Minutes	Chats				
5 Minutes	Individual (Alexander)	Individual (Grayson)	Individual (KayLynn)	Individual (Xander)	Individual (Paisley)
5 Minutes	Individual (Reagan)	Individual (Brooklyn)	Individual (Wyatt)	Individual (Abigail)	Individual (Elijah)
5 Minutes	Chats or open for student-requested conference				

Sample 3:	Monday	Tuesday	Wednesday	Thursday	Friday
5 Minutes	**Observation:** After the mini-lesson, move about the room to observe the students' writing, noticing and noting what they are attempting, how much they are writing, and who needs support with the targeted skill.				
5 Minutes	Individual (Jacklynn)	Individual (Akeem)	Individual (Trent)	Individual (Ryder)	Individual (Gianna)
10–15 Minutes	Individual (Gracie) Individual (Samuel)	Small group Skill/strategy	Small group Skill/strategy	Small group Skill/strategy	Follow up w/ Trent Gracie Samuel

Sample 4:	Monday	Tuesday	Wednesday	Thursday	Friday
2–3 Minutes	Chats and settling into writing				
10–15 Minutes	Small group Table 1	Small group Skill/strategy	Small group Table 2	Small group Skill/strategy	Small group Table 3
5 Minutes	Individual (Kai)	Individual (Cole)	Individual (Keira)	Individual (Darrel)	Individual (Vivian)

Strategy 3: Follow a Conference Structure

Understanding and following a routine during the conference helps make the process more manageable and efficient. Although predictable, it is a conversation between writers and the content is determined by the responses students share about their writing.

There are four phases to focus on during the conferring process: Observe and Question, Praise, Guide, and Connect. Each phase plays an important role in developing "writerly" conversations with our students. During the first two phases, Observe and Praise, look at the student's work as a writer. As you move into the Guide and Connect phases, the focus shifts to providing support that helps the student become a better writer.

1. **Observe and Question** the writer(s) and decide on the writing strategy, skill, or element of writer's craft to address during the conference. Consider conversation responses, what you know from student(s) writing, anecdotal notes, and observations.

2. **Praise** the writer(s) by giving a compliment about something he or she accomplished.

3. **Guide** the writer through introducing the concept in the following ways:

    - modeling through explicit language and strong examples from literature or writing samples

    - engaging students in conversations that explain the process

    - allowing student(s) time to practice the skill with teacher feedback and guidance

    - following up with students to determine if they apply the concept in writing

4. **Connect** what the writer(s) accomplished during the conference and the importance of using it in their future writing.

Observe and Question the Writer

During the Observe phase, focus attention on the student as a writer. Quickly recall what you know about the writer, review the current work of the writer, and explore through questioning and listening to what the student is working on as a writer at this time. Keep focused on two things: what to teach and what to compliment. Sounds easy enough! However, when reviewing a student's piece of writing seemingly thick with errors, it can be difficult to determine where to begin in the quest for a single teaching point or a constructive compliment.

The key to accomplishing this task is focus. Focus on the writer, not the writing.

When deciding what to teach, ask:

- What do I know about this student's writing development from previous conferences and observations?

- Looking at the student's current work, what strengths, needs, and patterns do I notice in the writing?

- Based on this information, what is one strategy, skill, or element of writer's craft that can help this student grow as a writer?

Engage the student writer in deciding the writing focus by starting a conversation about his/her writing and asking clarifying questions such as:

- How is your writing going today?

- What are you planning to do in your writing time today?

- How will you go about doing that in your writing? Would you like to try ___ or ___?

- Tell me how your writing is going today. What parts do you like best? What parts do you think need work?

- How might I help you with your writing?

- Tell me about your goals or questions you have about this piece.

The Observe phase looks somewhat different when working with a small skill group. Most of the observation takes place prior to the conference. Gathering information from students' writing and anecdotal notes from conferences identifies students with similar strengths and needs. Small groups may also be formed as a new genre study is introduced to generate ideas, develop, organize and analyze text/genre structure, create topic vocabulary, develop characters, revise, and edit. These collaborative guided writing groups are fluid and short term.

Here is a snapshot from a first grade classroom, demonstrating how one teacher used questions to support her observations.

Classroom Snapshot: Grade 1

After explaining the conferring process to her students, with conference log in hand, Mrs. R sat down to confer with one of her first graders. Looking at a page full of possible options for a teaching point, she finally decided on a compliment. She asked Jake, "How is your writing going today?" He replied, "Great, Mrs. R! You should probably go help somebody else today!" Not knowing what to say, she politely moved off to assist another student.

Sometimes it is not enough to just ask an opening question. As Mrs. R develops her conferring skills, she will recognize the need to "respond to children's first answers with questions that probe and explore their responses" (Calkins, Hartman, and White 2005, 52). Teachers sometimes find the need to encourage and extend the conversations when asking a student how it's going and they answer, "Okay," or they tell you about the content of their writing. Respond by reminding them about what good writers do or what they were doing the last time you talked together (e.g., "At our last conference you were working on using more action verbs in your writing. How's that working out?"). When a student's response centers around content—"I'm writing a story about me and my brother."—redirect the conversation. "I enjoy writing stories about my family, too. Now let's talk about what you are doing as a writer today." The main purpose with the Observe phase is to gather information about what the writer is capable of doing, attempting to do, and almost doing.

Praise the Writer

While observing the student to identify a focused teaching point, note the student's writing, behaviors, and attitude to search out what the writer is doing well. Remember part of a teacher's role is to encourage and build confidence in our writers so they will take risks in their writing and be more receptive to our suggestions. One way to look beyond errors is to listen and focus on the content as students read their writing. Think about the development of ideas, the organizational structure, the flow of sentences, word choice, and voice used in the writing. Then, give the student a specific and focused compliment.

The compliment focuses on one valuable writing skill the student is doing or attempting to do really well. Although positive, "Great job!" and "Good writing!" are not specific and focused compliments. After you reread a sentence or section of the writing aloud, point out and state the obvious, such as:

- Your _____ really makes me want to just keep on reading. Nice work on _____.

- The _____ you included here makes me feel like _____. You have painted a very clear picture of _____ for your reader!"

- What? You wrote two pages and are working on the third! You certainly know a lot about _____, just like the author, _____.

- I really like how you _____. That's exactly what good writers do!

So how do you go about giving compliments to three or four students in a skill group? As you preview their writing during the first phase, you are searching out strengths as well as needs. Similar strengths unfold and you may give a compliment such as:

- As I looked through your writing, one thing I noticed you all had accomplished is _____ (name and describe the strategy, skill, or element of writer's craft).

- During our chat time today, I was excited to see you were all _____ (name and describe the strategy, skill, or element of writer's craft).

- Let me say congratulations to all of you for being such hard workers! I am amazed at the way you all are _____ (name and describe the strategy, skill, or element of writer's craft).

A compliment starts the conference on a positive note, creating an eagerness and energy to continue working through the writing process. It lets writers know that someone notices their efforts and is proud of the results. As you compliment, provide a model for students to use as they begin to confer and compliment the writing of their classroom peers.

Guide the Writer

In this phase of conferring, use the information gathered to identify the instructional focus of the conference. Keep three key points in mind as you guide the writer:

1. **Choose only one strategy, skill, or element of writer's craft as the instructional target.** Teachers often look at the writing of a student and think, "Oh my, there is so much to teach this writer!" Ask yourself, "Of all that this writer needs, what will help the writing at this time and will support this writer in the future?" That is the one strategy or skill to focus on for today.

2. **Choose an instructional focus appropriate for the student's writing development.** It is important to consider what the writer is capable of accomplishing at this stage in his or her writing and what the writer is trying to do. Focusing on a teaching point far beyond a student's understanding lessens the opportunity for this student to grow as a writer. In the same way, interjecting a strategy that has no purpose or meaning also undermines the productivity of the conference.

3. **Scaffold instruction to meet the writer's needs, looking closely at the amount of support to provide and how to release that support to the student.** Similar to the whole-group mini-lesson instruction, move through by modeling and demonstrating, practicing and guiding the writer, and then encouraging independent practice.

   - First, explicitly state what you will teach, demonstrate, and/or model. For example: "One strategy I use when I write is..." "I'd like to share something that good writers do.", "Think back to our mini-lesson about _____ when we... You might try...", or "Let's take a look at the way _____(author's name) goes about..."

- Next, model the skill or use a mentor text to show a student how to accomplish the skill.

- Then, practice the skill, either together or while guiding the student along.

- Finally, encourage students to try it on their own. Restate the strategy, skill or craft and set expectations like, "Now let's see if you can...", "I'll be back and when I return, I expect to see...", or "Let's all use [name the strategy] in our writing today" It is important to follow up with the student(s) before the conference time ends to provide feedback to the writer(s).

Connect with the Writer

This final phase of the conference is brief. It serves as a means to share the work accomplished during the conference and restate the learned information. Also, to connect means to encourage writers to add the strategy to their growing collection of tools to be used in future writing. You might have students add the strategy to a list in a writing folder or notebook as a reminder.

- "You have added a number of details to your writing today just by asking questions. Always remember, your readers need to see what you are thinking and writers can ask themselves questions to give readers a clearer picture."

- "Writers, now you know another strategy to use in your writing from now on: adding different kinds of hooks/leads! Nice work today."

Most importantly, end the conference on a positive note with students eager and enthusiastic about the writing that awaits them. Use this conference structure as a guide to support you as you begin conferring with writers. Although this common structure works for many teachers, everyone must have their own conference variations that work for themselves, their students, and their classroom environment. Over time, as you discover what works for you, what you are comfortable doing, and how your students respond, the structure will become your own. Figure 4.2 provides additional questions/prompts you can use to support the implementation of writing conferences.

Figure 4.2 Prompts to Guide the Writing Conference

Observe and Question Decide What to Teach	• "How is your writing going today?" • "What are you planning to do in your writing time today?" • "Tell me how your writing is going today. What part do you like best? What part do you think needs work?" • "How might I help you with your writing?" • "Tell me about your goals or questions you have about this piece."
Praise Give a Compliment	Point out and state what it is the writer is doing well. • "One strategy you are trying is using transition words to link your text together. This strategy is helping you get better at organizing your thinking and your writing. Nicely done!" • "The action verbs you are using in your writing here and here (point out the specific action verbs) really help your reader visualize what the character is doing!"
Guide Teach and Support	State what you will teach: • "Today, I will show you how..." • "I want to remind you about how authors..." Support through demonstration and sharing: • "Let's look back in our writer's notebooks..." • "Notice how I use..." • "Let's explore this step-by-step..."
Connect Link to Writing	Celebrate hard work and restate the strategy. • "You worked diligently to revise _____ today. Remember you can take what we learned today and use it anytime you are writing." • "Writers, you are working so hard to _____ in your writing. Always remember to ...."

Strategy 4: Communicate Conference Expectations

When both the teacher and student(s) take an active role during a conference, writing conferences can be the most successful at addressing student needs. However, it is important to explicitly teach students their roles in the conference structure. This chart includes some examples of teacher, student, and class responsibilities. It is important to share this information with students—anchor charts are one way to do so—so that expectations are clearly communicated. By establishing a predictable conference structure and helping students understand that both teacher and student take responsibility for their roles during the conference, it becomes a valuable instructional tool.

Figure 4.3 Conferring Roles and Responsibilities

	Teacher's Role	Student's Role
Observe and Question	**I will...** • ask you to share what you are working on as a writer • sometimes read your writing • listen when you read your writing • ask questions about your writing • look for strengths—what you are doing well as a writer • look for things you might want to practice • ask for help if you need support explaining/articulating what you are doing as a writer	**I will...** • share my writing • be ready to talk about what I'm doing as a writer • listen and answer questions about my writing • tell about my pictures
Praise	• tell you what you are doing well as a writer	• listen and be proud
Guide	• suggest a writing strategy, skill, or element of writer's craft that will help you as a writer • only focus on one teaching point at a time • give you a task to improve your writing and time to try it • be your guide, but also your challenger	• listen and watch carefully • commit to trying out your suggestions • give it a try • tell you when I do not understand • ask questions to better understand
Connect	• check back with you to see how the new work is going • remind you to use what you learned in your future writing	• remember to try new things in my writing • write notes about what I learn in my writer's notebook • continue to work hard on my writing
The Class's Role		

We will...
- respect the teacher and other students during conference time
- work together to problem solve by asking a friend and using our resources instead of interrupting a conference to ask the teacher for help
- stay focused on our own individual writing

Strategy 5: Prepare a Conferring Toolkit

The writing conference provides opportunities for targeted instruction to meet students' individual needs. Preparing a toolkit for conferring allows us to be productive and efficient during the limited time available for conferences. Here is some information about how to create a successful toolkit.

What is a Conferring Toolkit?

Just as a carpenter or sculptor has unique sets of tools to refine their crafts, teachers also need a collection of tools to meet the individual writing needs of our students. A conferring toolkit is a place to keep all the conferring resources organized and easily accessible. These toolkits can change over time and no two are exactly the same.

Why prepare a Conferring Toolkit?

A conferring toolkit helps us to be more prepared and organized, thus the conference becomes more efficient and productive. When the materials needed are close by, the necessary resources are available to "show" students how to write, and not just "tell" them what to do.

What kind of Conferring Toolkit is best?

Whether you develop an electronic toolkit, a small tote, a file box, or a three-ring binder, keep it simple, organized, and portable. When making that decision, keep these tips in mind:

- **Think minimalistic:** What are the resources and tools essential to support my student? There are many resources and tools to choose from that can be used for instruction. Soon the toolkit can be overflowing with "stuff," some of which is probably not all that important. Conferring with students is a valuable yet brief teaching moment best filled with conversation and writing, not stuff.

- **Think genre:** Many teachers organize their conferring toolkits based on the genre they are teaching. The writing samples, mentor texts, and revision checklists. all relate to a specific genre. This helps minimize the amount of material needed when trying to locate a specific resource.

- **Think convenience:** Develop a toolkit where resources are easily accessible and portable. Having everything readily available and handy creates efficiency and prevents interruptions of conferring conversations. The second you have to run over to a desk or cabinet to find something, you lose the focus of your instruction. When moving from an individual conference at a student's desk to a small-group conference at a table, having a toolkit that is portable is key to efficiency.

What resources and tools should be included in a Conferring Toolkit?

The resources that are included in a conferring toolkit should support the overall writing development of your students. No two toolkits will be the same, but here is a list of recommended resources:

- **A checklist, rubric, targeted skills list, or writing development chart:** Focusing on goals that are clearly articulated in some form of chart or list guides our teaching. It is a reminder of the teaching points that are the focus of a specific genre of writing and the essential strategies, skills, and crafts that students need to be successful. A checklist helps teachers remain tuned in to the writer, not the writing.See pages 126–132 for sample checklists that can be used in your toolkit.

Time to Write and Confer

- **Examples of teacher and student writing:** These are exemplar writing pieces created by the teacher to mirror the phases of writing students may encounter while developing their own writing. For example, a narrative draft that may be without details, dialogue, or character development can be used to show students how to elaborate in those skill areas. If punctuating dialogue is a targeted skill, provide writing demonstration pieces with dialogue lacking commas and quotation marks, etc. Place these pieces in plastic sleeves and use dry erase markers to mark them. This allows for the exemplars to be used again and again.

  Similarly, a modeled writing piece created during whole-group mini-lessons or student work collected from previous classes can be shared as exemplars of genre expectations. Use sticky notes to identify specific writing techniques you wish to highlight.

- **Mentor texts:** Using favorite authors as mentors is another means of sharing examples of quality writing, as well as inspiring student writers. When selecting a mentor text, search the text for multiple strategies that can be used for demonstrations. Once you select the mentor texts for a writing genre, identify and tag the strategies and crafts you want to target and teach for easy access. Write down exactly what the skill/craft is and how to state it in conversations. For example, "Let's look to see how Jane Yolen uses similes and metaphors to add rich language to describe the moment. How might you try that in your writing today?" Then, demonstrate the skill and guide the student in using the technique. Figure 4.4 provides a list of favorite mentor texts for the various writing genres. Additional lists of mentor texts may be found in Appendix B.

Figure 4.4 Favorite Mentor Texts

	Grades K–2	Grades 3–5	Grades 6–8
Opinion	*I Wanna New Room* by Karen Kaufman Orloff *Can I Have a Stegosaurus, Mom? Can I? Please!?* by Lois Grambling and H.B. Lewis *Red is Best* by Kathy Stinson	*Earrings!* By Judith Viorst *Hey, Little Ant* by Hannah Hoose and Philiph Hoose	*The Great Kapok Tree* by Lynne Cherry *The Snow Walker* by Farley Mowatt *The Best Town in the World* by Byrd Baylor
Informative	*How to Lose All Your Friends* by Nancy Carlson *One Tiny Turtle* by Nicola Davies *If You Were a Penguin* by Florence Minor	*Animals Nobody Loves* by Seymour Simon *The Pumpkin Book* by Gail Gibbons *Eye to Eye: How Animals See the World* by Steve Jenkins	*Tornadoes* by Seymour Simon *A Drop of Water: A Book of Science and Wonder* by Walter Wick *Airborne: A Photobiography of Wilbur and Orville Wright* by Mary Collins
Narrative	*The Snowy Day* by Ezra Jack Keats *Shortcut* by Donald Crews *Come On, Rain!* By Karen Hesse	*Fireflies!* By Julie Brinckloe *Owl Moon* by Jane Yolen *The Pain and the Great One* by Judy Blume	*The Table Where Rich People Sit* by Byrd Baylor *Marshfield Dreams* by Ralph Fletcher *Thank You, Mr. Falker* by Patricia Polacco

	Grades K–2	Grades 3–5	Grades 6–8
Poetry	*I Love You the Purplest* by Barbara M. Joosse *Creatures of Earth, Sea, and Sky* by Georgia Heard *Here's a Little Poem: A Very First Book of Poetry* by Jane Yolen and Andrew Fusek Peters	*Twilight Comes Twice* by Ralph Fletcher *Water Dance* by Thomas Locker *Love That Dog* by Sharon Creech	*Ubiquitous* by Joyce Sidman *Joyful Noise: Poems for Two Voices* by Paul Fleishman *The Place My Words Are Looking For: What Poets Say About and Through Their Work* by Paul B. Janeczko

- **Mini-charts:** Having a mini version of classroom anchor charts provides a familiar starting point during the conference and a visual resource for students as they work independently. Digital photos of classroom charts can be resized and printed to give to students to add to their writing folders or notebooks. Many teachers store these supportive resources in tablet apps like Penultimate, Dropbox, or Google docs for easy access during conferences. When stored on a classroom website, students gain immediate support for their writing.

For younger students, mini versions of an alphabet chart, as well as spelling charts including blends, digraphs, and vowels are all useful to developing writers. A list of high-frequency words can be helpful as well.

Additional Conference Tools:

- **Sticky notes:** Sticky notes are versatile tools that make them a favorite for conferences. They can be arranged one way, then rearranged another—stuck, unstuck and re-stuck to create just the right sequence of a story or structure of a sentence. Many teachers use them to jot down anecdotal notes during the conference that will later be added to a student page in their conferring notebooks.

- **Student checklists:** Just as a teacher has a rubric or goal sheet, a student-friendly checklist helps writers stay tuned in to the task at hand. Checklists may be targeted to a specific phase of the writing process such as editing or publishing. Or, they may reflect the genre of writing. See samples of student checklists on pages 126–132.

- **Blank paper:** Always include blank copies of the writing paper students are using for "in the moment" teaching.

- **Revision tools:** Revision tools, such as a mini-stapler, scissors, glue, and highlighting tape always seem to come in handy. But, be careful to include only those items that are essential to instruction, so as not to clutter up your toolkit.

- **Writing implements:** Pencils, pens, colored pens for editing, highlighters, markers, and crayons are important to include.

- **Conferring Notebook:** The conferring notebook is included as a valuable tool because it needs to be accessible during every conference. It is used during the conferring time to record specific notes regarding students' strengths and needs. It helps us keep track of which students we have conferred with and reminds us of what skills we may need to reteach. The conferring notebook is fully described in Chapter 7.

How-To/Procedural Checklist

☐ Write about something you are an expert on.

☐ Write a clear title.

☐ List the materials needed. (You will need...)

☐ Use pictures or drawings. (Step 1, Step 2...)

☐ Add words that match the pictures or drawings.

☐ Use order words.

first	next	then
before	after	finally

☐ Include action words.

bake	color	cut	cut
dip	draw	eat	glue
kick	lick	mix	paint
pour	pull	roll	run
stir	spread	shake	trim
walk			

☐ Start each sentence with a capital letter.

☐ End each sentence with punctuation.

Emergent Writer Narrative Checklist

How's My Writing?

 I can tell and draw about a small moment from my life.

 I can draw and write about what happened first in my story (beginning).

 I can draw and write about what happened next (middle).

 I can draw and write about what happened last in my story (end).

 My drawing and writing tell who is in my story.

 My drawing and writing tell where the story takes place.

 My drawing and writing share the feelings of the characters in my story.

Early Writer Narrative Checklist

How's My Writing?

Not Yet ☐ Yes ☐	**Beginning** I included a "hook." I described the setting (where, when). I introduced the characters (who).
Not Yet ☐ Yes ☐	**Middle** I shared the events in the story and introduced the problem (if there was one). The events are in an order that makes sense. I added details and action verbs. I used linking/transition words to show time and order.
Not Yet ☐ Yes ☐	**End** I described what happens to my characters and how the problem was solved. I wrote about how my characters feel or what lesson my characters learned.
Not Yet ☐ Yes ☐	**Editing** All my sentences began with a capital letter. All my sentences end with punctuation. I used the word wall and my word lists to check my spelling. I reread my story to make sure it makes sense.

Opinion Essay Checklist

Ideas/Purpose

☐ I clearly named the topic/text and stated my opinion.

☐ I focused on the topic throughout my writing.

☐ I attended to the audience and purpose of my writing.

Organization/Structure

☐ I introduced my topic in a way that grabs the reader's attention. (Can you believe...? Did you know...?)

☐ I introduced my reasons and evidence in paragraphs/sections.

☐ I used linking words and phrases that connect my opinion and reasons.

☐ I provided a concluding statement or section that stresses the value of my opinion.

Evidence/Resources

☐ I included facts, reasons, and evidence that support and strengthen my opinion.

☐ I listed sources that support evidence of my opinion.

Word Choice/Sentence Fluency

☐ I selected language relative to the audience and purpose of the writing.

☐ I used content-specific vocabulary when necessary and appropriate.

☐ I began my sentences in different ways.

☐ I completed my sentences without any run-ons.

☐ I included different types and lengths of sentences in my writing.

Conventions

I edited my writing for:

☐ capitalization   ☐ punctuation

☐ grammar usage   ☐ spelling

Informative/Explanatory Essay Checklist

Ideas/Purpose

- [ ] I named the topic and clearly stated the main idea.
- [ ] I focused on the topic throughout my writing.
- [ ] I attended to the audience and purpose of my writing.

Organization/Structure

- [ ] I introduced my topic in a way that grabs the reader's attention.
- [ ] I organized my facts and examples into logical progressions of paragraphs/sections.
- [ ] I used a variety of transitional words and phrases to link ideas.
- [ ] I provided a concluding statement or section that relates to my audience and purpose.

Evidence/Resources

- [ ] I included facts, examples, and details that support and strengthen my main idea.
- [ ] I integrated sources that support my facts in a way that continues the flow of the writing.

Word Choice/Sentence Fluency

- [ ] I selected language relative to the audience and purpose of the writing.
- [ ] I used academic and domain-specific vocabulary when necessary and appropriate.
- [ ] I began my sentences in different ways.
- [ ] I completed my sentences without any run-ons.
- [ ] I included different types and lengths of sentences in my writing.

Conventions

I edited my writing for:

- [ ] capitalization
- [ ] punctuation
- [ ] grammar usage
- [ ] correct spelling

Narrative Writing
(Real/Imaginary) Checklist

Introduction

☐ I opened with a strong lead (action, dialogue, inner thoughts, question, description).

☐ I established the setting to orientate the reader.

☐ I introduced the narrator and/or main characters.

☐ I gave details that initiate the plot of the story.

Structure/Organization

☐ I organized my story using a traditional narrative sequence (e.g., introduction, build-up, complicated action/problem, resolution, conclusion).

☐ I included transition words, phrases, and clauses to manage the sequence of the story.

☐ I ended with a strong conclusion that resolves the problem, reaches a goal, teaches a lesson, or changes feelings/beliefs.

Elaboration/Craft

☐ I elaborated on the storyline through narrative techniques such as actions, descriptions, dialogue, inner thoughts, pacing, flashbacks, etc.

☐ I used precise word choice, sensory details, and figurative language to illustrate the story for my reader.

☐ I used character traits and emotions to develop characters.

☐ I varied sentence lengths and structures to create pacing and tone in the story.

Conventions

☐ I used punctuation to emphasize meaning, pacing, and/or emotions.

☐ I edited my paper for spelling, grammar, punctuation, and capitalization.

Argumentative Writing Checklist

Introduction

☐ I developed a lead statement that connects all sources of information. (This should be a statement and not an opinion.)

☐ I used a thesis statement that includes wording from the prompt. (It explains who, when, how many, which ones, where, and uses a debatable phrase: does, does not, should, should not.)

☐ I explained the significance to the audience (proving that..., resulting in..., making us doubt..., reminding us that...).

Structure/Organization

☐ I used transition words or phrases to link ideas and paragraphs.

☐ I paraphrased the evidence that addresses my thesis statement. (Paraphrase using your own language when talking about evidence from the text.)

☐ I added several sentences to elaborate using bits of evidence from the text.

☐ I cited references from the source/article and included title and paragraph number.

☐ I presented supporting points from weakest to strongest.

☐ I ended paragraphs with a statement that wraps up the main idea of the paragraph.

Elaboration/Craft

☐ I varied sentence structure, type, and length.

☐ I used precise word choice relative to my topic and audience.

☐ I involved my audience by using rhetorical questions.

☐ I included an analogy, simile, or metaphor for clarity (if appropriate).

Conclusion

☐ I restated my thesis statement.

☐ I paraphrased each main idea chunk from the body paragraphs.

☐ I wrote a concluding sentence that captures the overall main idea of the work, not my opinion.

Conventions

☐ I capitalized proper nouns, proper adjectives, words in titles, first words in quotations, and first words in sentences.

☐ I used correct punctuation (question mark, exclamatory mark, period, commas in series) before quotation marks, dates, city/state, and linking sentences with a conjunction.

☐ I used apostrophes and quotation marks correctly.

☐ I used resources to edit spelling.

Tips for Successful Writing Conferences

In this chapter we've given you the strategies you need to implement individual and small-group conferences in Writing Workshop effectively. As you use these strategies the power packed tips that follow will help ensure your success.

- **Focus** on the development of the writer, not just the writing.

- **Talk** *with* writers, not *at* writers. Become comfortable with the language and vocabulary of writing through holding student-led conversation—writer to writer.

- **Be patient** with the writer. Our fast-paced world means that teachers are often trying to just fit it all in. During the conference slow down, listen, and allow students the time they need to gather their thoughts, capture a moment, or think of just the right word.

- **Praise** and celebrate student accomplishments with words of kindness. The finished product is never as valuable as the feeling of self-confidence, pride, and joy in the writing itself.

- **Practice** with a colleague. Visit each other's classroom during the conference time and notice, note, and share what you observed about the conversation and teaching method. Study student writing together, identifying writing strengths, needs, and goals for the writer. "If you have even one colleague with whom you can share ideas, readings, and questions, you can draw from that enough energy to maintain your motivation and ability to grow professionally" (Graves 2002, 9).

- **Be efficient.** Make a commitment to organize materials and to use a timer. When materials and resources are disorganized and hard to find, it can take time from student learning. Until you are comfortable with the flow of the writing conference, use a timer. It helps to stay focused on the teaching point. When given more time, teachers often over-confer and over-explain—leaving students confused.

- **Read** a variety of writing texts and literature. Explore and find the authors and texts that best support your instruction as you guide students through the strategies, skills, and crafts of writing genres.

- **Write** for your students and with your students. Be an active writer by practicing a teaching point in your own writing. Mem Fox (1993, 163) tells us, "If you are not a writer, you will not understand the difficulties of writing. If you are not a writer, you will not know the fears and hopes of the writers you teach. If you are not a writer, you will not be aware of the needs of a writer..."

- **Set goals** for both you and your students. There is so much to be done in the teaching and learning of writing. By establishing a goal, you can master one valuable piece at a time.

- **Mess up!** Yes, you have official permission. Even when the conference doesn't go quite as expected, it's really okay. Just by talking and showing you are genuinely interested in how a student is doing helps him or her become a more confident writer. There's always the next time.

- **Reflect** about your student's learning as well as your conferring. Notice and note the strengths and needs of your student to monitor development and utilize during planning for future writing instruction. Reflect on your conferring skills by asking yourself: "How did I impact this writer today? Did he or she leave excited and eager or deflated and empty?"

- **Keep it simple.** Conferring is an art that develops through commitment and continued practice. What is important? Not to have the best conferring toolkit, conference logs, or resources, but to let students know the importance and value you put on writing in your everyday life. Giving students time, attention, and guidance goes a long way to getting that same principle across to them.

Conclusion

Remember, "Time to Write and Confer" is one of the legs of our three-legged stool model for implementing strategies for Writer's Workshop. Conferring both individually and in small groups is an essential part of the Writing and Conferring leg. When you take the time to have "writerly" conversations with your students that acknowledge their accomplishments, support their weaknesses, and lift and motivate them as writers, you become *that* special teacher who values them as writers; who strives to provide differentiated instruction; who observes, listens, and asks questions that help them become better writers; and who enables them to reach their writing goals.

Michelangelo is famously quoted as having said, "Every block of stone has a statue inside it and it is the task of the sculptor to discover it." Likewise, there is writer inside every one of your students. By conferencing with individuals and in small groups, you will enable those students to discover the writer inside.

Strategies for Writing in the Content Area

A new era of state and national standards intended to get students ready for college and careers has created new focus on writing in the content areas. At every level—federal, state, and local—there is renewed emphasis on teaching content-area writing beginning in primary school and continuing through middle school and beyond. Why is this necessary? No one explains it better than the following quote:

> *Adolescents entering the adult world in the 21st century will read and write more than at any other time in human history. They will need advanced levels of literacy to perform their jobs, run their households, act as citizens, and conduct their personal lives. They will need literacy to cope with the flood of information they will find everywhere they turn. They will need literacy to feed their imaginations so they can create the world of the future. (Moore et al. 1999, 3)*

Content-area researchers as well as classroom innovators have demonstrated how reading and writing go hand in hand and that students need instruction in writing strategies for deep learning with texts and writing in the content areas covering genres such as narrative, informational, opinion/argumentative, and poetry (Vacca 1998; Robb 2000).

A paper from the Educational Policy Improvement Center entitled "Redefining College Readiness" based on the last two decades of research lists specific content knowledge, including skills in writing and specific content areas, as one of four key components for college success (Conley 2011). It reports that students are expected to write extensively in college and to do so within short time frames. This research follows the Writing Workshop model as it reports that students need to know how to pre-write, edit, and rewrite a piece before it is submitted. Once a piece of writing has been submitted and feedback has subsequently been provided, students often must repeat this process (Conley 2007). Beyond that, as reported in *The New York Times*, "Writing is the single most important skill for success in college" (Atkinson and Geisermay 2015).

In a synthesis of research as well as examples based on best practices from their own experience, researchers Douglas Fisher and Gay Ivey (2005) created six foundational principles for writing in the content areas. They argue that the goal of content-area literacy is to help students learn and that writing and reading are foundational for thinking. To be a successful and strategic content-area writing teacher, follow these six guiding principles below based on Fisher and Ivey (2005) and include narrative, informational, opinion/argument, and poetry writing in the discipline.

1. Expect students to read and write every day in every class.

2. Select texts and writing engagements that span a range of difficulty levels including casual, semiformal, and formal pieces.

3. Teach students strategies for reading and writing increasingly complex text.

4. Link students' reading and writing to what they already know, what they are interested in, and contemporary issues.

5. Dedicate instructional time to self-selected reading and writing in the content areas.

6. Give students ownership and autonomy by allowing them to select their own writing topics.

Figure 5.1 Six Principles for Effective Content-Area Writing

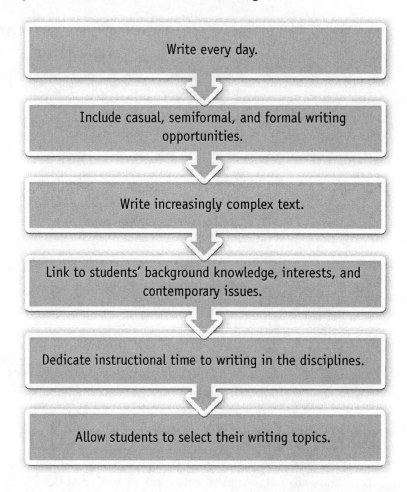

In this chapter, you will find six strategies for teaching students writing in the content areas:

- Write every day
- Include casual, semiformal, and formal writing opportunities
- Write increasingly complex text
- Link to students' background knowledge, interests, and contemporary issues
- Dedicate instructional time to writing in the disciplines (including sample graphic organizers for grades K–8)
- Allow students to select their writing topics

Strategy 1: Write Every Day

Writing is fundamental. It's key to sharpening the critical and analytical capacities of our minds, in our worlds of work, and in our worlds of civic commitment, so we should recommit ourselves in intensified fashion to the study and teaching of writing. (Baucom 2014)

Teachers who lecture from notes to dispense content knowledge might be reminded of the old proverb: give a man a fish and you feed him for a day; teach a man to fish and you feed him for a lifetime. Move from a delivery stance to a "learn by writing" stance. When you teach students to learn information from the curriculum in your content area by writing you are giving the student a tool he or she can use for a lifetime. That is to say, it's more worthwhile to teach students to learn by writing in your content area than to simply give them facts or knowledge to pass a test.

Susan Sturock, a seasoned educator and national education consultant, writes about how the content areas and learning by writing are inseparable:

Science attempts to explain the phenomena of our Earth and the galaxies. Math attempts to quantify and manipulate the phenomena. Technology attempts to deliver the manipulations and imaginings. History attempts to codify events unfolding.

Writing across these inseparable content areas is how students learn about them at the deepest level. The literature that comes out of content area writing is a human record of the writer's journeys and learning outcomes. It is the voice, eyes and souls of those both present and far removed resonating and offering the possibility of wisdom. (Sturock 2015)

Both writing and reading are vehicles for teaching your students to learn. You can't foresee what obstacles or opportunities your students will face in life, but if you teach students the foundational skill of writing to learn, they will be ready to use these tools in all content areas for lifelong learning.

Use a Sports Model for Repeated Practice

Think of your favorite sport—football, baseball, basketball, soccer. Now consider the time your favorite sports star spends playing the game on the field in front of an audience versus the time spent practicing.

Here's an example: A college football player spends a significant amount of time preparing for the season and for each game. There are summer training camps, practices with pads and without, sessions to study videotape of their own and their opponents' performance, weight training, and even some days where they practice twice. There can be up to 29 practices before the first game!

Students should expect a similar "time spent" ratio for a formal writing project. You might plan five or six formal writing projects in your content area or in your self-contained classroom each year. A formal writing assignment due each six weeks in the content area is like the big game schedule. It's the piece that is in front of an audience. And if the piece is to represent the best work of the writer, it's likely that a lot of casual writing and semiformal writing has been happening behind the scene (just like weight training and football practice), before the final product.

Ask students: "Do professional athletes spend more time in practice or more time in games?" Use this analogy to help your students understand why it's important for them to be writing every day. Let them know ahead of time what "big game pieces" (formal writing assignments) they will be doing this year in your classroom. Explain to them that most student writing will be like practice before a "big game."

Strategy 2: Include Casual, Semiformal, and Formal Writing Opportunities

In his popular online article, Steve Peha (2013) introduced us to three easy-to-follow strategies to help disciplinary teachers ease students into writing by moving from "casual," everyday writing, to "semiformal" writing for more expansive pieces, and finally to "formal" writing for major writing projects. Using the "Dress for Success" strategies not only eases students into content-area writing but it also helps them develop routines, gain confidence, avoid feelings of anxiety about writing, develop ownership, and, most importantly from a motivational standpoint, makes writing in the content areas fun and enjoyable for both you and your students.

There are many ways to move from the casual samples to the semiformal and the formal samples that are listed in Figures 5.2–5.4. For example, a list of people in a kindergartner's family might lead to drawings with speech bubbles about one fun thing that happened with that family member and that might finally lead to a little eight-page kindergarten book entitled "A Fun Day at the Beach with Dad!" A grade 3–5 journal response might lead to a draft of a piece that the student turns into a report for the class newsletter. In grades 6–8, a free write about the student's feelings about the developer who cut down the 50-year-old trees in the city's historic district might lead to a draft of an opinion piece that could eventually lead to a formal opinion piece for the local newspaper. The possibilities are endless when you invite students to choose their own topics and give them ownership in deciding who their audience is going to be. The writing becomes easier when they move from casual, to semiformal, to formal.

Figure 5.2 Sample Casual Writing Ideas

Grades K–2	• Lists • Labels • Sticky notes to highlight target features in a mentor text (e.g., "It made me laugh when…")	
Grades 3–5	• Lists • What I think…Why I think it • Sticky notes • Drawings with speech bubbles	• Free writes • Notebook entries • Journal/log responses • Brainstorms
Grades 6–8	• Lists from readings • Field notes from observations • Free writes	• Notebook entries • Journal/log responses • Brainstorms

Figure 5.3 Sample Semiformal Writing Ideas

Grades K–2	• Drafts • Responses • Drawings with speech bubbles	
Grades 3–5	• Summaries • Responses • Drafts	• Field notes from observations • Informal letters, notes, emails • Reading/dialogue journals
Grades 6–8	• Summaries • Responses • Drafts	• Field notes from observations • Informal letters, notes, emails • Reading/dialogue journals

Figure 5.4 Sample Formal Writing Ideas

Grades K–2	• Fairy tale • Poem • Autobiography	• Letter • Little books (e.g., eight-page books illustrated by the student)
Grades 3–5	• Fairy Tale • Poem • Autobiography/biography • Letter	• Little books with chapters (e.g., chapter books written by the student.) • Magazine article • Newsletter report
Grades 6–8	• Editorial • Poem/play • Autobiography/biography • Formal letter • Book with chapters (fiction and nonfiction)	• Magazine article • Newsletter report • Blog • Formal interview • Brochure

Chapter 5

Show Students How to Take Structured Notes

Taking notes is a study habit that requires explicit instruction. Note-taking helps students think about and analyze text material, a lecture, or an interview more deeply and comprehensively. It is also a way to have students engage in interleaved practice, which is variable or mixed practice. Instead of using notes in one way such as simply reviewing notes for a test, cognitive scientists and neuroscientists have found that students learn better by mixing, or interleaving, their practice (Dunlosky et al. 2013). With note-taking, for example, students might mix using their notes by first reviewing the notes, then creating questions to be answered from their notes, followed by using the notes to create a graphic organizer to show *how* new information in their notes is related to known information.

Incorporate note-taking in your teaching by showing students how to use a structured system, such as Cornell notes (Fisher, Frey and Williams 2002; Spires and Stone 1989). In this model, students search for main ideas and key words that are supported by details or quotes. At the bottom of the note-taking page, ask students to write a brief summary from the notes or remind themselves how to apply the notes.

Although many people have begun to use computers or tablets to take notes, it may be better for students to physically write notes because research shows that the brain *learns* better when things are written by hand (Berninger et al. 2009; Berninger et al. 2014).

Figure 5.5 Sample Cornell Notes Structure

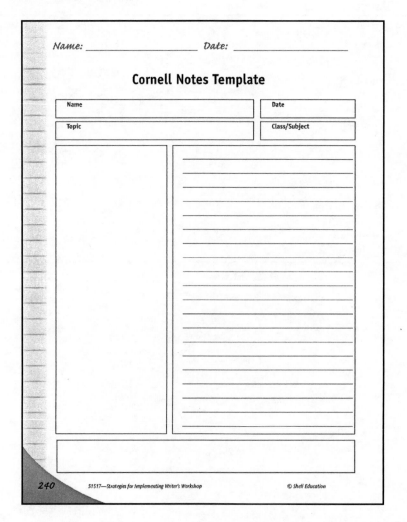

Strategy 3: Write Increasingly Complex Text

Read Like a Writer

Students should read and reread to dig deep into the writing of a recognized author and explore the "read like a writer" strategy (Harste 1993, Smith 1998, Ray 2006). This strategy helps reinforce writing skills by reading the genre that you want students to practice writing.

To implement this strategy, begin with any mentor text appropriate for the grade level and genre you are teaching and ask students to think about, "What makes this author a good writer?" One way to help students think about examining texts is to ask them to think about the way a mechanic inspects a car. Students can "open the hood and look deep inside." This means they are looking at a text from a writer's perspective. Here are questions to get the class started:

- How long is the text?

- What is the purpose of the text?

- Who do you think is the audience?

- How is the text organized?

- What text features (bolded words, headings, diagrams, charts, photos) are used?

- What are different alternatives for writing a text like this?

After students have examined the text, ask them to brainstorm about what they could do to make their own writing more like this author. Tell them we call this strategy "Reading Like a Writer." Make a wall chart with their suggestions for your focus author. Note that their suggestions will vary depending upon the author, the genre, and the grade level.

For example, if you want students to write paragraphs to express their opinions about a topic, gather samples of opinion pieces and study the text features for them. Did the author use underlined, bold, italicized, or highlighted words? What headings and subheadings were used? How long (or brief) is the piece? Did the author use diagrams, charts, graphs, maps, or tables to support his or her opinions? Are there photographs, illustrations, sidebars, captions, bullets, or numbered lists? Did the author use parentheses or footnotes? As a class, list the text features that are identified. Then, allow students time to create their own pieces using qualities of the studied text/author.

Sample Teacher Talk

"Now that we have thought about reading like a great author, practice reading like a writer yourself. All good writers read a lot and pick up tips from other writers. You have to read to become a writer because reading helps you think like a writer!"

Time to Write and Confer

Use Pictures and Diagrams to Understand Complex Ideas

Graphic organizers are useful tools for writers of all ages because they help students organize their thoughts and plan their ideas. They also help authors convey complex ideas in ways that are easier for the reader to understand.

I discovered the power of drawing and learned that when you draw something, you get closer to it and know it better. (LaMarche 2001, 4)

1. Show students that making a drawing is a form of thinking. If they draw something they see it better.

2. Model how to use diagrams and drawings in both reading and written texts. For example, use a sketch and labels to explain the cycle of photosynthesis or any complex process.

3. Use a balance of teacher-planned diagrams and curricular pictures and diagrams along with student-initiated pictures and diagrams that meet curricular standards and content. For example, show how pictures of the trait characters such as Ida the Idea Creator and Wally Word Choice Detective help students remember the traits of quality writing. (See Appendix C for trait posters.)

4. Allow student choice for pictures and diagrams. Have them explore ideas for pictures and diagrams by finding examples of how authors have used pictures and diagrams to help the reader understand complex texts in their science, history, math texts, or other subject areas.

5. Model options students may choose from: a mural, map, chart, computer graphics, photography, illustration, painting, cartoons, and the like.

"Use drawing to develop and share thinking." (Gray 2006, 228)

Model Graphic Organizers that Represent Text Structures

Graphic organizers are useful tools for writers of all ages because they help students organize their thoughts and plan their ideas.

Figure 5.6 provides a variety of graphic organizers that can be used to demonstrate text structure and help students plan and create their own writing using those structures. Graphic organizers make different sense to different kinds of writers. Not all students use them in the same way (or even need them in the same way). Consider encouraging older students or more advanced writers to design their own organizers that work for them.

Figure 5.6 Sample Graphic Organizers that Represent Text Structures

Text Structure	Graphic Organizer	Example(s)
Sequence or Chronological Storyboard/Sequence Chain/Timeline This can be easily adapted for younger writers with simple beginning/middle/end, or made more complex to challenge students.	1 ➡ 2 ➡ 3 4 ➡ 5 ➡ 6 7 ➡ 8 ➡ 9	Students enjoy writing personal narratives. Storyboards help organize their ideas and details. How things happen, such as how a star is formed or how food is digested, and how-to topics, like brushing your teeth or harvesting grapes, are possible topics for sequence chains.
Compare and Contrast Venn Diagram Venn diagrams visually represent attributes that are similar in the overlapping area and different in individual circles.	(two overlapping circles)	Venn diagrams may be used when identifying similarities and differences between animals, such as a lion and tiger or two presidents. Often, consumer reports compare and contrast different product brands to inform the public.
Cause and Effect Event-Cause or T-chart Either chart serves to support students in planning writing.	**Effect/Event** **Cause** | **Cause** | **Cause** **Cause** **Effect**	Changes in weather patterns (causes) may explain the unexpected hurricane (effect/event), or the hurricane (effect/event) could be explained as the cause of a number of hardships.
Problem Solution Flow Chart A simple flow chart can support writers of different developmental levels by simply increasing or decreasing the number of events in the organizer.	**Problem** ↓ **Event** ↓ **Event** ↓ **Event** ↓ **Solution**	Problem and solution can be used to persuade the reader that motorized transportation is a problem, offering alternatives and then recommending solutions like riding a bike. Younger writers can relate to mentor texts when identifying the problem and solution and then creating their own writing.
Description Detail Web/Sensory Web The topic is in the center and descriptive details are listed in each circle. Additional stems may branch out to represent more related details.	**Topic** (central circle with branching circles)	A book about Italy (main topic) and the culture, people, and land (subtopics) is an example of a detail web. The subtopics would then each contain details represented by additional web lines. Brochures often contain examples of descriptive writing.

(Gentry, McNeel, and Wallace-Nesler 2014)

     51517—Strategies for Implementing Writer's Workshop

Chapter 5

Teach Vocabulary to Help Support Genre Writing

Knowing vocabulary inspires students to do their best writing on daily assignments and builds an understanding of terminology that provides a choice of words to communicate their thinking. When specific genres are introduced within classroom instruction, provide the examples either as an anchor chart or as an insert in a writing folder. The following sample sentence stems will help your students understand and use the kind of vocabulary needed to develop organizational skills and flow of specific text.

Sample Sentence Stems to Support Opinion Writing Grades K–2

Introduction	Body	Conclusion
I agree...	According to...	To sum up...
I disagree...	In fact...	It is obvious...
It is my belief...	Besides...	As I have noted...
I believe...	In my experience...	As you can see...
I think...	For instance...	In conclusion...
My point is...	Although...	After all...
	In support of...	
	Next...	

Sample Sentence Stems to Support Informative Writing Grades K–2

Introduction	Body	Conclusion
First...	Eventually...	After all...
Experts tell us...	During...	To sum up...
To begin with...	At this point...	In the final....
It is true that...	Prior to...	To summarize...
Did you know...	Although...	To close...
No doubt!	Immediately...	Finally...
	Likewise...	
	Additionally...	
	Furthermore...	

Sample Sentence Stems to Support Narrative Writing Grades K–2

Introduction	Body	Conclusion
Long ago...	All at once...	As you can see...
One summer day...	Later...	Finally...
One foggy morning...	The next day...	Fortunately...
In a log cabin...	Meanwhile...	To this day...
On my first day of school...	Since we...	After all...
On my family vacation...	After that...	As it turned out....
On the playground...	That afternoon...	So the next time...
Once upon a time...	Since we were ready for school...	

Sample Sentence Stems to Support Opinion Writing Grades 3–8

Introduction	Body	Conclusion
In my opinion...	According to...	To sum up...
I disagree...	For instance...	In conclusion...
It is my belief that...	In support of this...	All things considered...
I question whether...	In addition...	Given these ideas...
I believe...	Moreover...	In any event...
From my point of view...	In fact...	As I have explained...
I agree...	In my experience...	After all...
I maintain that...	Although...	As I have noted...
There is no doubt that...	I personally believe...	To summarize...
	On the other hand...	As shown above...
	Similarly...	As you can see...
	I believe...	In the final analysis...
	As evidence...	Without a doubt...
	Consequently...	Summing up...
	For example...	As a result...
	Despite...	
	Furthermore...	
	Besides....	

Time to Write and Confer

Sample Sentence Stems to Support Informative Writing Grades 3–8

Introduction	Body	Conclusion
To begin with...	Based on the text...	To sum up...
Authorities say...	Although...	In conclusion...
It is a fact...	My inference is...	Given these ideas...
Did you know?...	An example is...	After all...
Experts tell us...	Furthermore...	As you can see...
For hundreds of years...	Nevertheless...	In the final analysis...
According to the text...	The author stated...	To summarize...
Born as a famous...	In addition...	Summing it all up...
Scientists say...	In fact...	All things considered...
Many challenges...	For instance...	As a result...
It is true that...	Despite...	As I have explained...
Three things I know...	Instead...	In brief...
	At this point...	As I have noted...
	Additionally...	Obviously...
	According to the text...	Without a doubt...
	Equally important...	In summation...
	Why else...	In other words...
	To demonstrate...	In any event...

Time to Write and Confer

Sample Sentence Stems to Support Narrative Writing Grades 3–8

Introduction	Body	Conclusion
Long, long ago…	All at once…	When I think back…
Early one morning…	As time went on…	Fortunately for me…
One foggy day…	Suddenly…	As it all turned out…
My best friend…	Out of nowhere…	To this day…
I loved walking…	As usually happens…	So the next time you…
Help! Come quickly!…	Later in the day…	It is obvious that…
Squish went the mud…	The very next day…	And wouldn't you know…
It was a splendid day…	Meanwhile…	And as it usually happens…
Not so long ago…	At this point…	Would you believe that…
Long before…	At that moment…	It wasn't long before…
On the first day…	Since we are…	In any event…
Once upon a time…	When I stepped outside…	After all of this…
One fall day…	After that…	Right to this day…
Crash! …	Lo and behold!…	As time ticked by…
On a dark night…		As luck would have it…

Strategy 4: Link to Students' Background Knowledge, Interests, and Contemporary Issues

Write Real-World Texts

When students write about themselves and the topics that matter personally to them, they are more invested in their writing and can better explore the ideas they have. It helps motivate students and also helps teach students that their own experiences and backgrounds are valid, interesting, and worthy of examination in their writing.

Listen to what students are excited to talk about when they enter the room to pick up on good real-world topics. In addition, brainstorm ideas as a group, discuss and identify school and community issues, find age-appropriate current event articles to share, etc. Real-world texts can take many forms, such as the following:

- lists
- memos
- greeting cards
- directions

- book/movie reviews
- poetry
- letters
- journals

- recipes
- personal narratives
- newspaper articles
- editorials

Figure 5.7 shares some sample writing prompts that will allow students to use their real-world knowledge in their writing.

Figure 5.7 Sample Writing Prompts for Real-World Texts

Grades K–2	• Write directions for how to take care of a pet in the classroom.
	• Write directions for how to get from school to your house.
	• Write an opinion piece for the school newspaper about how to improve the school cafeteria. Include sample menus and reviews of students' favorite foods.
Grades 3–5	• Be a reporter and write an article for the school newspaper about a school event, such as field day.
	• Publish a class magazine with stories about student athletes and community teams or write about students' favorite sports stars.
	• Write about a problem in the school or community that needs to be solved.
Grades 6–8	• Write about a type of technology in your classroom that you like to use and why.
	• Write a campaign speech for a favorite local or national election candidate.
	• Instead of a traditional book report, write a book review, a book jacket description, or an endorsement.
	• Write a movie/TV review, giving it a positive or negative review and explain why.

Teach Students to Write their Own K-W-L Charts

K-W-L Charts (Know—Want to Know—Learn) were created by Donna Ogle (1986) to engage readers in deeper levels of reading of text. They are useful for any content area as well as for literary and informational text.

Three questions are related to the reading material before, during, and after the lesson/reading:

1. **What do you know about the topic?** This helps the reader activate prior knowledge and consider what they already know about a topic.

2. **What do you want to know about the topic?** This helps the reader make predictions while reading and focuses attention on encouraging the reader to read deeper.

3. **What did you learn about the topic?** This helps the reader summarize the information (Fisher, Frey, and Williams, 2002).

The K-W-L graphic organizer is a great example of semiformal writing because it's easy to set up and requires little explanation for students. They simply make three columns and answer the three questions. It can be a daily or weekly activity that extends the lesson or unit. Display the K-W-L chart for students and demonstrate how it use it. You may want to do shared writing where the teacher and students compose K-W-L charts together until beginning writers can do them on their own. Figure 5.8 shows a sample K-W-L graphic organizer.

Figure 5.8 Sample K-W-L Graphic Organizer

K **What I Know**	W **What I Want to Know**	L **What I Learned**
(Before reading/the lesson) Activate the student's background knowledge: In this space students relate what they already know about the topic by generating a list.	(Before and during reading/ the lesson) Set goals for learning and add new questions: In this space students relate what they want to know about the topic by generating a list.	(After reading/the lesson) Summarize and review the learning: In this space students summarize what they learned and list the questions that have been answered.
I know that... I learned about this when... I saw this when I...	I want to know... I am curious about... I wonder...	In summary, the most important things I learned are: My study answered these questions:

 Strategy 5: Dedicate Instructional Time to Writing in the Disciplines

Writing across the disciplines is an important skill to prepare students for college and career. Explicit attention within Writer's Workshop should be given to developing students' abilities to write narrative text, informational text, opinion/argument text, and poetry in all of the content areas.

Narrative Writing in the Content Areas

Many state standards are explicit regarding expectations for having students write in a range of genres. For example, Common Core State Standards for fiction and nonfiction narrative state that a range of text types may be selected from a broad range of cultures and periods. These include children's adventure stories, folktales, legends, fables, fantasy, realistic fiction, dramas, and myth (Common Core State Standards Initiative 2015). Grades 5–8 include the subgenres of adventure stories, historical fiction, mysteries, myths, science fiction, realistic fiction, allegories, parodies, satire, and graphic novels (Common Core State Standards Initiative 2015).

Creative uses of these genres make writing in the content areas challenging and fun. For example, in science or mathematics, a student might create a story about how a main hero or event solved a problem without a determinable basis of fact or a natural explanation and dispelled a myth. A student-written drama might reenact a famous historical event.

Successful writers often receive support through graphic organizers whether they are a proficient writer or need simple words of encouragement. A graphic organizer that can be drawn or handed to students with completed words and phrases encourages writing success. The resources that follow (pages 150–154) can be used to support students as they write narratives in any content area.

Name: _____ Date: _____

Beginning, Middle, and End

Directions: Tell a story using the boxes below. Touch each box in order as you tell it. Make sure that your story has a beginning, middle, and end. Then, draw a picture that tells your story in each box.

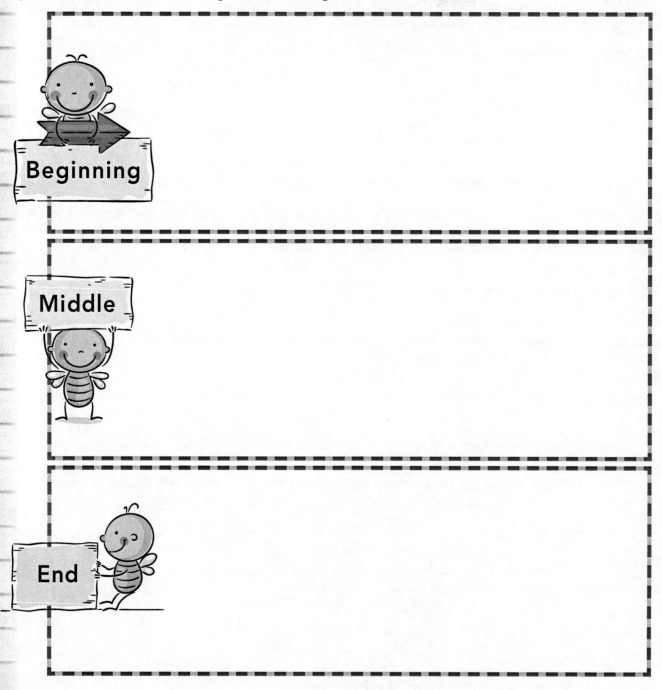

(Gentry, McNeel, and Wallace-Nesler 2012c)

51517—*Strategies for Implementing Writer's Workshop*   © *Shell Education*

Name: _____ Date: _____

My Story Mountain

Directions: Use the boxes below to plan your story.

Problem:

What's the trouble?

_____

_____

Build-Up:

What are your characters doing?

_____

_____

_____

Fix-Up:

How does this problem get solved? Who helps?

_____

_____

_____

Title:

_____

Introduction

Characters: Who?

Setting: When/Where?

_____

_____

Wrap-Up:

What happens at the end of the story?

_____

_____

(Gentry, McNeel, and Wallace-Nesler 2012c)

Name: _____ Date: _____

Telling a Story

Narrative writing may be a fictional story like *The Wizard of Oz* or a personal story about something that happened to you. The purpose is to entertain the reader. Both have characters, settings, and sequenced events.

Beginning/Introduction The introduction may be one or two paragraphs. It will "hook" your reader and introduce the topic of your story. These paragraphs will include the characters and setting.	**Brilliant Beginning (BB)** • Hook • Characters: Who? • Setting: Where? When?
Middle/Body The middle paragraphs tell the events in the order in which they happened and give the story suspense. They should include enough details to make the experience come to life for the reader.	**Mighty Middle (MM)** What happened? How did it happen? Why did it happen? • Event 1 • Event 2 • Event 3
End/Conclusion The final paragraph sums up the story. It may share your feelings about the experience or event and why it was important to you.	**Excellent Ending (EE)** • Wrap-up • Feelings/Importance

(Gentry, McNeel, and Wallace-Nesler 2012d)

Steps to Success

Directions: Complete the story steps below by filling in each section of the graphic organizer to support the development of your story.

The Big Event/Climax

The Build-Up

Events for Resolution

Getting Started
(characters, setting, when/where, mood)

The Ending

Hook/Lead/Grabber

Wrap-up/Conclusion

The Story coaster

A **story plot** is a series of linked events connected by a problem, which is eventually resolved by the character(s). It can move through a story much like a roller coaster ride.

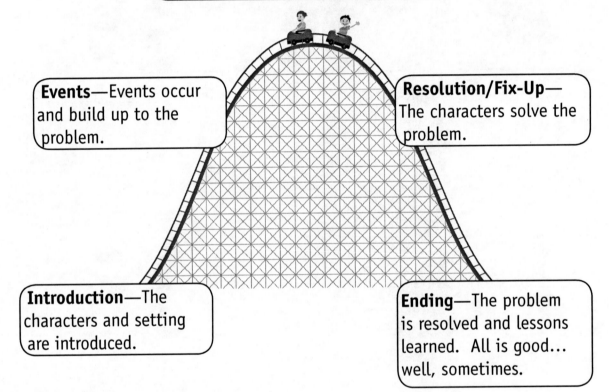

Dilemma/Climax—Something goes wrong or a mystery occurs. It is the most exciting part of the story!

Events—Events occur and build up to the problem.

Resolution/Fix-Up—The characters solve the problem.

Introduction—The characters and setting are introduced.

Ending—The problem is resolved and lessons learned. All is good... well, sometimes.

Your Turn:

Use what you know to create your own story coaster planner. Remember to revisit favorite authors and explore features of their story plots.

(Gentry, McNeel, and Wallace-Nesler 2012f)

Informative Writing in the Content Areas

Today's standards are explicit regarding expectations for having students write in a range of genres. Informational writing may cover a range of text types selected from a broad range of cultures and periods encompassing nonfiction, historical, scientific, and technical texts. For example, Common Core State Standards lists the following subgenres for informational texts which writers may use as models for their own writing: biographies and autobiographies; books about history, social studies, science, and the arts; and technical texts, including directions, forms, and information displayed in graphs, charts, or maps (Common Core State Initiative 2015).

Figure 5.9 provides some high-interest informative writing topics for each grade range.

Figure 5.9 Recommended Writing Topics

Grades K–2	Grades 3–5	Grades 6–8
Holidays	Animal Communication	History of Cartoons
Animal Habitats	Ocean Life	Atmospheric Conditions
Community Workers	Mammals	Westward Expansion
Transportation	Animal Migration	American Revolution
Animal Life Cycles	American History	Civil War
Healthy Snacks	Scientific Experiments	Hazards in the Environment
Safety	Creative Inventions	Overcoming Shyness
Weather	Living with Disabilities	How to Attend a Formal Event
Healthy Habits	Reduce and Recycle	The Economy
Other Cultures	Renewable Energy	Animal Rights
Historical People	Systems of the Body: Nervous, Circulatory, Skeletal, Muscular	TV Propaganda
Superheroes	Inspirational People	Analyzing the Past to Plan for the Future
Rights and Rules	Exploring Hiccup Preventions	Civil Rights Movement
Being a Good citizen		
Environmental Cleanup		
Woodland Preservation		

The resources that follow (pages 156–159) can be used to support students as they write informational text in any content area.

Name: _____ Date: _____

Hand Plan

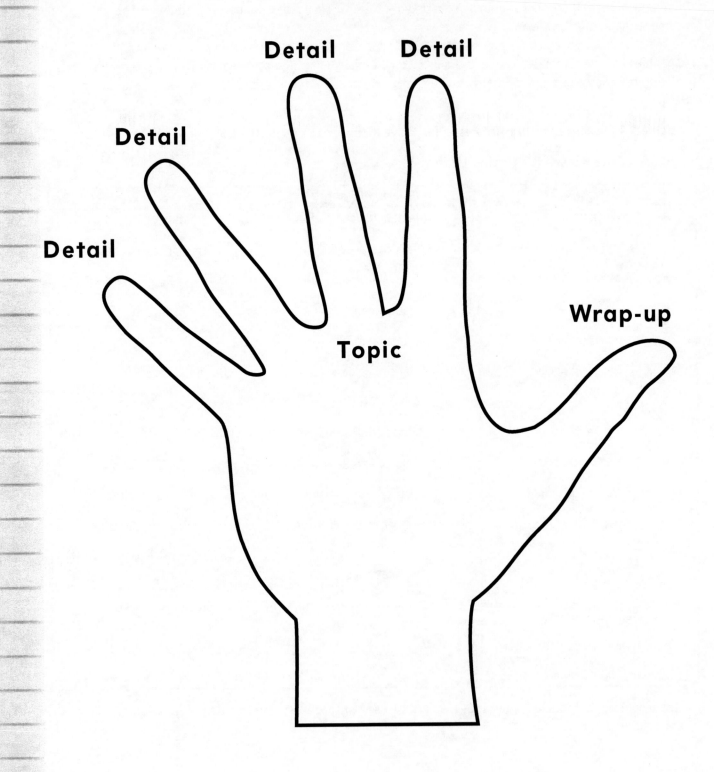

Detail   **Detail**

Detail

Detail

Wrap-up

Topic

(Gentry, McNeel, and Wallace-Nesler 2012b)

Researching from A to D

A **research report** provides factual information and informs the reader about a specific topic.

Writing research reports includes basic steps that you can use at any grade level and with any report topic. Although it may sound challenging, it is really as simple as ABCD!

Ask a question: What do I want to know more about? Think about the topic and narrow it down.

Be a researcher: Gather information from at least three resources (e.g., books, Internet). Take notes on index cards: bibliographic information on one side, your notes and quotes on the other. Remember, use your own words!

Complete an outline: The outline helps organize your information and subtopics in a logical sequence. Sort your index cards into subtopics to create paragraphs.

Draft your paper: Include a title page, introduction, body (the largest, most informative section), conclusion, and bibliography.

Your Turn:

Use the ABCD steps to write your own research report. Choose from these general topics, or select one of your own. Remember to narrow them down.

- Animals
- Environment
- Inventors
- Nutrition
- Solar System

- Authors
- Explorers
- Musicians/Artists
- Presidents
- States/Countries

(Gentry, McNeel, and Wallace-Nesler 2012f)

123 Paragraphs: Informing

An **informative paragraph** informs, describes, explains, or defines a specific subject for the reader.

There are three parts to an informative paragraph—a hook and topic sentence, the body, and a closing statement.

1. The **hook** grabs the reader and the topic sentence or main idea tells the reader what you are going to write about.
Did you know our country, America, is covered by forests? Our trees are one of our greatest natural resources.

2. The **body** gives information the reader needs to understand the topic, such as facts, procedures, and examples.
Two trees produce enough oxygen to support a family of four for a year. Ninety-five percent of homes in our country use lumber (wood) for construction. On average, Americans use approximately 750 pounds of paper products each year. Think of all the paper plates, cups, notebooks, and notebook paper! Even the sap from trees can be used to make syrup, chewing gum, and crayons.

3. A **closing statement** summarizes the information within the paragraph.
Here's a reminder to all that we need to protect and replenish our trees, one of our greatest natural resources.

Your Turn:

Try writing your own informative paragraph. Think about a topic related to health, science, space, nature, animals, history, or presidents.

(Gentry, McNeel, and Wallace-Nesler 2012d)

Name: _____ Date: _____

Triple-Decker Sandwich

Think about a triple-decker sandwich to help support your paragraph development. The bread represents your main ideas. The meat, cheese, and veggies are your details supported by source information. Remember to check your notes as you write. Remember to use sentence stems: The text says... In source one... According to the text....

Directions: Organize an informational article that can be read by other students, teachers, parents, and possibly submitted to a newspaper. Use the three sources of information to support your main ideas. Then, write a text that is several paragraphs long citing evidence that supports your thinking. Use your own words, paraphrasing information from each source. In addition to the sources of information from your text, remember to add an interesting introduction and a paragraph to wrap-up your thinking.

Main Idea: Source #1	Main Idea: Source #2	Main Idea: Source #3
Details: Evidence to support	Details: Evidence to support	Details: Evidence to support

Opinion/Argument Writing in the Content Areas

Many state standards have placed more emphasis than in the past on opinion and argumentative writing. For example, Common Core State Standards expect students to "Write arguments to support claims in an analysis of substantive topics or texts using valid reasoning and relevant and sufficient evidence" (Common Core State Initiative 2015). Opinion writing begins in kindergarten. Here is a simple technique that can be used across the grade levels to help students begin to write opinions/arguments and support their thinking with specific claims (adapted from Peha 2013).

What I Think…Why I Think It

Present students with a procedural activity such as the following:

- a math problem

- a recipe

- a science lab

- a problematic event (e.g., a storm approaching)

Then, ask them to briefly describe their thought processes in step-by-step procedures for how to solve or complete the activity. Students should then write down what they think and why they think it.

I think _____because _____(list the points)_____ (point 1, point 2, point 3, etc.).

This is the beginning process for defending a point of view or solution path. The additional resources that follow (pages 161–167) will enable you to delve into opinion/argumentative writing effectively.

Name: _____ Date: _____

In My Opinion . . .

Directions: Complete the chart below to plan your writing.

Title of Book _____

| I think . . .
I feel . . .
It's my opinion that . . .
In my opinion . . .

_____
_____
_____
_____
_____
_____
_____
_____
_____ | → | Because . . . |

My Point of View

Directions: Complete the chart below to plan your writing.

Title or topic your opinion or point of view is based upon:

_____

State your opinion or point of view: I think, I feel, I believe, It is my opinion...

_____

_____

Strongest rationale (reason) that supports your opinion:	Second strongest rationale (reason) that supports your opinion:	Use these transition words and phrases to connect your rationale (reason) to your opinion: *because, therefore, since, for example, for instance, in order to, in addition, consequently, specifically*

Concluding sentence or paragraph that ties rationale to opinion or point of view: "For these reasons, it is my opinion that..."

Name: _____ Date: _____

Opinion Writing Tree

Topic:

↓   ↓   ↓

Reason #1:	Reason #2:	Reason #3:

My Reasons:

_____

_____

_____

_____

_____

_____

_____

(Gentry, McNeel, Wallace-Nesler 2012f)

TREES Graphic Organizer

Directions: Complete the graphic organizer below, using strong reasons, evidence, and examples.

Topic:

↓

Reason #1:	Reason #2:	Reason #3:

↓   ↓   ↓

Evidence:	Evidence:	Evidence:

↓   ↓   ↓

Example:	Example:	Example:

↓   ↓   ↓

Summary:

(Gentry, McNeel, and Wallace-Nesler 2012f)

Name: _____ Date: _____

It's Newsworthy

Journalists have the responsibility to inform their readers through their writing. However, some newspaper writers write opinion pieces. A reader has to be able to distinguish between the two.

Article: Gives information

- Captures reader with opening sentence
- Gives concrete details
- Sometimes uses quotes from interviews
- May include illustrations
- Specifically answers questions: Who? What? When? Where? Why? How?
- May include charts and graphs
- Uses a formal style of writing
- Includes a concluding statement

Editorial: Gives point of view

- Captures reader with opening sentence
- Gives point of view
- Provides an understanding about a topic
- Generally relates to current events, recent happenings, economics, or political views, etc.
- Subjects need to address the targeted audience.
- Requires asking questions
- Must research and find information
- Requires accurate and factual information to persuade
- Provides a concluding statement about the argument presented

Your Turn:
Draft an article or editorial. Your task is to decide how to inform the reader or to share your opinion.

(Gentry, McNeel, and Wallace-Nesler 2012g)

Organizing Thinking for Expository Writing

Writing frameworks offer writers support. Frameworks can help writers become familiar with content-area writing structures such as compare and contrast, cause and effect, or chronological texts.

Your Turn:

Select and research two topics you wish to compare and contrast. Create a Venn diagram in your writer's notebook to record similarities and differences. Then, complete this writing framework to summarize your information.

Compare and Contrast Framework

_____ and _____ are similar because they _____.

They both _____. In addition, each _____.

_____ and _____ are different because _____.

Furthermore, they _____. For example, the _____,

but _____.

Circle the concluding transition that makes sense in your framework.

- In conclusion,
- To summarize,
- As a result,
- As shown above,

- In the final analysis,
- Consequently,
- To clarify,
- For this reason,

(Gentry, McNeel, and Wallace-Nesler 2012g)

My Argument Planning Frame

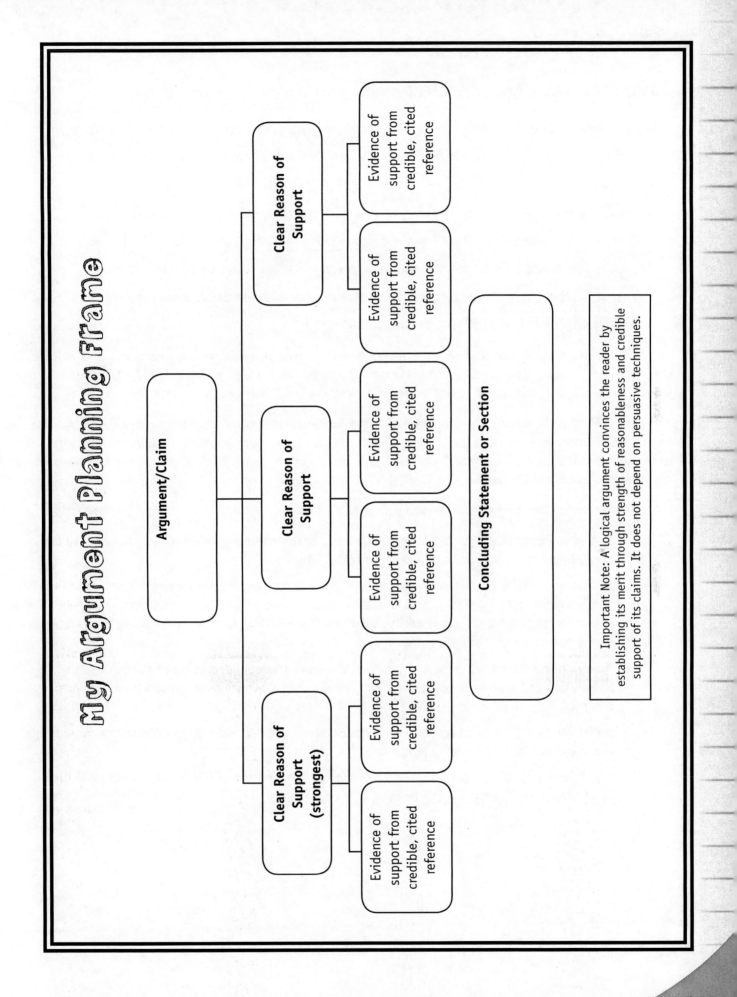

Argument/Claim

Clear Reason of Support (strongest)

Clear Reason of Support

Clear Reason of Support

Evidence of support from credible, cited reference

Evidence of support from credible, cited reference

Evidence of support from credible, cited reference

Evidence of support from credible, cited reference

Evidence of support from credible, cited reference

Evidence of support from credible, cited reference

Concluding Statement or Section

Important Note: A logical argument convinces the reader by establishing its merit through strength of reasonableness and credible support of its claims. It does not depend on persuasive techniques.

Chapter 5

Incorporate Poetry into all Content Areas

Students who don't like writing essays may like poetry, with its dearth of fixed rules and its kinship with rap. For these students, poetry can become a gateway to other forms of writing. It can help teach skills that come in handy with other kinds of writing—like precise, economical diction, for example. When Carl Sandburg writes, "The fog comes/on little cat feet," in just six words, he endows a natural phenomenon with character, a pace, and a spirit. All forms of writing benefit from the powerful and concise phrases found in poems. (Simmons 2014, 1)

If you are finding that your students are struggling with content-area information, poetry can be a welcomed shift in the curriculum. Using precise, efficiently crafted poems with patterns makes it easy for the brain to remember the content. Poetry can be written about almost any topic in any content area.

Certain poetry patterns may rhyme and be whimsical, while others may not rhyme and yet still be emotional and moving. Writers may choose ideas for poetry based on their background knowledge, people they admire, or something that presents thoughtful moods. Patterns that require knowing parts of speech require more sophisticated words and phrases.

In our experience four things happen when you write poetry:

- Just as music speaks to you on an emotional level, poetry naturally speaks directly to the head and heart. Even very young students respond to nursery rhymes.

- The sound of poetry is pleasant. Often the ear can easily discern if your poem is discordant and will psychologically jar your senses. Some students, such as some English language learners, may not respond to the natural sounds of poetry, but through scaffolding and lots of examples, the cadence of poetry becomes more natural and understood.

- Poetry can fill the written page with different shapes and sensory details that can stimulate the imagination and provide powerful metaphors, similes, and illustrations of important content-area concepts.

- Poetry can flourish with an economy of words. Short, simple text is a way to differentiate for students who may have difficulty reading longer texts.

Reading and writing poetry is a powerful tool to motivate. Here are some of our favorite forms for writing poetry. Many of these recommendations can be used at any grade level.

Powerful Poetry Types

Acrostic: This poem uses the letters of a name or a word or short phrases to begin each line in the poem. It integrates nicely with content for science or social studies curriculum. The acrostic example below was written by a first-grade student after a mini-lesson on onomatopoeia.

Kites in April

Kites are fun!

It's Spring! Yipee!

Thump! It's in the lake!

Eeek!

Splash! You weird kite!

It fell in the water!

Nooooo, this can't be happening!

Always fun to fly kites!

Puff!

Reel the string! Very tired! Yawn.

It's getting late!

Love flying kites.

Time to Write and Confer

Five W's Poetry: This poem answers the questions: who, what, where, when and why. It's an easy poem format that we have used effectively across the content areas with students of all ages. For example, once we introduce the narrative version below, students may use Five W's Poetry to describe a historical figure, scientist, or mathematician.

Who: JuShawn

What: Loves to watch soccer matches,

Where: At the United Arena Stadium,

When: During Spring soccer season,

Why: To prepare for tournaments.

Who: Thomas Jefferson

What: Famous third president of the USA,

Where: Lived in Virginia,

When: Founding father at the birth of our nation,

Why: "Author of the Declaration of American Independence of the Statute of Virginia for religious freedom and Father of the University of Virginia"—which he put on his tombstone!

Haiku: This is a three-line poem about nature. The first line is five syllables. The second line is seven syllables. The third line is five syllables.

> The snow was falling
>
> Gently onto the cold ground,
>
> Forming soft shadows.

Limerick: A limerick poem can be traced back to early English history. Short and easy to compose, a limerick is a nonsense poem that consists of five lines. The first, second, and fifth lines rhyme. Lines three and four have five to seven syllables and also rhyme. You can't go wrong with a limerick! The limerick could be patterned A, A, B, B, A.

> (A) There once was a mineral named quartz.
>
> (A) Optics, abrasives, and glass it supports,
>
> (B) Found in computer chips.
>
> (B) And dazzling rings for courtships.
>
> (A) It has many uses of all sorts.

Tercet: This is a poem that has three rhyming lines together.

> How beautiful is the full moon tonight!
>
> How round and curved and ghostly white!
>
> When full, the moon is a gorgeous sight!

Diamante: A diamante is a poem in the shape of a diamond using this specific format:

Noun

Adjective, adjective

A three-word sentence

Four verbs ending with ing

A three-word sentence

Two adjectives

A synonym for line one

Sahara

Frigid, harsh

Camels live there.

Surviving, searching, living, dying

Food is scarce.

Hot, dry

Desert

Couplet: When two lines rhyme, one after the other, we call the two lines a couplet. Couple means "two." Poets sometimes write rhyming poems using many couplets.

(A) In this winter time we go,

(A) Walking through the fields of snow:

(B) Where there is no grass at all,

(B) Where the top of roofs and walls,

(C) Every fence, and every tree,

(C) Is as white as white can be.

Quatrain: Quatrains appear throughout ancient history and remain popular today. A variety of stanza forms may be used but the easiest remain ABAB or AABB.

An ecosystem is like no other.

Some systems require a surrogate mother.

Systems work together in order to survive.

Without these systems no one can thrive.

Strategy 6: Allow Students to Select Their Writing Topics

Student choice and autonomy is important when developing independent writers. As students have more power in choosing the topics about which they write, they become more engaged and invested in the content, structure, coherence, and overall presentation of their work.

Students should have the opportunity to self-select topics for all genres of writing, but choice is especially powerful when writing informational text and conducting their own research.

Have Students Choose a Research Topic

It is important to teach the research process to students of all ages. When students are given freedom to delve deeper into topics that they are personally interested in, their engagement in the research process is enhanced. Student choice builds motivation to be a writer (Graves 1983).

Have students choose a topic to research. This can be as specific or as structured as needed for what the class is studying. For example, if the class is studying the solar system, students can choose something specific within that topic to learn more about and research.

Research can be completed in a number of ways. Putting students into pairs or small groups for researching can help them share ideas and work collaboratively to organize information. This is particularly helpful for younger students. Most research projects include at least some of the following steps:

1. **Ask students to consider what they want to know about the topic they have selected.** They may write "I wonder" sentence stems or complete K-W-L charts.

2. **Have students collect resources to use for their research.** These may include classroom books, library books, newspaper articles, videos, or websites.

3. **Provide students time to gather their information.** They may take notes on sticky notes or note cards about anything that is related to their guiding "I wonder" questions or about facts that are interesting, surprising, or important (Minkel 2013).

4. **Provide explicit instruction in how to read for information gathering.** They have to read in order to write. Students may need to know how to use certain text features—a table of contents or an index—in order to do this.

5. **Provide mini-lessons during the research process to help guide students through their work.** These lessons may include:

   - how to find the main idea for note-taking

   - how to organize information into subtopics

   - how to use visuals and text features (e.g., photographs, maps, diagrams, captions, or subheadings) during research

   - how to take structured notes

6. **Allow time for students to write several drafts during the research process.** They may also choose to include their own diagrams, maps, pictures, and captions.

7. **Provide time for students to share their final drafts in some way with the class.**

Develop a Vision for Writing by Planning Ahead

The objective of this strategy is to make sure students have a clear vision for the formal writing they will do.

First, show examples of the kind of writing that is expected. Choose quality texts and examples to anchor the project. Allow students to discover a vision for their piece by reading several anchor texts.

Explain the timeline for the stages of the project. Create a due dates sheet (Ray 2006) with the following types of items customized for the particular formal assignment. A sample is provided in Appendix C and the Digital Resource CD so that customization is possible.

Figure 5.10 Sample Due Dates Template

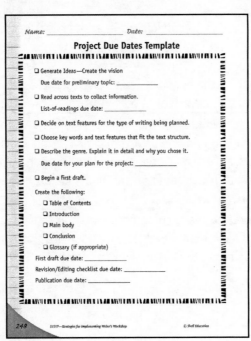

Peha (2013) created a chart that allows students to individualize their formal writing project by choosing a Role, a Format, an Audience, a Purpose, and an Approach (R-F-A-P-A Chart). Using this chart helps students take ownership and develop content that is meaningful for them personally.

Figure 5.11 R-F-A-P-A Chart

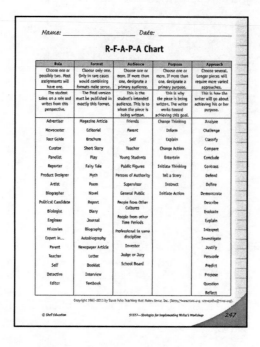

Figure 5.12 includes examples for social studies, science, and mathematics.

Figure 5.12 R-F-A-P-A Chart Examples Across the Content Areas

Content Area	Assignment
Social Studies	You have been invited to participate in an archaeological dig at the site of Droop Mountain Battlefield, site of an intense battle between the North and the South during the Civil War. At the conclusion of the dig, every artifact is cataloged and placed in the Droop Mountain Museum. Reflect on the artifacts found and their place in the history of the battle. Summarize your experience with an editorial placed in the local newspaper, *The Pocahontas Times*.
Science	You are a dietician working in the school system. You know the effects of influential advertising on young minds. Commercials appear on APPs, TV sports programming, even cartoons. Collect advertising from Sunday newspapers and create a poster that shows the effects of sugary drinks (sodas) on the body. (phosphoric acid, caloric intake without providing nutrition, etc.)
Mathematics	Your family is getting ready to go on a vacation to the beach. Each family member must earn money, and you must plan a budget. Use your imagination to brainstorm possible ways to earn income and plan possible expenses you might incur. **Ways to earn income:** **Possible Expenses:** allowance movies mowing grass snacks babysitting video games other other

Conclusion

Follow our research-based overarching foundational principles and bring narrative, informational, opinion/argument, and poetry writing into your content-area classroom. Not only will you meet rigorous new standards, your students will write more, learn more, and amaze you as writers in the disciplines. We have found strategic writing in the content-area classroom to be one of the most rewarding aspects of teaching—both for students and for teachers.

Strategies for Publishing Student Writing

We all have an innate need to be accepted and valued by others, which includes being recognized for our accomplishments. Each time teachers offer opportunities to share student writing, from a simple author's chair or work displayed on a bulletin board or during a celebration of writing, they recognize and respect the student and acknowledge the efforts made to create the writing piece. We see the smile, the pride, and the confidence as each of our students begins to recognize themselves as "real" writers. Magic happens...and that's why students publish.

So why do teachers ask students to practice and practice their writing strategies and crafts, yet think that they cannot find the energy or time to let students share their accomplishments? The answers we hear most often are summarized here:

I know publishing is important. I know my students love it. I also know it's a lot of work and with everything else, I just can't find time to fit it all in."

Publishing takes on many faces in the classroom. It holds many rewards, and we invite you to explore a variety of options until you find what works best for your classroom. For just as athletes practice hours for the big game and musicians play the same scores over and over until the final concert, after our students work diligently on their writing craft, they also deserve opportunities to share their successes.

The benefits of publishing are many. Here are some of the most significant reasons for finding the time and energy to include publishing in your classroom:

- **Students write with purpose for an authentic audience.** Writing is communicating, relaying a message, telling a story, expressing thoughts and opinions. The degree of effort differs when students write for the teacher or computer assessment scorer than when they write for a peer in the other sixth-grade classroom, to share with parents, or to put on display in the hallway or class blog. When teachers offer an authentic audience, writers get a sense of value and an understanding that someone, besides the teacher, recognizes and values their learning and achievement. Consequently, they work hard to improve their skills and strive to produce their best work.

- **Students make connections between reading and writing.** When teachers ask students to publish writing, they not only enhance learning in writing, but also in reading. While reading, developing writers soon recognize the way authors use structure, voice, sentence variety, etc. In the same way, as writers gain knowledge about the use of figurative language, text features, leads, etc., they read with greater awareness of the writing itself, which enhances the meaning of text. It is the awareness of the reciprocal nature between reading and writing that moves students to begin "reading like writers" and "writing for readers."

- **Students are motivated and excited about writing.** Without question, providing opportunities for students to write for real purposes and for authentic audiences motivates students to write. In addition, as teachers offer occasions for students to receive praise and feedback (not just from the teacher), self-confidence and pride create the momentum for writers to continue learning, practicing, and preparing for the next writing challenge. Think about the first time your paper was selected to be read aloud or displayed for all to see; the proud moment you became a writer. Taking the time to publish, no matter the form, gives your students the gift of seeing themselves as "real" writers.

This chapter covers three strategies for publishing student writing:

- Follow guidelines for publishing

- Explore options for publishing (including sample checklists for grades K–8)

- Writing celebrations

 ## Strategy 1: Follow Guidelines for Publishing

In Chapter 4, we shared the importance of keeping the focus of our conference conversations on the writer and not the writing. We stand by that same message as we talk about the process of publishing. These foundational principles or guidelines can help you to guide publishing with students.

- **Focus on the writer.** No matter what form publishing takes on in your classroom, the product is never more important than the learning that takes place along the way. Many teachers view publishing only as that perfect, polished, error-free writing project completed after a unit of study. That is one form of publishing. However, student writing, especially that of young writers, can easily become "the teacher's paper," and the student is lost in all the fixing up. A kindergarten student, Alisha, expressed this so well when I complimented her after she shared her story: "Oh, that's not mine. The teacher did that one. I did draw the pictures. Do you want to see my 'real' story?" Remember the writer and that it's all right for their writing "to look like the work of children who are learning how to write" (Ray 2004, 79). Each time a student publishes, we are not looking for the writing to be perfect; we are looking for it to be better. We hope to see glimpses of our teaching and hints of new learning in each piece of writing.

- **Remember that publishing has many faces.** Any act of sharing writing publically fits our definition of publishing. Publishing can exist in two forms: informal and formal. Informal publishing is writing students have refined and readied to be shared with the class, a small group, another class, hung on the bulletin board, displayed in the hallway, or the like. This form of publishing is frequent and does not require extraordinary time and effort to be readied for sharing, though it has been teacher edited. Formal publishing places more demands upon the student to ready the piece to be shared and takes more time, perhaps only publishing one or two formal pieces per month. Formal publication may be the end product of a unit or special project. It may be a polished piece that represents a student's best penmanship, creativity, art, or illustration. This kind of publishing demonstrates the student's best efforts as a writer and best efforts at presenting the craft publicly. Both formal and informal published pieces are in keeping with the writer's age and developmental level.

- **Keep it practical.** When creating a writing plan for the year, include a timeline and the type of publishing that best suits your instructional focus. Do not feel obligated to take every writing piece to formal or even informal publication. It is not necessary and you, your students, and any classroom volunteers may become frustrated with the whole process. Students will write many stories that stay in rough draft. Do consider how to include a mixture of informal and formal publishing throughout the year. Continued opportunities to publish and share learning rejuvenate and inspire writers.

- **Confer along the way.** Engaging writers in consistent conferences is key to successful publishing. Spending time with students every week fosters their writing development and leaves fewer issues to address during publishing. Conferring also keeps us informed of the writer's skill level so we can establish appropriate expectations for publications.

- **Keep writers' development as the goal.** Keep in mind that time to write is essential in developing writing skills. Publishing should not take too much time and energy away from writing. Focus on student learning and the writing process, not the product.

 ## *Strategy 2:* Explore Options for Publishing

Publishing can be formal or informal, simple or complex. Team with your students to explore the best options for publishing. In the words of Judy Green, think of yourself as "an editor—nurturer, supporter, prodder, and prompter. You are also there to model the process—to demonstrate for your students how to read, write, proofread, illustrate, and talk about stories" (Green 1999, 10). Explore the following list as you give students the opportunity to publish their work. This list is not intended to be all-inclusive but rather a starting point of ideas for your publishing projects.

- **Oral Publications:** When considering that the dictionary definition of "publish" is "to make public," the simple act of reading the writing piece aloud is a form of publishing. Examples include:

  - **Author's Chair:** A designated seat where students read their writing to others in the classroom

  - **Audio Recordings or Podcasts:** Students make an oral recording of the writing that can be listened to in the classroom or from an online source.

  - **Collaborative Programs:** Students read their writing or a selection of their writing to their classmates, another class, the principal, support personnel, or even during announcements and over closed circuit TV. These sharing opportunities can have a name, such as "Project Listen!", "Authors' Share," or "Writers Express."

- **Bulletin Boards:** Make student writing public by creating a bulletin board or hallway display. An "Authors at Work in Room 212," "Look Who's Writing!" or "Growing Writers!" display sends the message that the class is proud of the achievements they are making in writing. Displays near the library, cafeteria, and school entryway allow opportunities to share with a wider audience. Leave an area with blank paper or sticky notes and a pen for others to post compliments. Remember, the writing does not have to perfect, but reflect the developmental level of the students. For younger writers, you may want to attach notes that point out the exceptional features in their individual piece like, "Look how Isabella is adding labels to tell her story!" or "Did you notice the descriptive details Zachery has added to his writing?"

- **Postcards, Notes, and Letters:** Who doesn't like getting a personal handwritten letter? Audiences might include a family member, a classmate, or another class in the school, district, state, or country. Some celebrities and authors respond to student letters as well. Don't forget email. Teach students that email is a form of communication and can be used formally and informally depending on the purpose and the audience.

- **Daily/Weekly News:** Begin by modeling how to create a short piece or paragraph that captures the news from the classroom or community. Share the information with other students, parents, and administrators. Even the youngest writers can write and draw a representation of class activities. Eventually, challenge groups and/or individuals to create weekly newspapers. As students develop their skills, expand beyond the classroom through interviews of other classes, teachers and students and extend the text.

- **All Kinds of Books:** Publishing books can be as simple as folding paper and adding a title and illustrations. You can also add a cover to a class collection of writing and staple it together. A bound anthology of writing, such as class poetry, is another idea for a class book. Some may be individual texts or class collections with each student contributing a page or section. Here are just a few ideas for book publishing.

- **ABC Books:** These are easy to use at all levels and in any content area. Students can create individual, group, or class pages on a topic of their choice. Text may include simple labels, phrases, sentences, or even paragraphs. Share published alphabet books to spark ideas for other teachers.

- **Acrostic Books:** Acrostic poetry is a popular writing piece in school, so extending the format to book form is easy and fun. Just as with poetry, students can use one word, a phrase, a sentence, or a topic to develop text related to each letter of a word. The book can be poems about a single topic (All About Me or the Civil War) or a variety of topics.

- **Big Books:** Big books are typically created as a class and added to classroom libraries to be enjoyed by all. Some formats include ABC, sentence frames, mentor mimic (mimicking the style of a mentor text), story retells, and poems.

- **Biographies/Autobiographies**: Make reading biographies and autobiographies interesting and creative by having students create and publish the life of a historical figure, a current celebrity, a veteran, a special person of interest, or their very own life story.

- **Compare and Contrast Books:** Students use comparing and contrasting as a reading skill. Make an authentic connection to the strategy by inviting students to publish books based on the strategy. Be sure to provide modeling and support along the way. Compare and contrast topics to explore include: frogs/toads, cats/dogs, cars/trucks, morning/night, city/country, home/another country, baseball/basketball, hurricanes/tornadoes, one version of a story/another version of the same story, book/movie, and more!

- **How-To Books:** Procedural books require writers to create explicit, sequential directions. Writers also focus on the purpose and audience for the text. Recipe books and step-by-step books are fun formats for publishing how-to writing. Topics to consider include how to: be a good friend, grow pumpkins, build a snowman, clean your room, make a free-throw, plant a garden, play a sport or game, give a dog a bath, stay healthy, multiply fractions, or conduct a science experiment.

- **Repetition Books:** This book form has a repeated line or phrase, such as "I like..." or "My mom can...", throughout the text and is used frequently in the K–2 classroom. Older students also create repetition books mimicking language from mentor texts such as, *Honey, I Love* by Eloise Greenfield or *In November* and *When I Was Young in the Mountains* by Cynthia Rylant. Other texts to share: *No David!* by David Shannon, *Pete the Cat: I Love My White Shoes* by Eric Litwin, *When I Am Old With You* by Angela Johnson, *That's Good! That's Bad!* by Margery Cuyler, *Fortunately* by Remy Charlip, *The Bus Ride That Changed History* by Pamela Duncan Edwards, and *Up North at the Cabin* by Marcia Wilson Chall.

- **Topic Books:** In this type of book, the content evolves around a specific subject, such as a book of friendship or family, a whale book, a weather book, a book of similes or rhyming words. Most of the time the topics for these books are nonfiction, but fiction can take center stage in a published class collection of fractured fairy tales, tall tales, or ghost stories.

- **Additional Types:** book of riddles, cause and effect, photo essay books, book of letters, book of lyrics, poetry books, question and answer books, shape books, or trifold/brochure booklets.

The following (pages 181–183) are publishing checklists to use with students. You may use these general guides when initially modeling the steps of publishing with students. However, as your writers develop, include them in the development of class publishing lists based on the genre of writing and the type of publication.

My Publishing Checklist

 ☐ I can get my materials.

 ☐ I can print or type neatly.

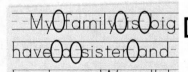 ☐ I can leave spaces between my words.

 ☐ I can draw illustrations to match my words.

 ☐ I can make a title page.

 ☐ I can put my book together or ask a friend to help.

☐ I can share my writing with others.

My Publishing Checklist

☐ Include main idea with interesting and important details.

☐ Check organization of writing to include an introduction, body, and conclusion.

☐ Read your writing aloud to yourself and someone else. Listen carefully for parts that may be confusing or where something may have been left out.

☐ Edit for capitalization, grammar, punctuation, and spelling.

☐ Use your best handwriting to create a final copy or type a final copy.

☐ Place page numbers at the bottom of each page.

☐ Add illustrations/pictures/photographs to your writing for the final copy.

☐ If making a cover, select the materials for the cover and back of your publication.

☐ Design the cover page. Remember to capitalize the title and include the names of the author and illustrator.

☐ Develop an "About the Author" page.

☐ Arrange all pages in order.

Consider these optional pages:

    ☐ Dedication page

    ☐ Table of contents

    ☐ Glossary

My Publishing Checklist

☐ Main idea is clear with interesting and supportive details.

☐ Criteria for project met including:

- page length
- margins
- medium/platform
- Table of Contents

- word count
- design features
- audience/purpose
- Other _____

☐ Flow and clarity established by rereading your writing and sharing it with a peer.

☐ Final edit for capitalization, grammar, punctuation, and spelling is completed.

☐ Handwriting/Typing is easy to read with balance of text and white space.

☐ Page numbers and/or page heading meet project criteria.

☐ Visuals, photographs, diagrams, graphs, and/or illustrations added for clarity of text.

☐ Project cover meets project criteria and may include: title, date, teacher, design, etc.

☐ Author biography and photograph is included.

☐ All sources are cited and any necessary permissions have been gathered.

☐ Pages arranged in order.

☐ Final project is shared.

Publishing with Mentor Texts

Mentor texts are a valuable resource for teaching the craft of writing and modeling publication. Additionally, mentor texts are just as useful during the publishing phase of the writing process. We use them to "show" students text structures for writing and specific styles, layouts, and types of publishing. Here are examples of mentor texts we have used to teach students text structures for publishing, text styles for publishing, and publishing layouts, along with various types of publishing.

Structure

Text structure refers to how the writer's ideas are organized to convey the meaning and message to the reader. Well-structured texts guide the reader through the content with the use of specific patterns, signal words, and phrases that create cues that support comprehension. As students decide to publish their writing, they need to determine the text structure that will best deliver the information to their reader. Sharing mentor texts with different story patterns and text structures gives students a set of blueprints to support them as they create different genres and types of texts. Students also need to be aware that many texts hold more than one specific text structure within, for example, *The River Ran Wild* by Lynne Cherry has several elements woven together including: cause and effect, chronological order, and problem and solution.

Exploring a variety of mentor texts gives students support and guidance to try writing with different text structures. For example, once students share the text *The Escape of Marvin the Ape* by Caralyn Buehner, they may mimic the episodic structure to create a sequel entitled, "The Escape of Helvetica the Hippo." Students might create a compare and contrast text following the structure of author Jerry Pallotta's *Who Would Win?* book series or even a chronological journal mimicking that of the boy from *Diary of a Wimpy Kid* by Jeff Kinney.

A list of mentor texts with eight story patterns that authors use are listed in Chapter 3. Mentor texts to support additional structures may include:

Figure 6.1 Sample Mentor Texts for Text Structure

Text Structure	Grades K–2	Grades 3–5	Grades 6–8
Chronological Sequence	*A Dandelion's Life* by John Himmelman	*Lights! Camera! Action!* by Gail Gibbons	*Castle* by David Macaulay
Cause and Effect	*Ira Sleeps Over* by Bernard Waber	*The Frog Scientist* by Pamela Turner	*Beetle Busters* by Loree Griffin Burns
Compare and Contrast	*Are You a Grasshopper?* by Judy Allen	*Outside and Inside Trees* by Sandra Markle	*We the People* by Peter Spier
Description	*The Skeleton Inside You* by Phillip Balestrino	*Why Do Volcanoes Blow Their Tops?* by Melvin and Gilda Berger	*"Imagine"* by Alex Porter and Kristin Lewis (nonfiction article)
Problem and Solution	*A Place for Birds* by Melissa Stewart	*When the Wolves Returned: Restoring Nature's Balance in Yellowstone* by Dorothy Hinshaw Patent	*If You Traveled on the Underground Railroad* by Ellen Levine
Combination	*The Popcorn Book* by Tomie dePaola	*Digging Up Dinosaurs* by Aliki	*Face to Face with Dolphins* by Flip and Linda Nicklin

Layout

Layout of the text on the page is important to consider when publishing. Mentor texts can show students models of font choice, size, and location, as well as how the text fills the page. Is the font choice formal or more script-like? Does the text run across the top of the page, the bottom of the page, or through the middle of the page? Are some words larger or bolder than others?

Art layout is also important to consider. Where are the images located in the book and what is the medium (photography, painting, drawings) of the art?

The mentor text *The Best Part of Me* by photographer Wendy Ewald is a great layout model for a photo book with text. A class can create its own book by having students take their own photos and write essays for a photo book entitled "The Best Parts of Us!" A sample photo essay could be written like this:

My Feet

Thump, thump, thump, that's my beautiful beautiful little feet. My shiny feet!

I like them because I get to show off my nail polish. My beautiful sparkling nail polish.

Style

Exposing students to a variety of text styles in mentor texts provides additional choices and options when publishing. For example, in Byrd Baylor's text *"Everybody Needs a Rock,"* students could explore the unique style she uses to create text matched with pen and ink art. Her text flows down the left side of the page and pauses, helping the reader almost literally feel the text visually. In addition, the placement of the text flowing down or across the page adds to her distinct style of writing. Students consider these elements when they decide how they want the style of the text to be read in their work.

Types

Remember to bring in authentic published writing that represents different forms of publishing, such as posters, brochures, newspapers, magazines, newsletters, blogs, emails, and postcards. Showing students physical examples promotes interests and motivation.

Publishing with Technology

Traditional publishing allows students to create one copy of a writing project for a very limited audience. Online publishing provides students opportunities to share their work with an authentic audience far beyond the boundaries of the classroom. With the use of classroom technology and the Internet, teachers are taking advantage of electronic publishing to post student writing on school and classroom webpages, intranet systems, classroom wikis and blogs, and much more. In addition to providing an extended authentic audience, publishing with technology motivates and engages student writers, increases opportunities to collaborate and communicate, and strengthens technology skills.

We suggest starting to publish with technology by trying a general method of access for online publishing.

- Use tools such as Keynote, Microsoft Word, PowerPoint and Adobe PDF to transform student work to a digital format.

- Try using web-based publishing sites where text and images are developed on the site creating a final published product, such as a virtual book. This may also be used in combination with creating a PowerPoint or Word document and then uploading it to a web-based publishing site.

- Create a classroom blog or individual student blogs for sharing writing. As a reminder, before submitting any student writing for online publication, obtain written parental consent.

The following projects represent a sampling of the myriad of publishing activities using technology.

Amazing Animals A-Z: Students use a graphic organizer to gather information. Each student adds research onto a PowerPoint slide. Each slide is printed and bound into a classroom book and added to the classroom library.

Figure 6.2 Amazing Animals Sample

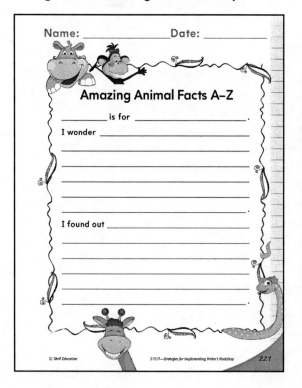
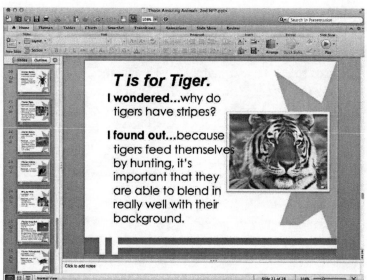

All About Me: Students prepare drafts of a story about themselves and transfer the information into a PowerPoint template. Students then have the option to add transitions, special effects, and audio to enhance the information. After their story is complete, the presentation is printed into a book; saved as an ebook and/or iMovie; and shared with classmates, friends, and family. Here are suggestions for the content of the book:

- My Favorite: (One page or individual pages)
  - Vacations/Trips/Places to Visit
  - School Subject(s)
  - Books to Read/Authors
  - Sports/Teams
  - Foods (liked or disliked)
  - Color
  - Books
  - Movies
  - Songs
  - State
  - Hobbies
- Best Day Ever/Proud Moments
- When I Grow Up/My Future

- Three Words That Describe Me
- Three Wishes
- Things That Make Me Crazy
- Pets
- Most Interesting Fact About Me
- All About Me cover page (if applicable)
- Table of Contents (if applicable)
- On the Day I was Born
- My Family (describe family members)
- Fun with Family
- Friends
- School Days (by grade)
- Birthdays

Figure 6.3 Sample All About Me Pages

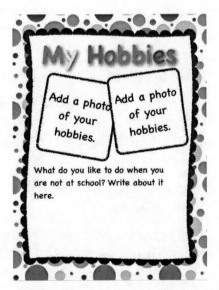

Planet Poster: Students work to create an informational poster highlighting a planet. After modeling, students use the Internet to research images and information to develop their poster. Each includes a title, an interesting subtitle, two images, and an informational paragraph. Students print their posters and they are posted on the classroom website to be shared with others.

Time to Share

Figure 6.4 Sample Planet Poster

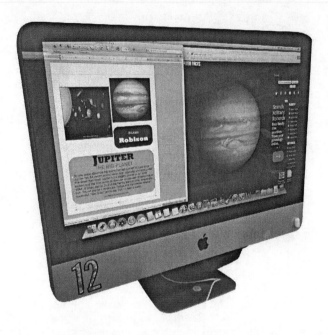

Commercial Project: Students use persuasive writing skills, along with acting and speaking, to create an iMovie commercial convincing their audience to do something, buy something, or go somewhere, such as visit their state.

Research Project: Students conduct research on a specific topic and then create a digital presentation to share the information. For example, in a state research project information about the state such as state facts, natural resources, physical features, parks, landmarks, tourist attractions, and famous people who came from the state could all be included in the presentation. Students can easily use the information in their presentations to create other writing pieces such as brochures, posters, or oral presentations.

Five Tools for Publishing with Technology

Publishing tools abound on the Internet, making it easy and available for publishing student writing. Explore these five tools and select one to get started publishing in the classroom. Encourage students to stay focused on the content and the process—the meat of the learning—so that they don't get distracted by the final product.

- **Tablet Apps** like *My Story* and *StoryBuddy 2* give student writers a simple format to create or import images, add text, add audio, and publish their writing as iBooks to share with family and friends.

- **Storybird** uses illustrations from artists around the world as the stimulus for student writers. The fun and simple format makes it an ideal online publishing option. Teachers can set it up in their classroom for free and students' work is saved as public or private. Writing can be shared through links.

- **ePubBud** has been referred to as the "YouTube for ebooks." Students can easily create text, upload images, photographs, and videos, add links, and then publish in epub format to be shared as digital books. Like many online publishing resources, books can be identified as private or public and hard copies purchased for a fee.

- **PowerPoint and Keynote** are great for creating student books. Many teachers and students are familiar with these programs and find them an easy way to introduce publishing with technology. Once students revise and edit their presentations, they simply save them as PDFs and use a program like *ePub* or *Calibre* to create ebooks to be shared. Other options might be to transfer the presentation to iMovie and save to a DVD or flash drive, or print out the presentation as full pages and bind into a physical book.

- **iBooks Author** gives teachers and students the tools to create and publish text with options for images, video, shapes, charts, tables, 3D objects, and more. Students are engaged while exploring new features like interactive diagrams and popup widgets that bring their writing to a whole new level when published. Although this resource is highly motivating, publications can only be viewed on Apple devices.

These publishing tools are a very small sampling of what is available to educators. To be successful, take the time to work through the application you choose to use with your students and publish a piece yourself first. Knowing the process and being familiar with the use of tools within the resource makes publishing more productive. Explore and be adventurous! Start with one or two free applications and have some fun. You may also like to explore:

- Book Creator
- ComicLife3
- Creative Book Builder
- Flipsnack
- Google+
- Kidblog

- Kindle Kids' Book Creator
- Poetry.com
- Scribble My Story
- Shutterfly
- SlideShare
- TikaTok

Strategy 3: Writing Celebrations

Writing celebrations are not the result of completing a project. They are celebrations of all the learning that takes place from the first idea of prewriting, through drafting, revising, reflecting, editing, and finally publishing. Classes celebrate the diligence and resilience students exhibit daily in Writer's Workshop. They are celebrations where students stand proud of their accomplishments and look for affirmation of a job well done. They are celebrations of authors! These celebrations move students to "continue writing with expertise and energy" (Ayres 2013, 15).

There are a number of ways to celebrate student writing that span from very simple to huge productions. Do not feel pressured to put on some big bash that ends up being overwhelming for you and your students, while the actual joy of writing is lost in the hoopla. Most students are just happy to have a "special" identified time and day when they have an audience and are recognized for their hard work. Whatever type of celebration you choose, be sure to include a means for complimenting and responding to the writer. The following are a few suggestions for celebrating student writing.

- **Author's Chair:** Many teachers use author's chair in their daily Writer's Workshops as one or two students present their writing or a selection from their writing to the class. To create a larger event—an Author's Chair Celebration—set aside a special time of day, put a sign on the door, "Author Celebration in Progress," roll out a red carpet, and take a snapshot of the author with their newly released text. Once he or she is at the designated chair, use a projector spotlight or a background celebration screen to honor the new author. Simply adding a pretend microphone is enough to spark enthusiasm and capture the attention of the audience.

- **You Are Invited!:** Send special invitations created by students, to the principal, support staff, or another class announcing the celebration of authors. These celebrations can be as simple as the unveiling of a bulletin board full of newly published writing pieces, presented similar to the author's chair, or planned as a buddy share. Younger students are thrilled to share their writing with older peers, and older students enjoy the sharing of their writing as writing mentors.

- **The Read Around:** This type of celebration saves a bit of time, yet still gives everyone an opportunity to share. Each student selects his or her best sentence to share with the whole group. Then, students divide into small groups and share their entire pieces. The audience in each group offers compliments to the author. This can also be reversed: moving to small groups, identifying the strongest sentence and/or section, and then sharing it with the whole group.

- **Video Conferencing:** With a little guidance, using a tool to talk over the Internet is a great way of sharing and celebrating writing with those outside of the classroom. Class books are one type of published writing that works well with video conferencing.

- **Authors' Signing Session:** After a class book is completed, each student signs his or her name to their designated page of the text. Afterward, the book might be presented to the classroom or school library to be checked out and enjoyed by others.

- **Author's Tea or Poet's Party:** This type of celebration can be as simple or lavish as you like. Students can assist with planning and organizing the event by writing and delivering invitations, meeting and greeting visitors, announcing authors, arranging the room, and even distributing comment cards and pens. Involving students creates ownership and further develops the writing community.

- **Growing Writers Celebration:** This event is a family favorite. Here, students display writing from earlier in the year alongside a current published piece. Students and families look at the writing together and discuss/record all the learning they notice. Provide a guide for adults so attention is on content as well as mechanics.

- **Celebration of Experts:** After completing and publishing a nonfiction writing project, students are quite knowledgeable about the topic—experts in their field. Use this celebration to highlight their new learning. Project the covers of books behind authors as they give an oral summary of their writing including their name, topic/title, and one or two facts about their topics. Afterwards, invite visitors to browse student publications and encourage them to ask questions and leave compliments.

- **Gallery Walk:** Gallery walk celebrations are particularly effective for older students and when celebrations involve a large number of classrooms or a school-wide event. Like an art gallery, writing is displayed in a way that readers can browse, read, and leave meaningful comments for the writer. Adding "All About the Author" information next to the writing adds a special touch. This might be a photograph or self-portrait along with their name, age, and favorite writing topics.

- **Authors' Film Festival:** And why not? After working through publishing digitally, invite others to a special viewing of presentations including popcorn and drinks. Students create their own "Walk of Fame" by lining the hallways with "headshots" and author information. At the conclusion, have visitors offer "Kind Critics' Comments."

- **KISS (Keeping It Simple Share):** This idea is excellent for lengthier pieces of writing and older students who may be hesitant about sharing their writing. Each student selects one section of their writing that creates a memorable image, sends a strong/important message, or just simply sounds great. They write only that selection on a colored sheet of paper with pen or marker and lay it on their desks. Next, turn on a little soft music as students move around the room and simply read the text without any oral or written comments. Then, students get a note card to copy one favorite writing selection and add two explanations for their selection. Students move into groups of three to four to share their selections and reasoning. The class is brought back together for a few group shares.

Writing celebrations, no matter how large or small, are important to students and their overall development as writers. Here are a few tips when planning your festivities:

- Plan celebrations throughout the year.
- Give guests 1–2 weeks advance notice of the event.
- Ask for help from students, co-workers, and families.
- Explain students' writing goals to visitors.
- Provide opportunities for compliments.
- Decide how students will share.
- Keep it simple, if providing refreshments.

Conclusion

Making a cake can be messy and it takes many attempts to create Grandma's chocolate layer cake. Layers might be different sizes or a bit lopsided, and perhaps the icing sticks to the spatula and cake crumbs spread across the top. But when we sit down to eat a slice of the cake, none of that seems important. In spite of its imperfect appearance, the rich, creamy taste brings smiles to everyone's face and one is proud he or she made the effort to make this special treat for their family.

Publishing and celebrating student writing is the "icing on the cake." Even if there are imperfections in the writing, students and everyone around them share the joy and delight in their efforts.

Strategies for Assessment

Assessment is gathering data and using it to measure students' learning outcomes. Wiggins and McTighe (2005) tie the term assessment to curricular goals: "By assessment we mean the act of determining the extent to which the curricular goals are being and have been achieved. Assessment is an umbrella term we use to mean the deliberate use of many methods to gather evidence to indicate that students are meeting standards" (4).

As writing teachers we gather data of student learning from many different sources to increase the validity of assessment. A single standardized writing test may not really show what a writer can do. Other assessment sources include ongoing daily classroom observations, conferences, students' self-assessments, and crafted writing products, as well as both high-stakes and low-stakes writing tests from the state/district.

Evaluation/assessment systems can be divided into two categories: formative assessments and summative assessments. *Formative assessments* are ongoing and occur during the learning process. In general, formative assessments provide feedback throughout the teaching cycle and enable teachers to plan instruction. State standards and efforts to reform schools have made formative assessments more popular in America during the last two decades. For example, writing researcher Lucy Calkins and her co-authors say: "If there is a magical solution to reforming schools in line with CCSS—and we think there is—that magic will come from an increased attention to formative assessments in the richest and best sense of the word, and from instruction that is increasingly assessment based" (Calkins, Ehrensworth, and Lehman 2012, 193).

Summative assessments evaluate student learning by comparing learning against some standard or benchmark at the end of a period of time. The "summary" evaluation may come at the end of a unit, end of chapter test, end of a grading period, or end of a school year. In an era when high stakes testing seems to drive many educational decisions and policies, it's important to remember the words of Regie Routman: "The best test preparation is excellent teaching" (2005, 244).

Strategic writing teachers use a balance of formative and summative assessments. For example, they have students do a lot of writing rather than spend too much time teaching to the test or engaging in days and days of test prep exercises. Too much test prep can be burdensome for both students and teachers and make everyone anxious. When test preparation becomes the main focus, students often become disinterested and lose the motivation to write.

Wiggins (2006) compares summative assessments such as high-stakes state tests to an annual checkup by a physician. It's important to get a good overall report. But it's equally important to gather data, assess one's health status, measure progress, and live a healthy lifestyle day by day. This day-by-day routine is analogous to formative assessment.

Formative assessments help us to gather data and note outcomes of our teaching while we are doing it. We collect data and target our instruction to achieve certain outcomes just like the healthy person pays attention to diet, exercise, and does what's necessary to achieve a healthy lifestyle. Formative and summative assessments go hand in hand to achieve the desired results.

Time to Share

Figure 7.1 Sample Formative and Summative Assessments

Grade Range	Formative Assessment Ideas	Summative Assessment Ideas
K–2	Observation notes Evidence of developmental phases of writing Checklist of writing behaviors Records of letter formation Records of knowledge about letters and sounds Traits of quality writing assessments	Narrative progress report End of reporting period writing samples Evidence of research projects Required assessments such as DIBELS (Dynamic Indicators of Basic Early Literacy Skills®)
3–5	Observation notes from conferring notebook Checklist of writing behaviors Evidence from reflection logs Small guided writing groups Discussion groups Whiteboard question/answer Think-Pair-Share opportunities Traits of quality writing assessments	End of thematic unit writing projects Performance tasks matched to state assessments Beginning, middle, and ending benchmark data End of year state assessment
6–8	Lab reports Letters (friendly and business) Dialogue journaling with peers Conventional spelling errors Brainstorming activities Traits of quality writing assessments	Benchmark writing samples Research projects Writing assessments to determine end of reporting period grades (if applicable) End of genre study writing sample State-mandated assessments

Ten Tips for Formative and Summative Assessments

1. Use a teacher's conferring notebook for formative assessment and collecting data on student learning all day long. Use the data collected to plan instruction.

2. Teach students how to score their own work using rubrics for self-assessment. The modeling component for teaching students to examine their own work using the 10-point writing rubric can be found at the end of this chapter.

3. Show samples of high-scoring writing.

4. Provide regular and focused time for vocabulary development to support students' writing. For example, use strategies for teaching transition words for opinion, narrative, and informative genres.

5. Communicate with families so that all parents are familiar with the language of assessment such as informational, opinion, and narrative genres.

6. Provide clear expectations for assessments to help build test-taking and writing stamina.

7. Integrate writing into all content areas to provide authentic practice for the content-area writing skills that will be tested both during writing exams and in tests in the respective content areas.

8. Set up a station in the classroom where students without technology at home can practice keyboarding skills to get ready for digital assessments. Remember, a valid writing test should measure a student's writing ability, not keyboarding ability.

9. Let students know what to expect when the summative writing test is computer scored. For example, teach students not to use abbreviations or slang.

10. Make sure students are well informed of the importance of standardized assessments. Make a big deal of the upcoming assessments, but make it fun.

Five Types of Formative Assessment

There are five types of formative assessment that we often use to collect data on students to improve instruction and student learning *while it is happening* in the everyday activity in the classroom: performance based, product/project, portfolios, personal communication, and anecdotal observation of students.

Performance Based: This type of assessment often includes some type of real-world problem or scenario that students have to solve. Students are expected to use multiple sources of information (technology, photographs, diagrams), explain information from the sources, and give details to support their explanation. Often this assessment requires group collaboration. Within this scenario, embed performance-based responses and text-based responses during instruction, and provide opportunities for prompted writing.

Product/Project: This form of assessment requires students to create visual displays, charts/graphs, and written and oral reports, which may be presented for public viewing. Examples include social studies, science, and literature fair projects.

Portfolios: Portfolio assessments celebrate and document students' progress over time and should represent what a student can do. Portfolios are often used to showcase student work for family involvement, open house, and parent/student conferencing night. Work sampling may include finished assignments as well as work in progress.

Personal Communication: In this form of assessment, teachers conduct personal interviews; complete surveys on interests; and keep records of personal communication between student/teacher, parent/teacher, and self-scoring of student writing using rubric scales.

Anecdotal Observation of Student: Anecdotal observation is a powerful form of assessment for making an independent plan for students. Focus on the following:

- specific patterns of behavior
- weaknesses and interests
- ability to work independently
- ability to work with small groups

There are four strategies within this chapter that cover strategies for assessment with students:

- Observe student behaviors to gather formative assessment data
- Provide effective feedback in conferences
- Gather evidence of student learning from different sources
- Involve students in self-assessment and setting learning goals

 ## Strategy 1: Observe Student Behaviors to Gather Formative Assessment Data

Using a variety of assessment measures allows teachers a more open window into understanding each student as a writer. The examples that follow support all writers, both struggling and advanced. They are easy to implement, require few resources, allow assessment of the quality of learning, and provide immediate feedback in your classroom!

Four Corners: Place colors or shapes or both colors and shapes in the corners of the classroom. For example, you might use a blue triangle, a red square, a yellow rhombus, and a green circle. Students count off based on shape or color, and that dictates where in the room they will move. This allows for movement, collaboration, deep conversations, and an indication of students' ability to follow directions and work together. Use the Four Corners strategy as students discuss a writing topic, tips for conventions, or an opportunity to share writing. Keep your class conferring log in hand and move around, making notes about students' strengths, possible misconceptions, and areas of growth.

Parking Lot: A "parking lot" is chart paper placed in a visually appealing and accessible location in the classroom. Label the chart "Parking Lot!" Students are provided with sticky notes to respond to some kind of instruction. For example, if a modeled lesson on close reading and note-taking is complete and you expect students to use a graphic organizer, students can use sticky notes to indicate their understanding—ready to roll, need more information, need to work with a partner for support, or need to confer with teacher. Sticky notes are placed on the "Parking Lot." You can organize the "Parking Lot" with students. Use your imagination! The "Parking Lot" can be used throughout the day for all content areas and can reflect the success of your mini-lessons.

Learning Response/Reflection Logs: Students stop and reflect on their learning by writing their thoughts in a response log. This strengthens the classroom writing program, increases metacognition, and provides the teacher with evidence of learning. Students can use words, pictures, or graphic organizers to express knowledge gained.

Appointment Clock: An appointment clock is used to observe students' ability to meet and discuss their writing. It provides the opportunity for both movement and observation of students when appointments are set up for self-assessment. Students keep a completed clock at their desk. The clock is filled with names of classmates at each hour, completed earlier through an activity called "Complete Your Appointment Clock." The clock can be used for multiple weeks or can be revised. Students move to their specific appointments (1:00 p.m., 2:00 p.m., 3:00 p.m.) to self-assess during that particular session. As the students move through their appointments, the teacher notes movement, work ethic, use of time on task, focus, and student engagement.

Self-Questioning/Self-Assessment Technique: With this strategy, the teacher moves around, talking and making observations as students create questions about a current piece of their writing. Students generate questions to self-assess their current piece by explaining to themselves "how" a piece can be improved, or students explain to themselves "why" a change they need to make improves a piece of writing.

Steps for Self-Questioning/Self-Assessment

1. Students take out a writing piece to self-assess.

2. Students generate questions for how a piece they are working on can be improved. For example, "Can this piece be improved with better word choice?"

3. Students generate questions explaining why a change needs to be made: "Why is my voice not coming through in this piece?"

4. Students prioritize questions. For example, do they decide to focus on the "how" questions or the "why" questions to further improve the piece?

5. Groups share questions.

6. Students reflect on the process. For example, they might create question stems to use for further self-assessment such as "Did I think about ...?" "How can I clarify this part?" "Did I remember to...?" "How or why did my assessment questions require me to think deeply?"

 ## Strategy 2: Provide Effective Feedback in Conferences

Formative assessments provide multiple opportunities for conversations between the teacher and a student or small group. These conversations offer feedback to improve students' performance. They can motivate and inspire or deflate and defeat. When used effectively, feedback serves as "one of the most powerful influences on learning and achievement" (Hattie and Timperley 2007, 81). As teachers, we are ultimately responsible for engaging students in a learning experience where feedback offers clear and specific guidance to improve writing.

Consider these principles for providing students with effective feedback.

- **Feedback is timely and consistent:** Providing feedback sooner rather than later increases comprehension and the probability of using the writing strategy, skill, or craft in future writing. With timely and routine opportunities for feedback through individual, group, and peer conferences, teachers give students guidance throughout the learning process so they can reflect and adapt their writing. If responding in writing, it is just as important to return feedback promptly to keep interest and momentum in the writing project. "Effective feedback occurs during the learning, while there is still time to act on it" (Chappuis 2012, 41).

- **Feedback is relevant and specific:** Feedback is most effective when it is related to learning goals and focused on the quality of writing and specific strategies. The feedback is least effective when used as isolated praise to the student, vague comments, or is difficult to interpret. "Great job!" and "Word choice" written in the margins provide little information to the student as to what was done well or what words to reconsider. Effective feedback emphasizes the strengths of the writer and includes "information feedback about a task and how to do it more effectively" (Hattie and Timperley 2007, 84). For example: "Great job! Your main idea is very clear here in your introduction." Or, "You have included very specific steps for your reader to follow. Good effort. However, I'm a little confused about the sequence. How can you use your diagram to help you?"

- **Feedback = Thinking:** As teachers, we are helpers and we are fixers. So when giving feedback, we tend to observe, identify, and "help" our students when they are struggling with their writing. Unfortunately, often "helping" students leads to doing for students or just telling them exactly what to do, leaving them to simply mimic our steps. This type of feedback does not allow students to think through the concept being taught. If our goal is to create independent writers, we must scaffold the instruction and guide our students toward metacognition and self-efficacy.

Modeling and thinking aloud when demonstrating is a valuable instructional tool for teaching writing. When providing feedback for students during conferences, it certainly is useful to "show" a writing strategy or craft, and not just "tell" a student what to do. What is even more effective is combining the think-aloud modeling with feedback that "causes thinking and metacognition" (Miller 2015, 1). The use of open-ended questions and strategy prompts encourages students to think about how and why they made specific choices in their writing and if they need to reconsider those choices.

- **Feedback requires response:** Feedback is only effective when students listen to it, take a risk, and use it. Effective feedback gives students the means and opportunities to deepen their understanding of writing and use that new learning to revise and improve their writing. After encouraging, informing, questioning, listening, and guiding, are students responding to the feedback? We recognize our success in using effective feedback when:

  - students' writing reflects improvement

  - students recognize themselves as writers

  - students are motivated to learn

  - students value feedback as a productive tool in the process of writing

  - students are engaged, energized, and focused on improving their writing performance

 Strategy 3: Gathering Evidence of Student Learning from Different Sources

In order to get a full view of each student as a writer, gather data from different sources based on expectations from local, state, and national standards. Putting local, state, and national standards at the center of your assessment model assures that assessment of each student's learning outcomes is aligned with the writing and language arts standards you are expected to teach.

Triangulation Model of Assessment

Three essential data sources of student learning comprise the triangulation model presented in Figure 7.2: first, ongoing classroom observations; second, products and tests; and third, conferences and student self-evaluations. Each of these data sources helps you see the complete picture of each student as a writer. Gathering data from ongoing classroom observations, students' products, formal and informal testing, and through conferences and student self-evaluation not only helps you know what each student is learning but also increases both reliability and validity of student assessment (Davies 2000; Mathison 1988; Sammons 2013).

Figure 7.2 Triangulation Model of Assessment

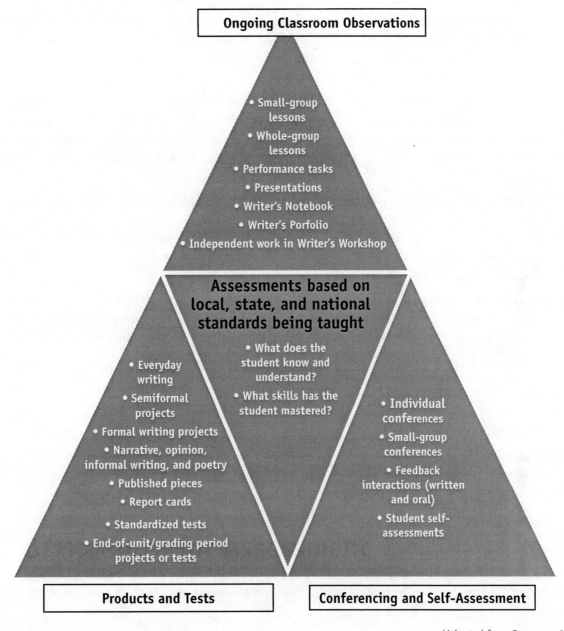

Ongoing Classroom Observations

- Small-group lessons
- Whole-group lessons
- Performance tasks
- Presentations
- Writer's Notebook
- Writer's Porfolio
- Independent work in Writer's Workshop

Assessments based on local, state, and national standards being taught

- What does the student know and understand?
- What skills has the student mastered?

- Everyday writing
- Semiformal projects
- Formal writing projects
- Narrative, opinion, informal writing, and poetry
- Published pieces
- Report cards
- Standardized tests
- End-of-unit/grading period projects or tests

- Individual conferences
- Small-group conferences
- Feedback interactions (written and oral)
- Student self-assessments

Products and Tests

Conferencing and Self-Assessment

(Adapted from Sammons 2013)

Use a Conferring Notebook

Just the act of sitting alongside a student, talking writer to writer, guiding their writing process is in itself an invaluable instructional and assessment method. The conferring notebook is a resource used to record the strengths and instructional focus during conferences that reaps benefits for both teacher and student. However, teachers may feel they don't have time to jot down notes during the conference and convince themselves they will add notes later. They don't because they still don't have time, they don't remember what to write, and/ or they don't understand the true value in using a conferring notebook. Why should teachers take the time to "notice and note" student accomplishments and needs in a conferring notebook?

Here are four principle reasons we include conferring notebooks in our writing conferences:

1. **The conferring notebook holds teachers responsible for meeting and conferring with every writer.** It serves as a record and a reminder of which students teachers have met with for conferring and who they have yet to see. Although teachers may meet more frequently with some students based on need, it is important to meet with all students for individual conferences.

2. **Teachers can identify the strengths of all writers from the conferring notebook.** The logs in the notebook give information about students' writing development. When using a genre checklist or rubric, look for those skills the writer has accomplished. Having them in the notebook also helps to not repeat the same compliment in the conference; as kindergarten student Gianna once explained, "I must be really good at using color words, 'cause you just keep on telling me over and over!"

3. **The conferring notebook serves as teaching and learning data for Writer's Workshop.** Not only do logs keep track of a student's strengths, but teachers can also note the instructional focus of the conference. Skimming the notes prior to the next conferring session gives teachers information to start the conversation and to see if the student made progress with the last teaching point. This data is useful when sharing student information with colleagues and parents.

4. **The conferring notebook is a valuable source of reflection.** By searching the notebook for clues and patterns, teachers can identify areas of writing instruction that have proven to be successful and those areas that were unsuccessful. Based on findings, teachers can identify areas of need that can lead to a small skill group or revisiting a writing strategy in whole-group instruction.

Contents of the Conferring Notebook

Mini-Lesson Log

Keep a list of the mini-lessons taught to the whole group in the notebook. This serves as a reminder of what has been taught, so that teachers can remind writers during a conference. Record the date and the topic or name of the mini-lesson. (See Appendix C, page 249.)

Class Conference Frequency Record

This documentation gives at-a-glance information about how often teachers are conferring with each student. It includes the names of all students in the class and the dates of each conference. Some teachers add the letter "I" or "G" or use different pen colors to indicate the type of conference—individual or group. (See Appendix C, page 250.)

Calendar

Including a calendar provides a place to plan for individual and group conferences, as well as a place to schedule a student-requested conference. Teachers are also less likely to forget to follow up with a writer if they quickly add an appointment to a conferring calendar.

Class Conferring Log

Teachers are always searching for the "just right" recording form. Many teachers use a weekly conferring grid that includes boxes for each student in the class. (See Appendix C, page 251.)

The anecdotal observations in Figure 7.3 are shown as a representation of one teacher's class conferring log. The P (praise) indicates strategies the student is using successfully, and TP (teaching point) is the strategy, skill, or craft the teacher selected to use as the instructional focus during the conference. Use the log to collect data from roving and individual conferences, and search for patterns of behavior to plan future instruction.

Figure 7.3 Sample Excerpt from a Class Conferring Log

Name: Leily **Date:** 3/1 **P:** Multi-syllabic words and pacing good **TP:** Use talk time wisely	**Name:** Jonah **Date:** 3/1 **P:** On-task during guided writing. Handled quick pacing **TP:** Conventional spelling Whent/went wuz/was	**Name:** Marcus **Date:** 3/1 **P:** Excellent use of anchor chart on adjectives **TP:** Sentence variety: complex, compound
Name: Shanice **Date:** 3/1 **P:** Pair share, intense and focused **TP:** Letter confusions: sound/symbol and order	**Name:** Brandon **Date:** 3/2 **P:** Deep discussion to elaborate from sources of information **TP:** Some difficulty holding on to sentence	**Name:** Omar **Date:** 3/2 **P:** Beginning a new story without prompting **TP:** Serial order and penmanship issues
Name: Aliyah **Date:** 3/2 **P:** Work pacing excellent. Started quickly. **TP:** Use of capital letters	**Name:** Hayley **Date:** 3/2 **P:** Giving partner information on fingers **TP:** Saying and stretching words for sound/symbol	**Name:** Roberto **Date:** 3/2 **P:** Confidence evident. Moved into text format quickly. **TP:** Use of conventions: ending punctuation
Name: Monique **Date:** 3/3 **P:** Using appropriate transitions for "how to!" **TP:** Conventions: spelling frist/first, thin/then	**Name:** Peyton **Date:** 3/3 **P:** Rereading for meaning **TP:** Elaborate with more evidence	**Name:** Kathryn **Date:** 3/4 **P:** Tightly focused introduction **TP:** Include more rigorous word choice.
Name: Martin **Date:** 3/4 **P:** Uses resources wisely/mentor text **TP:** Organize facts and evidence	**Name:** Laron **Date:** 3/4 **P:** Use of math transition words controlled for content writing **TP:** Reteach narrative writing for math story problems	**Name:** Mina **Date:** 3/4 **P:** Whispery discussion on brain function + (excellent) **TP:** Use mentor text to reteach introductions for informative.

Time to Share

The teacher can easily look at the grid to see which writers to schedule for conferences. Teachers who prefer more space for recording can use a log with headings at the top. They record information and simply draw a line to separate the notes on individual students, allowing varied space for each conference session (see page 252). Preprinted labels or sticky notes are also a popular method of logging. These are easily transferred to the individual student conference page. Some teachers prefer to record notes directly onto the individual student page in the student section of the conference notebook (see page 253). These pages may serve as a confidential format for IEP, 504, and classroom parent/teacher conferences.

There are numerous variations of the conferring log and teachers should try a few out or even create one until they find the record system that works best. Keep it simple and keep in mind the four principle reasons for using a conferring log.

Individual Student Section

This section of the notebook has a page(s) for each student where successive conference notes are recorded and/or collected. (See Appendix C, page 253.) Additional pages can be added for each student as needed. This serves as a comprehensive file of the student's writing goals and progress over time.

Digital Conferring Tools

The number of digital options for conference logs continues to grow. Applications like *Confer, Evernote, Penultimate,* and *CAFÉ Conferring Pensieve* allow quick documentation, data organization, and sorting options to identify students with similar needs, etc. Storage and access to photos, audio, and video clips of student writing makes sharing with parents and collaborating with support personnel easy and productive. Most offer options to "try before you buy."

 Strategy 4: Involve Students in Self-Assessment and Setting Learning Goals

Self-testing and self-explanation have been shown by cognitive psychologists to be among the best learning strategies that students can use (Dunlosky et al. 2013). Self-assessment engages students in their own learning and helps both the teacher and the student identify and focus on specific learning goals (Davies 2000). A student assessment profile binder is the perfect venue for collecting and utilizing student thinking to communicate their ideas with their teacher, their families and as documentation of learning. In the profile binder you might include: opinion, informational, and narrative self-reflections; self-assessments on peer conferencing; and other self-reflections depending on local, district and state mandated goals. Use the following guidelines for increasing student involvement in self-assessment and learning (adapted from Sammons 2013):

1. **Model the self-assessment process.** Self-assessment can seem like an intangible concept to many students. They need to understand the process and the types of questions you ask yourself as you wonder. Located at the end of this chapter you will find a complete set of steps for modeling self-assessment using a writing rubric. You need not limit your modeling to this example of self-assessment. You can also model how to write a self-reflection from your own writing sample, as well as a self-assessment of your thinking during a peer conference through the use of self-assessment checklists and rubrics.

2. **Teach students how to set learning goals.** It's not enough to simply ask students to evaluate or reflect on the quality of their work. No matter what the process for self-assessment—checklists, traits of quality writing rubrics, evaluations of writing notebooks or writing portfolios—the purpose is to set new learning

goals. Develop appropriate targets depending on grade level and learning expectations. Build these targets with students through the use of anchor charts. Figure 7.4 shows sample learning goals divided by grade range.

Figure 7.4 Sample Learning Expectations/Target Goals

Grade Range	Learning Expectations/Target Goals
K–2	• Control grade-appropriate, high-frequency words. • Use phonetic spellings and spelling patterns when appropriate. • Effectively use a variety of sentence patterns. • Recognize and use ending punctuation. • Introduce topic, use transition words, and provide a conclusion.
3–5	• Use conventional spelling of grade-level, high-frequency words and patterns. • Attempt phonetic spellings of multi-syllabic words. • Demonstrate appropriate word choice connected to audience and purpose. • Effectively use simple, compound, and complex sentences. • Use prepositional phrases to extend and enrich sentence variety. • Use correct capitalization as mandated in state curriculum. • Maintain effective organizational structures with ideas linked using words and phrases. • Use a strong introduction and conclusion.
6–8	• Appropriately use grade-level spelling. • Effectively use correct punctuation, grammar, and capitalization. • Effectively use sentence formation in a variety of sentence types. • Paragraph structure should include main idea statement, supporting details, a logical progression of ideas, and a conclusion. • Transition between paragraphs using smooth and fluid phrases. • Use vocabulary appropriate to audience and purpose.

3. **Make self-assessment and goal-setting a daily routine.** Self-assessment and goal-setting should become a habit of mind (Sammons 2013). For example, it can be a daily part of the student's editing and revision processes in Writer's Workshop. It can be a daily part of the conferencing process: you will observe, praise, guide, and connect, and the students will self-assess and set goals for learning. A strong habit for self-assessment during the writing process utilizes a shared writing wrap-up in primary grades Writer's Workshop. Using chart paper and markers, pull writers into a community wrap-up session. Divide the chart paper into two columns with headings: "What went well today!" and "What do we need to strengthen for tomorrow?" Students are to partner talk, reflect, and discuss as you act as the scribe and take notes on their reflections. On the next writing day, begin the session with a review of the wrap-up chart.

For intermediate and middle-school writers, have students keep a writing reflection log in a pocket of their writing folders. At the end of the day or class period, create a relaxing environment in your classroom (e.g., turn on twinkly lights, play classical music) and have students spend three minutes in reflection on their productivity, writing stamina, and accomplishments.

4. **Use checklists and rubrics to prompt students to reflect on their own work and progress.** Develop a variety of checklists and rubrics, but use them judiciously to avoid having instruction become formulaic.

5. **Debrief with students after their self-assessments.** Debriefing sessions are required in real experiences; therefore, let's make them authentic. The goal is to make the learning experience more meaningful and give the process authenticity. Develop debriefing rules with all students having a vested interest in the process. Make decisions about proper debriefing etiquette as a community of learners where all ideas are valued. You might try the following:

   - **Whip Around:** Students form a circle and say a word or phrase to express their thinking about a completed writing project or daily writing experience. All students share quickly to "whip around" the room.

   - **Give and Get:** Students play a memory game and move around the class, giving an idea from a classmate and getting an idea. This can be done orally or with paper and pencil. This is the perfect debriefing activity that requires movement and reflection. You might also try the following:

   - **Synthesize:** What do you know now that you didn't know before?

   - **Attitude:** How have your feelings changed since...?

   - **Contribute:** What have you contributed to writing today?

   - **Change:** What would you suggest we do to improve our debriefing sessions?

6. **Use Self-Assessments from the Triangulation Assessment Model:** Self-assessments may range from simple to complex, and from informal to formal. They include reflections based on products and tests, conferences, self-assessment checklists and rubrics, and even reflections on ongoing classroom observations such as the following:

   - Was I on task today?

   - Did I do my best work?

   - Did I set my learning goals?

   - What can I do to meet my goals?

7. **Share Student Self-Assessments:** As students move out into their careers, companies often require employees to measure their contributions to the business community through the process of writing self-assessments. Let's prepare students for college and career and begin the process early. Have students generate their own written self-assessments and allow them to share. Start the share process with partner pairs to eliminate apprehension. Move to a small-group share after you've demonstrated how successful people work together in a group setting. Remember you may have students in the early phases of writing all the way to proficient writers. Create heterogeneous groups. Your struggling writers will grow exponentially as they share their thinking and listen to the thinking of others.

Students may also share their self-assessments during peer conferencing meetings. To eliminate anxiety, post expectations for sharing in the peer conferring area. At the beginning of a writing session, have students meet in small groups and share a thought or idea from the previous day's self-assessment. At the end of the writing session, ask students to meet in triads to self-assess, share relevant information, and provide facts from their writing sample to support their thinking.

Assessment is about the conversation. It fits throughout the writing program. The conversation should always be about the writer. When asking pertinent, open-ended writing questions, students are assessing themselves. Questions might include the following:

- How do you plan to get your draft started?
- Can you say more about that?
- What revision work have you done?
- How have you used information from today's mini-lesson in your writing?
- What new vocabulary words have you tried?
- Why did you decide to use this quote in your introduction?

Remember to respond with a sense of joy and awe as your students respond to these questions. Jot your thinking down in your conferring notebook and return to answers on another writing day.

Involve not only students but parents as well in self-assessment. Allow self-assessments to be shared as you build a community of learners where students are not afraid to fail. Use self-assessments to allow students to learn, to feel okay about making mistakes, and to create a mindset of setting goals for lifelong learning, building grit and stamina, but not always expecting to achieve perfection. When sharing assessments with parents heed the the words of *New York Times* Op Ed columnist Frank Bruni: "While we sometimes point students toward markers of achievement, we don't want to deny them time to fail" (2015, SR3). Bruni shares psychiatrist Adam Strassberg's wise words to parents and puts it best: "Want the best for your child, not for your child to be the best" (Bruni 2015, SR3).

Closing Thoughts

In the introduction of this book we challenged you to adopt one clear goal: teach your students how to write. This book has given you strategies for Writer's Workshop built upon our three-legged stool model for Writer's Workshop: Time to Teach, Time to Write and Confer, and Time to Share. Keep them handy and refer to them often.

We hope that you are achieving the goals we set forth in the introduction and that you are gaining confidence in all these goal areas:

- Building a community of writers
- Motivating student writers
- Maximizing good instruction
- Having students writing every day and in every class
- Having students share writing publicly
- Monitoring writing outcomes through assessment

If you are doing these things, you aren't just a good, strategic writing teacher. Indeed, *you are amazing*!

51517—*Strategies for Implementing Writer's Workshop*

References Cited

Allen, Patrick A. 2009. *Conferring: The Keystone of Reader's Workshop*. Portland, Maine: Stenhouse Publishers.

Anderson, Carl. 2000. *How's it Going?: A Practical Guide to Conferring with Student Writers*. Portsmouth, NH: Heinemann.

Angelillo, Janet. 2008. *Whole-Class Teaching: Minilessons and More*. Portsmouth, NH: Heinemann.

Atkinson, Richard and Saul Geisermay. 2015. "The big problem with the new SAT." *New York Times*. Accessed December 5, 2015 http://www.nytimes.com/2015/05/05/opinion/the-big-problem-with-the-new-sat.html

Ayres, Ruth. 2013. *Celebrating Writers: From Possibilities Through Publication*. Portland, ME: Stenhouse Publishers.

Baucom, Ian. 2014. "'Making the Case for College?' an interview by Robert Viccellio." University of Virginia. 104 (4): 45.

Beers, Kylene, and Robert E. Probst. 2013. *Notice and Note: Strategies for Close Reading*. Portsmouth, NH: Heinemann.

Bellamy, Peter C. 2005. *Seeing with New Eyes: A Guidebook on Teaching and Assessing Beginning Writers Using the Six-Trait Writing Model*, 6th ed. Portland, OR: Northwest Regional Education Laboratory.

Berninger, Virginia W., William Nagy, Steve Tanimoto, Rob Thompson, and Robert D. Abbott. 2014. "Computer Instruction in Handwriting, Spelling, and Composing for Students with Specific Learning Disabilities in Grades 4–9." *Computers and Eductation* 81(1):154–168.

Berninger, Virginia W., Robert D. Abbott, Amy Augsburger, and Noelia Garcia. 2009. "Comparison of Pen and Keyboard Transcription Modes in Children With and Without Learning Disabilities Affecting Transcription." *Learning Disabilitiy Quarterly* 32(1):123–141.

Bruni, Frank, 2015. "Best, Brightest, and Saddest. *The New York Times*. Accessed April 27, 2015 http://www.nytimes.com/2015/04/12/opinion/sunday/frank-bruni-best-brightest-and-saddest.html

Calkins, Lucy. 2003. *The Conferring Handbook*. Portsmouth, NH,: Heinemann.

Calkins, Lucy. 1994. *The Art of Teaching Writing*. Portsmouth, NH: Heinemann.

Calkins, Lucy, Mary Ehrensworth, and Christopher Lehman. 2012. *Pathways to the Common Core: Accelerating Achievement*. Portsmouth, NH: Heinemann.

Calkins, Lucy, Amanda Hartman, and Zoe White. 2005. *One to One: The Art of Conferring with Young Writers*. Portsmouth, NH: Heinemann.

Chappuis, Jan. 2012. "How Am I Doing?" *Educational Leadership* 70 (1): 36–41.

Clackamas Education Service District. 2013. "Narrative Performance Task Rubrics." *Smarter Balance Assessment Consortium*. Clackamas Education Service District. Accessed April 27, 2015 http://www.clackesd.k12.or.us/cie/ccss/rubric/NEWNarrativeWritingRubricGrade3-8.pdf.

Clay, Marie. 1993. *An Observation Survey of Early Literacy Achievement*. Portsmouth, NH: Heinemann Education.

Cochrane, Orin. 1984. *Reading, Writing and Caring*. Katonah, NY: Richard C. Owen Publishers.

Appendix A

Coles, Martin and Christine Hall. 2002. "Gendered Reading: Learning from Children's Reading Choices." *Journal of Research in Reading*. 25(1):96–108.

Common Core State Standards Initiative. 2015. "Standard 10: Range, Quality, and Complexity." *English Language Arts Standards*. Accessed December 5, 2015 http://www.corestandards.org/ELA-Literacy/standard-10-range-quality-complexity/range-of-text-types-for-k-5

Conley, D. 2007. *Redefining college readiness*. Eugene, OR: Educational Policy Improvement Center.

Davies, Anne. 2000. *Making Classroom Assessment Work*. Courtney, Canada: Connections Publishing.

Denman, Gregory. 2013. *Think It, Show It, Mathematics*. Huntington Beach, CA: Shell Education.

Denton, Paula. 2015. *The Power of Words: Teacher Language That Helps Children Learn*. Turner Falls, MA: Northeast Foundation for Children, Inc.

Dunlosky, John and Katherine A. Rawson, Elizabeth J. Marsh, Mitchell J. Nathan and Daniel Willingham. 2013. "Improving Students' Learning With Effective Learning Techniques: Promising Directions From Cognitive and Educational Psychology. *Psychological Science in the Public Interest* 14 (1): 4–58.

Education Northwest. 2014. *Traits Rubric for Presentation K–12*. Portland, OR: Education Northwest.

Ernst daSilva, Karen. 2001. "Drawing on Experience: Connecting Art and Language." *Primary Voices K–6* 10 (2): 2–8.

Erlauer, Laura. 2003. *The Brain-Compatible Classroom: Using What We Know About Learning to Improve Teaching*. Alexandria, VA: ASCD.

Ferlazzo, Larry . 2012. Students Who Challenge Us: Eight Things Skilled Teachers Think, Say, and Do. *Education Leadership*, 70(2): 1.

Fisher, Douglas, Nancy Frey, and Douglas Williams. 2002. "Seven Literacy Strategies that Work." *Educational Leadership* 60 (3): 70–73.

Fisher, Douglas, and Gay Ivey. 2005. "Literacy and Language as Learning in Content-Area Classes: A Departure from 'Every Teacher a Teacher of Reading.'" *Action in Teacher Education* 27 (2): 3–11.

Fisher, Douglas, Nancy Frey, and Carol Rothenberg. 2008. *Content-Area Conversations: How to Plan Discussion-Based Lesson for Language Learners*. Alexandria, VA: ASCD.

Fletcher, Ralph. 1996. *A Writer's Notebook: Unlocking the Writer Within You*. New York, NY: HarperCollins.

Fletcher, Ralph, and JoAnn Portalupi. 1998. *Craft Lessons: Teaching Writing K-8*. Portland, ME: Stenhouse Publishers.

Fox, Mem. 1993. *Radical Reflections: Passionate Opinions on Teaching, Learning, and Living*. New York, NY: Mariner Books, Inc.

Gentry, Richard. 2013. "Will Common Core Wreck Writing in Schools?" *Psychology Today*. Accessed December 17, 2015 https://www.psychologytoday.com/blog/raising-readers-writers-and-spellers/201305/will-common-core-wreck-writing-in-schools.

Gentry, Richard and Steve Peha. 2013. "5 Ways to Motivate Young Writers and Readers." *Psychology Today*. Accessed December 5, 2015 https://www.psychologytoday.com/blog/raising-readers-writers-and-spellers/201310/5-ways-motivate-young-writers-and-readers.

Gentry, Richard, Jan McNeel, and Vickie Wallace-Nesler. 2012a. *Getting to the Core of Writing Level K*. Huntington Beach, CA: Shell Education.

———. 2012b. *Getting to the Core of Writing Level 1*. Huntington Beach, CA: Shell Education.

———. 2012c. *Getting to the Core of Writing Level 2*. Huntington Beach, CA: Shell Education.

———. 2012d. *Getting to the Core of Writing Level 3*. Huntington Beach, CA: Shell Education.

———. 2012e. *Getting to the Core of Writing Level 4*. Huntington Beach, CA: Shell Education.

———. 2012f. *Getting to the Core of Writing Level 5*. Huntington Beach, CA: Shell Education.

———. 2012g. *Getting to the Core of Writing Level 6*. Huntington Beach, CA: Shell Education.

———. 2014. *Fostering Writing in Today's Classroom*. Huntington Beach, CA: Shell Education.

Ginott, Haim. 1972. *Teacher and child: A book for parents and teachers*. New York, NY: Macmillan.

Graham, Steve, Alisha Bollinger, Carol Booth Olson, Catherine D'Aoust, Charles MacArthur, Deborah McCutchen, and Natalie Olinghouse. 2012. "Teaching Elementary School Students to Be Effective Writers: A Practice Guide." *Institute of Education Sciences*. Washington, DC: U.S. Department of Education.

Graves, Donald. 1983. *Writing: Teachers and Children at Work*. Portsmouth, NH: Heinemann.

———. 1994. *A Fresh Look at Writing*. Portsmouth, NH: Heinemann.

———. 2002. "The Energy to Teach." *Voices in the Middle* 10 (1): 8–10.

———. 2015. "Answering Your Questions About Teaching Writing: A Talk with Donald H. Graves." Accessed March 5, 2015 http://www.scholastic.com/teachers/article/answering-your-questions-about-teaching-writing-talk-donald-h-graves.

Gray, Esther Cappon. 2006. "Children's Use of Language and Pictures in Classroom Inquiry." *Language Arts* 83 (30): 227–237.

Green, Judy. 1999. *The Ultimate Guide to Classroom Publishing*. Ontario, Canada: Pembroke Publishers.

Harste, Jerome. 1993. "Inquiry-Based Instruction." *Primary Voices K-6*, 2–5.

Hattie, John, and Helen Timperley. 2007. "The Power of Feedback." *Review of Educational Research* 77 (1): 81–11.

Hindley, Joanne. 1996. *In the Company of Children*. Portland, ME: Stenhouse Publishers.

Ito, Carolyn. 1996. "Behavior Influence Techniques." *Challenging Behaviors*. William and Mary School of Education Training and Technical Assistance Center https://education.wm.edu/centers/ttac/resources/articles/challengebehav/behavinflutech/index.php.

Jensen, Eric. 2000a. *Different Brains, Different Learners: How to Reach the Hard to Reach*. San Diego, CA: The Brain Store.

———. 2000b. *Learning with the Body in Mind: The Scientific Basis for Energizers, Movement, Play, Games, and Physical Education*. Thousand Oaks, CA: Corwin Press.

———. 2005. *Teaching with the Brain in Mind*, 2nd ed. Alexandria, VA: ASCD.

Appendix A

Johnson, Peter H. 2004. *Choice Words: How Our Language Affects Student Learning*. Portland, ME: Stenhouse Publishers.

Konicovva, Maria. 2014. "What's Lost When Handwriting Fades." *The New York Times*. Accessed December 5, 2015 http://www.nytimes.com/2014/06/03/science/whats-lost-as-handwriting-fades.html?_r=0.

Lorain, Peter. 2015. "Teaching That Emphasizes Active Engagement." *National Education Association*. Accessed December 5, 2015 http://NEA.org/tools/16708.htm.

Marzano, Robert J. 2007. *The Art and Science of Teaching*. Alexandria, VA: ASCD.

Marzano, Robert J., and Julia A. Simms. 2013. *Vocabulary for the Common Core*. Bloomington, IN: Marzano Research Laboratory.

Mathison, Sandra, 1988. "Why Triangulate?" *Educational Researcher* 17 (2): 13–17.

Meyers, Chet, and Thomas B. Jones. 1993. *Promoting Active Learning: Strategies for the College Classroom*. San Francisco, CA: Jossey-Bass.

Miller, Andrew. 2015. "Feedback for Thinking: Working for the Answer." *Edutopia*. Accessed December 5, 2015 http://www.edutopia.org/blog/feedback-for-thinking-working-for-answer-andrew-miller.

Minkel, J. 2013. "Lions, Tigers, and Mating Polar Bears, Oh My! 2nd Grade Researchers Writing to Read." *Education Week: Teacher*. Accessed December 5, 2015 http://blogs.edweek.org/teachers/teaching_fortriumph/2013/12/lions_tigers_and_mating_polar_.html.

Moore, D. W., Bean, T. W., Birdyshaw, D., & Rycik, J. A. 1999. "Adolescent literacy: A position statement." Newark, DE: Commission on Adolescent Literacy of the International Reading Association.

Murray, Donald. 1982. *Learning by Teaching: Selected Articles on Writing and Teaching*. Portsmouth, NH: Heinemann.

———. 2005. *Write to Learn*. Belmont, CA: Wadsworth Thomson Learning Publishing.

Ogle, Donna M. 1986. "K-W-L: A Teaching Model that Develops Active Reading of Expository Text." *The Reading Teacher* 39 (6): 564–570.

Pappano, Laura. 2013. "'Grit' and the New Character Education." *Harvard Education Letter* 29 (1): 1.

———. 2015. "The 'New PE' Aims to Build Bodies and Brains." *Harvard Education Letter* 31 (1).

Peha, Steve. 2013. "Writing Across the Curriculum." *Teaching that Makes Sense*. Accessed February 28, 2014 http://www.ttms.org/PDFs/06%20Writing%20Across%20the%20Curriculum%20v001%20(Full).pdf.

Pink, Daniel. 2009. *Drive: The Surprising Truth About What Motivates Us*. New York, NY: Riverhead Books.

Ray, Katie Wood. 2006. "Exploring Inquiry as a Teaching Stance in the Writing Workshop." *Language Arts* 83 (3): 238–247.

———. 2004. *About the Authors: Writing Workshop with Our Youngest Writers*. Cleaveland Portsmouth, NH: Heinemann.

———. 2001. *The Writing Workshop: Working Through the Hard Parts (And They're All Hard Parts)*. Urbana, IL: National Council of Teachers of English.

Richardson, Jan. 2009. *The Next Step in Guided Reading.* New York, NY: Scholastic.

Richhart, Ron, Mark Church, and Karin Morrison. 2011. *Making Thinking Visible: How to Promote Engagement, Understanding and Independence for all Learners.* San Francisco, CA: Jossey-Bass Publisher.

Robb, Laura. 2000. *Teaching reading in middle school: A strategic approach to teaching reading that improves comprehension and thinking.* New York: Scholastic Professional Books.

Rockwell, Sylvia. 1995. *Back Off Cool Down, Try Again: Teaching Students How to Control.* Arlington, VA: Council of Exceptional Children.

Rothstein, Dan, and Luz Santana. 2011. "Harvard Education Letter." *Harvard Graduate School of Education* 27 (5).

Routman, Regie. 2005. *Writing Essentials: Raising Expectations and Results While Simplifying Teaching.* Portsmouth, NH: Heinemann.

Ruhl, Kathy L., Charles A. Hughes, and Patrick J. Schloss. 1987. "Using the Pause Procedure to Enhance Lecture Recall." *Teacher Education and Special Education: The Journal of the Teacher Education Division of the Council for Exceptional Children* 10 (1): 14–18.

Sammons, Laney. 2013. *Strategies for Implementing Guided Math.* Huntington Beach, CA: Shell Education.

Simmons, D. 2014. Why teaching poetry is so important. *The Atlantic.* Washington, DG: The Atlantic Media Company. Accessed April 8, 2014 http://www.theatlantic.com/eWhy%20Teaching%20Poetry%20Is%20So%20Importantducation/archive/2014/04/why-teaching-poetry-is-so-important/360346/.

Smith, Frank. 1998. *Joining the Literacy Club: Further Essays into Education.* Portsmouth, NH: Heinemann.

Spires, Hiller A., and P. Diane Stone. 1989. "The Directed Notetaking Activity: A Self-Questioning Approach." *Journal of Reading* 33 (1): 36–39.

Strauss, Valerie. 2014. "Seven Ways Schools Kill the Love of Reading in Kids." Reprinted with permission from Alfie Kohn. *The Washington Post Online.* http://www.washingtonpost.com/blogs/answer-sheet/wp/2014/12/06/seven-ways-schools-kill-the-love-of-reading-in-kids-and-4-principles-to-help-restore-it/.

Sturock, Susan. 2015. "Effective Writing In the Middle School Classroom," PowerPoint Presentation created for staff development, John Winthrop Middle School, Connecticut.

Tate, Marcia L. 2004. *Sit and Get Won't Grow Dendrites: 20 Engaging Learning Strategies that Engage the Adult Brain.* Thousand Oaks, CA: Corwin Press.

Vacca, R. T. 1998. Let's not marginalize adolescent literacy. Journal of Adult and Adolescent Literacy, 8, 604–609.

———. 2002. Reading and Writing in the Content Areas: From Efficient Decoders to Strategic Readers. Educational Leadership, 60(3) 6-11. Retrieved from the Internet November 2002. http://www.ascd.org/publications/educational-leadership/nov02/vol60/num03/From-Efficient-Decoders-to-Strategic-Readers.aspx

Weimer, Maryellen. 2012. "Faulty Focus: Higher Ed Teaching Strategies." *Magna Publications.* www.facultyfocus.com/articles/teaching-professor-blog/five-reasons-getting-students-to-talk-is-worth-the-effort/.

Wiggins, Grant and Jay McTighe. 2005. *Understanding by Design,* 2nd ed. Alexandria, VA: Association for Supervision and Curriculum Development.

Wiggins, Grant. 2006. "Healthier Testing Made Easy: The Idea of Authentic Assessment." Retried from *What Works* in Education, Edutopia http://www.edutopia.org/authentic-assessment-grant-wiggins.

Literature Cited

Aardema, Verna. *Bringing the Rain to Kapiti Plain*. New York, NY: Dial Books for Young Readers, 1981

Ahlberg, Allan, and Janet Ahlberg. *Each Peach, Pear Plum*. New York, NY: Puffin Books, 1986.

Aliki. *Digging Up Dinosaurs*. New York, NY: HarperCollins, 1988.

———. *My Five Senses*. New York NY: HarperCollins Children's Books, 1989.

Allen, Judy. *Are You a Grasshopper?* New York, NY: Kingfisher, 2002.

Appelt, Kathi. *Counting Crows*. New York, NY: Atheneum Books for Young Readers, 2015.

Archambault, John, and Bill Martin. *Chicka Chicka Boom Boom*. New York, NY: Simon & Schuster Books for Young Readers, 2012.

Balestrino, Phillip. *The Skeleton Inside You*. New York, NY: HarperTrophy, 1989.

Banks, Kate. *Max's Words*. New York, NY: Farrar, Straus and Giroux, 2006.

Bayer, Jane E. *A My Name is Alice*. New York, NY: Dial Books for Young Readers, 1984.

Baylor, Byrd. *The Best Town in the World*. New York, NY: Harcourt Children's Books, 1995.

———. *Everybody Needs a Rock*. New York, NY: Ateneum Books for Young Readers, 2011.

———. *The Table Where Rich People Sit*. New York, NY: Aladdin Paperbacks, 1998.

Beaumont, Karen. *I Like Myself!* New York, NY: HMH Books for Young Readers, 2004.

Berger, Melvin, and Gilda Melvin. *Why Do Volcanoes Blow Their Tops?: Questions and Answers about Volcanoes and Earthquakes*. New York, NY: Scholastic Reference, 2000.

Bishop, Claire. *Five Chinese Brothers*. New York, NY: Penguin Putnam Books for Young Readers, 1996.

Black, Holly. *Doll Bones*. New York, NY: Margaret K. McElderry, 2013.

Blos, Joan W. *Old Henry*. New York, NY: HarperCollins Publishers, 1990.

Blume, Judy. *The Pain and the Great One*. New York, NY: Atheneum Books for Young Readers, 2014.

Boelts, Maribeth. *Those Shoes*. Somerville, MA: Candlewick Press, 2009.

Bottner, Barbara, and Gerald Kruglik. *Wallace's Lists*. New York, NY: Katherine Tegen Books, 2004.

Brinckloe, Julie. *Fireflies!*. New York, NY: Aladdin Paperbacks, 1986.

Brown, Ruth. *A Dark, Dark Tale*. New York, NY: Puffin Books, 1992.

Buehner, Caralyn. *The Escape of Marvin the Ape*. New York, NY: Puffin Books, 1999.

Bunting, Eve. *Smoky Night*. New York, NY: Harcourt Brace & Company, 1994.

———. *The Wall*. New York, NY: Clarion Books, 1990.

Burgess, Matthew. *Enormous Smallness: A Story of E. E. Cummings*. Brooklyn, NY: Enchanted Lion Books, 2015.

Carle, Eric. *Does a Kangaroo Have a Mother, Too?* New York, NY: HarperCollins Children's Books, 2002.

———. *The Grouchy Ladybug*. New York, NY: HarperCollins Publishers, 1999.

———. *The Very Busy Spider*. New York, NY: Philomel Books, 1984.

———. *The Very Hungry Caterpillar*. New York, NY: Puffin Books, 2002.

Carlson, Nancy. *How to Lose All Your Friends*. New York, NY: Viking Juvenile, 1994.

Charlip, Remy. *Fortunately*. New York, NY: Aladdin Paperbacks, 1993.

Cherry, Lynne. *The Great Kapok Tree: A Tale of the Amazon Rain Forest*. New York, NY: HMH Books for Young Readers, 2000.

———. *The River Ran Wild: An Environmental History*. New York, NY: HMH Books for Young Readers, 2002.

Coffelt, Nancy. *Big, Bigger, Biggest!* New York, NY: Henry Holt and Company, 2009.

Colandro, Lucille. *There Was an Old Lady Who Swallowed a Fly!* New York, NY: Cartwheel Books, 2014

Collins, Mary. *Airborne: A Photobiography of Wilbur and Orville Wright*. Washington DC: National Geographic Children's Books, 2015.

Cooper, Melrose. *Gettin' Through Thursday*. New York, NY: Lee & Low Books, 1998.

Creech, Sharon. *Love That Dog*. New York, NY: HarperCollins Children's Books, 2001.

Crews, Donald. *Shortcut*. New York, NY: Greenwillow Books, 1996.

Cronin, Doreen. *Click, Clack, Moo: Cows That Type*. New York, NY: Simon & Schuster Books for Young Readers, 2000.

———. *Diary of a Spider*. New York, NY: Joanna Cotler Books, 2013.

———. *Diary of a Worm*. New York, NY: HarperCollins Children's Books, 2003.

Cuyler, Margery. *That's Good! That's Bad!* New York, NY: Henry Holt and Co., 1993.

Davies, Nicola. *One Tiny Turtle*. Somerville, MA: Candlewick Press, 2005.

Dawson Boyd, Candy. *Daddy, Daddy, Be There*. New York, NY: Philomel, 1995.

Defoe, Daniel. *Robinson Crusoe*. New York, NY: Aladdin Paperbacks, 2003.

dePaola, Tomie. *Nana Upstairs, Nana Downstairs*. New York, NY: Puffin Books, 2000.

———. *The Popcorn Book*. New York, NY: Holiday House, 1984.

Dickens, Charles. *A Christmas Carol*. Mineola, NY: Dover Publications, 1991.

Doctorow, Cory, and Jen Wang. *In Real Life*. New York, NY: First Second, 2014.

Duncan Edwards, Pamela. *The Bus Ride That Changed History*. New York, NY: Sandpiper, 2009.

Eastman, P. D. *Are You My Mother?* New York, NY: Random House, 1998.

Ewald, Wendy. *The Best Part of Me: Children Talk About their Bodies in Pictures and Words.* New York, NY: Little, Brown and Company Books for Young Readers, 2002.

Faruqi, Reem. *Lailah's Lunchbox: A Ramadan Story*. Thomaston, ME: Tilbury House Publishers, 2015.

Finchler, Judy. *Testing Miss Malarkey*. New York, NY: Walker Books for Young Readers, 2003.

Fleishman, Paul. *Joyful Noise: Poems for Two Voices*. New York, NY: HarperCollins Children's Books, 1992.

Fletcher, Ralph. *Marshfield Dreams: When I Was a Kid*. New York, NY: Square Fish, 2012.

———. *Twilight Comes Twice*. New York, NY: Clarion Books, 1997.

Fox, Mem. *Wilfrid Gordon McDonald Partridge*. San Diego, CA: Kane Miller Books, 1989.

Frasier, Debra. *Miss Alaineus: A Vocabulary Disaster*. New York, NY: HMH Books for Young Readers, 2000.

Frazee, Marla. *Roller Coaster*. New York, NY: HMH Books for Young Readers, 2003.

Geraghty, Paul. *Over the Steamy Swamp*. New York, NY: HMH Books for Young Readers, 1989.

Gerstein, Mordicai. *The Sun's Day*. New York, NY: HarperCollins, 1989.

Gibbons, Gail. *Apples*. New York, NY: Holiday House, 2000.

———. *Lights! Camera! Action!: How a Movie is Made*. New York, NY: Crowell, 1985.

———. *The Pumpkin Book*. New York, NY: Holiday House, 2000.

———. *The Seasons of Arnold's Apple Tree*. New York, NY: Sandpiper, 1988.

Grambling, Lois G. and H.B. Lewis. *Can I Have a Stegosaurus, Mom? Can I? Please!?* Mahwah, NJ: Troll Communications, 1998.

Greenfield, Eloise. *Honey, I Love*. New York, NY: Amistad Press, 2002.

Griffin Burns, Loree. *Beetle Busters: A Rogue Insect and the People Who Track It*. New York, NY: HMH Books for Young Readers, 2014.

Hakes Noble, Trinka. *The Day Jimmy's Boa Ate the Wash*. New York, NY: Puffin Books, 1992.

Heard, Georgia. *Creatures of Earth, Sea, and Sky*. Honesdale, PA: WordSong, 1997.

Hemingway, Ernest. *The Old Man and the Sea*. New York, NY: Charles Scribner's Sons, 1952.

Henkes, Kevin. *Chrysanthemum*. New York, NY: Mulberry Books, 2008.

Henson, Heather. *That Book Woman*. New York, NY: Atheneum Books for Young Readers, 2008.

Herrera, Robin. *Hope Is a Ferris Wheel*. New York, NY: Amulet Books, 2014.

Hesse, Karen. *Come on, Rain!*. New York, NY: Scholastic Press, 1999.

———. *The Music of the Dolphins*. New York, NY: Scholastic Signature, 1998.

Hill, Sandi. *A Great Attitude*. Huntington Beach, CA: Creative Teaching Press, 1998.

Himmelman, John. *A Dandelion's Life*. New York, NY: Children's Press, 1998.

Hinshaw Patent, Dorothy. *When the Wolves Returned: Restoring Nature's Balance in Yellowstone*. London, England: Walker Childrens, 2008.

Holm, Jennifer L. *Middle School is Worse than Meatloaf*. New York, NY: Atheneum Books for Young Readers, 2011.

Homer. *The Odyssey*. Translated by Robert Fagles. New York, NY: Penguin Books, 1997.

Hoose, Hannah, and Philip Hoose. *Hey, Little Ant*. Berkeley, CA: Tricycle Press, 1998.

Janeczko, Paul B. *The Place My Words Are Looking For: What Poets Say About and Through Their Work*. New York, NY: Simon & Schuster Books for Young Readers, 1990.

Jenkins, Steve. *Eye to Eye: How Animals See the World*. New York, NY: HMH Books for Young Readers, 2014.

Johnson, Angela. *When I Am Old With You*. New York, NY: Orchard Books, 1993.

Johnson, Crockett. *Harold and the Purple Crayon*. New York, NY: HarperCollins Children's Books, 2015.

Johnston, Tony. *The Harmonica*. Watertown, MA: Charlesbridge, 2004.

Joosse, Barbara M. *I Love You the Purplest*. San Francisco, CA: Chronicle Books, 1996.

———. *Mama, Do You Love Me?* San Francisco, CA: Chronicle Books, 1998.

———. *Old Robert and the Sea-Silly Cats*. New York, NY: Philomel Books, 2012.

Juster, Norton. *The Hello, Goodbye Window*. New York, NY: Hyperion Books for Children, 2005.

Kalan, Robert. *Jump, Frog, Jump!* New York, NY: Greenwillow Books, 1995.

Kaufman Orloff, Karen. *I Wanna Iguana*. New York, NY: Scholastic, Inc., 2005.

———. *I Wanna New Room*. New York, NY: G.P. Putnam's Sons Books for Young Readers, 2010.

Keats, Ezra Jack. *The Snowy Day*. New York, NY: Viking Books for Young Readers, 1996.

Kent, Jack. *Caterpillar and the Polliwog*. New York, NY: Aladdin Paperbacks, 1985.

Khan, Hena. *Golden Domes and Silver Lanterns: A Muslim Book of Colors*. San Francisco, CA: Chronicle Books, 2012.

Kinney, Jeff. *Diary of a Wimpy Kid*. New York, NY: Amulet Books, 2007.

Kitchen, Bert. *Somewhere Today*. Somerville, MA: Candlewick Press, 1994.

Lacamara, Laura. *Dalia's Wondrous Hair/El cabello maravilloso de Dalia*. Houston, TX: Piñata Books for Children, 2014.

L'Engle, Madeleine. *A Swiftly Tilting Planet*. New York, NY: Square Fish, 2007.

Levine, Ellen. *If You Traveled on the Underground Railroad*. New York, NY: Scholastic Paperbacks, 1993.

Appendix B

Litwin, Eric. *Pete the Cat: I Love My White Shoes*. New York, NY: HarperCollins Publishers, 2010.

Locker, Thomas. *Water Dance*. New York, NY: HMH Books for Young Readers, 2002.

Lowry, Lois. *The Giver*. New York, NY: Laurel-Leaf Books, 2002.

Macaulay, David. *Castle*. New York, NY: HMH Books for Young Readers, 1977.

MacLachlan, Patricia. *All the Places to Love*. New York, NY: HarperCollins Publishers, 1994.

Markle, Sandra. *Outside and Inside Trees*. New York, NY: Scholastic, Inc., 1993.

Martin Jr., Bill. *Brown Bear, Brown Bear, What Do You See?* New York, NY: Henry Holt and Co., 1996.

Mayer, Mercer. *I Just Forgot*. New York, NY: Random House, Inc., 1999.

Minor, Florence. *If You Were a Penguin*. New York, NY: Katherine Tegen Books, 2008.

Mowatt, Farley. *The Snow Walker*. Mechanicsburg, PA: Stackpole Books, 2004.

Muñoz Ryan, Pam. *Esperanza Rising*. New York, NY: Scholastic Inc., 2002.

————. *Hello Ocean*. Watertown, MA: Charlesbridge Publishing, 2001.

Murphy, Jim. *The Great Fire*. New York, NY: Scholastic Paperbacks, 2010.

Ness, Evaline. *Sam, Bangs, and Moonshine*. New York, NY: Square Fish, 1971.

Nicklin, Flip, and Linda Nicklin. *Face to Face with Dolphins*. Washington DC: National Geographic Children's Books, 2009.

Numeroff, Laura. *If You Give a Mouse A Cookie*. New York, NY: HarperCollins Children's Books, 2010.

O'Neill, Alexis. *The Recess Queen*. New York, NY: Scholastic Press, 2002.

Oppenheim, Joanne. *"Not Now!" Said the Cow*. New York, NY: Bank Street, 1981.

Palatini, Margie. *Bedhead*. New York, NY: Simon & Schuster Books for Young Readers, 2003.

Pallotta, Jerry. *Who Would Win?* New York, NY: Scholastic, Inc.

Peck, Richard. *The Year Down Yonder*. New York, NY: Dial Books for Young Readers, 2002.

Peppé, Rodney. *The House that Jack Built*. New York, NY: Longman Young Books, 1970.

Pérez, L. King. *First Day in Grapes*. New York, NY: Lee & Low Books, 2014.

Poe, Edgar Allan. *The Cask of Amontillado*. Brooklyn, NY: Sheba Blake Publishing, 2013.

Polacco, Patricia. *Chicken Sunday*. New York, NY: Philomel Books, 1992.

————. *Thank You, Mr. Falker*. New York, NY: Philomel Books, 2001.

Porter, Alex, and Kristin Lewis. "Imagine." *Scholastic Scope,* (March 12, 2012): 4–9. www.scope.scholastic.com.

Pulver, Robin. *Punctuation Takes a Vacation*. New York, NY: Holiday House, 2004.

Read Macdonald, Margaret. *The Old Woman and Her Pig: An Appalachian Folktale*. New York, NY: HarperCollins Publishers, 2007.

Robart, Rose. *The Cake That Mack Ate*. New York, NY: Little, Brown and Company Books for Young Readers, 1991.

Ross, Gary. *Bartholomew Biddle and the Very Big Wind*. Somerville, MA: Candlewick Press, 2012.

Rylant, Cynthia. *In November*. New York, NY: HMH Books for Young Readers, 2008.

———. *Missing May*. New York, NY: Scholastic, 2004.

———. *The Relatives Came*. New York, NY: Aladdin Paperbacks, 1993.

———. *When I Was Young in the Mountains*. New York, NY: Puffin Books, 1993.

Sachar, Louis. *Holes*. New York, NY: Yearling, 2000.

Say, Allen. *Grandfather's Journey*. New York, NY: HMH Books for Young Readers, 1993.

Schotter, Roni. *The Boy Who Loved Words*. New York, NY: Schwartz & Wade, 2006.

Seuss, Dr. *The Lorax*. New York, NY: Random House Books for Young Readers, 1971.

Seuss, Dr. *There's a Wocket in my Pocket!* Random House Book for Young Readers, 1974.

Shakespeare, William. *Hamlet*. New York, NY: New American Library, 1998.

Shannon, David. *No, David!* New York, NY: The Blue Sky Press, 1998.

Shelley, Mary. *Frankenstein*. Mineola, NY: Dover Publications, 1994.

Sidman, Joyce. *Ubiquitous: Celebrating Nature's Survivors*. New York, NY: HMH Books for Young Readers, 2010.

Silverstein, Shel. *A Giraffe and a Half*. New York, NY: HarperCollins, 2014.

———. *Where the Sidewalk Ends*. New York, NY: HarperCollins, 2014.

Simon, Seymour. *Animals Nobody Loves*. San Francisco, CA: Chronicle Books, 2002.

———. *Tornadoes*. New York, NY: HarperCollins, 2001.

Solheim, James. *It's Disgusting and We Ate It! True Food Facts from Around the World and Throughout History*. New York, NY: Aladdin Paperbacks, 1998.

Spier, Peter. *We the People: The Constitution of the United States*. New York, NY: Doubleday Books for Young Readers, 2014.

Steig, William. *Brave Irene*. New York, NY: Square Fish, 2011.

Stevens, Janet. *The Great Fuzz Frenzy*. New York, NY: Harcourt Children's Books, 2005.

Stewart, Melissa. *A Place for Birds*. Atlanta, GA: Peachtree Publishers, 2015.

Stinson, Kathy. *Red is Best*. Willowdale, ON: Annick Press, 2006.

Swinburne, Stephen. *Whose Shoes?: A Shoe for Every Job*. Honesdale, PA: Boyds Mills Press, Inc., 2011.

Tafolla, Carmen. *What Can You Do with a Paleta?/¿Qué Puedes Hacer con una Paleta?* New York, NY: Dragonfly Books, 2014.

Appendix B

The Matrix, directed by Andy Wachowski and Lana Wachowski. Burbank, CA: Warner Home Video, 1999. DVD.

The Terminator, directed by James Cameron. 1984. Beverly Hills, CA: MGM Home Entertainment, 2007. DVD.

The Wizard of Oz, directed by Victor Fleming. 1939. Culver City, CA: Warner Bros., 1998. DVD.

Thomson, Sarah L. *Imagine A Day*. New York, NY: Atheneum Books for Young Readers, 2005.

Tolstoi, Aleksei. *The Great Big Enormous Turnip*. Worksop, England: Award Publications Limited, 2013.

Truss, Lynne. *Twenty-Odd Ducks: Why, every punctuation mark counts!* New York, NY: G.P. Putnam's Sons Books for Young Readers, 2008.

Turner, Pamela. *The Frog Scientist*. New York, NY: HMH Books for Young Readers, 2009.

Twain, Mark. *The Adventures of Tom Sawyer*. Mineola, NY: Dover Publications, 1998.

VanDerwater, Amy. *Forest Has a Song*. New York, NY: Clarion Books, 2013.

Viorst, Judith. *Alexander and the Terrible, Horrible, No Good, Very Bad Day*. New York, NY: Aladdin Paperbacks, 1987.

———. *Earrings!* New York, NY: Aladdin Paperbacks, 1993.

Waber, Bernard. *Ira Sleeps Over*. New York, NY: HMH Books for Young Readers, 1987.

Ward, Cindy. *Cookie's Week* New York, NY: Penguin Putnam Books for Young Readers, 1997.

Watt, Melanie. *Scaredy Squirrel*. Toronto, ON: Kids Can Press Ltd., 2006.

White, E.B. *Charlotte's Web*. New York, NY: HarperTrophy, 2012.

Wick, Walter. *A Drop of Water: A Book of Science and Wonder*. New York, NY: Scholastic Press, 1997.

Wild, Margaret. *Fox*. San Diego, CA: Kane/Miller Book Publishers, 2006.

Williams-Garcia, Rita. *One Crazy Summer*. New York, NY: HarperCollins Children's Books, 2011.

Williems, Mo. *Knuffle Bunny: A Cautionary Tale*. New York, NY: Hyperion Books for Children, 2004.

Wilson Chall, Marcia. *Up North at the Cabin*. New York, NY: Lothrop, Lee & Shepard Books, 1992.

Wood, Audrey. *The Napping House*. New York, NY: HMH Books for Young Readers, 2009.

———. *Silly Sally*. New York, NY: HMH Books for Young Readers, 1999.

Woodson, Jacqueline. *Brown Girl Dreaming*. New York, NY: Nancy Paulsen Books, 2014.

Yolen, Jane and Andrew Fusek Peters. *Here's a Little Poem: A Very First Book of Poetry*. Somerville, MA: Candlewick Press, 2007.

Yolen, Jane. *Owl Moon*. New York, NY: Philomel Books, 1987.

Yousafzai, Malala. *I Am Malala: How One Girl Stood Up for Education and Changed the World (Young Readers Edition)*. New York, NY: Little, Brown and Company Books for Young Readers, 2014.

Zemach, Harve. *The Judge*. New York, NY: Farrar, Straus and Giroux, 1988.

Zullo, Allan. *10 True Tales: World War II Heroes*. New York, NY: Scholastic Nonfiction, 2015.

———. *10 True Tales: Vietnam War Heroes*. New York, NY: Scholastic, Inc., 2015.

Personal Word Wall

Aa	Bb	Cc	Dd	Ee
Ff	Gg	Hh	Ii	Jj
Kk	Ll	Mm	Nn	Oo
Pp	Qq	Rr	Ss	Tt
Uu	Vv	Ww	Xx	Zz
			Yy	

Topic Ideas for ABC Book Projects

A: Africa, African American history, America, the Arctic, authors, art/artists, astrology

B: baseball, basketball, beach, bears, birds, bugs, butterflies

C: candy, careers, cars, cats, celebrations, character traits, Christmas around the world, cities, colors, cooking, cowboys

D: daytime, dinosaurs, dogs, desert, desserts, dreams, Dr. Seuss

E: Earth, ecology, emotions, endangered animals, environment, explorers, extinct

F: fairy tale characters, fall, family, farms, food, fish, flowers, forests, friendship, frogs

G: games, gardens, geography, gymnastics

H: healthy habits, heroes, hobbies, holidays, human body

I: insects, instruments, inventions and inventors, Native American Indians

J: Japan, jazz, jobs, jungle

K: knights and knighthood, kitten, Martin Luther King Jr.

L: land formations landmarks, languages, Abraham Lincoln

M: mammals, math, me, medieval times, minerals, mountains, music, movies

N: names, national parks, nature, night, nursery rhymes, nutrition, nouns

O: ocean, orchestra, Olympics

P: pets, penguins, physical education, plants, princess, presidents

Q: quiet, quilt, queen

R: racing, rain forest, reptiles, rivers, rocks, running

S: safety, school, sea animals, seasons, shark, skateboarder, snakes, space, sports, spring, soccer, solar system, summer, sun

T: technology, telephones, Thanksgiving, theater, trains, transportation, trees

U: undersea exploration, underwater, United States, universe

V: vegetables, VIP (Very Important People)

W: Washington, D. C., weather, wetland, whales, White House, woodland

X: X-rays and other medical terms, X-Games, extreme sports

Y: Yankees, Yellowstone National Park, yoga, yucky (food/bugs)

Z: zoos, zoology

Name: _____ Date: _____

Amazing Animal Facts A–Z

_____ is for _____ .

I wonder _____

_____

_____

_____

_____

_____ .

I found out _____

_____

_____

_____

_____

_____ .

Ida

Idea Creator

What is my writing about?

✔ Did I choose an interesting topic?

✔ Did I focus on my idea?

✔ Did I include supporting details?

✔ Did I stick to my topic?

(Gentry, McNeel, and Wallace-Nesler 2012b)

Simon Sentence Builder

What kinds of sentences will I use?

✔ Did I use long, medium, and short sentences?

✔ Did I use statements and questions?

✔ Did I use different sentence beginnings?

✔ Do my sentences flow smoothly when I read them aloud?

Owen

Organization
Conductor

How do I plan my writing?

❧ Did I sequence my thoughts?

❧ Did I have a beginning, middle, and end?

❧ Did I hook my reader?

❧ Did I include transition words?

Wally
Word Choice
Detective

What words will paint a
picture for my reader?

✔ Did I use some *amazing*
   words?

✔ Did I use sensory words?

✔ Did I use action words?

✔ Did I use a variety of words?

Val and Van Voice

What is the purpose of my writing?

❥ Did I write to an audience?

❥ Did I share my feelings?

❥ Did I make my reader smile, cry, think?

❥ Does my writing sound like me?

(Gentry, McNeel, and Wallace-Nesler 2012b)

Callie
Super Conventions Checker

How do I edit my paper?

✔ Did I check my capitalization?

✔ Did I check my punctuation?

✔ Did I check my spelling?

✔ Did I use good spacing?

✔ Did I read over my story?

(Gentry, McNeel, and Wallace-Nesler 2012b)

Ida
Idea Creator

What is my writing about?

❥ Did I choose an interesting topic?

❥ Did I focus on my idea?

❥ Did I include supporting details?

❥ Did I stick to my topic?

(Gentry, McNeel, and Wallace-Nesler 2012b)

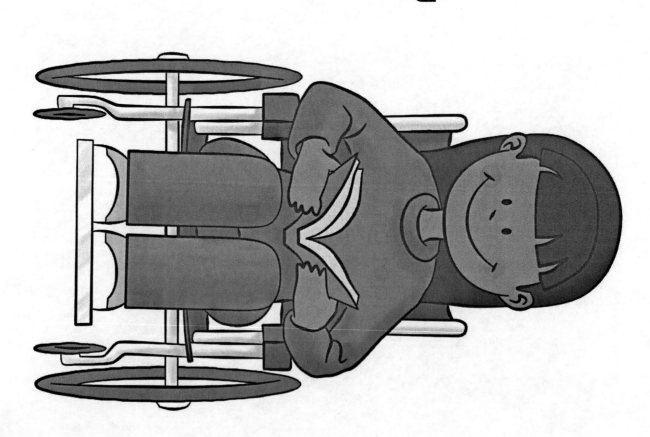

Simon
Sentence Builder

What kinds of sentences will I use?

✔ Did I use long, medium, and short sentences?

✔ Did I use statements and questions?

✔ Did I use different sentence beginnings?

✔ Do my sentences flow smoothly when I read them aloud?

(Gentry, McNeel, and Wallace-Nesler 2012b)

Owen
Organization Conductor

How do I plan my writing?

✔ Did I sequence my thoughts?

✔ Did I have a beginning, middle, and end?

✔ Did I hook my reader?

✔ Did I include transition words?

(Gentry, McNeel, and Wallace-Nesler 2012b)

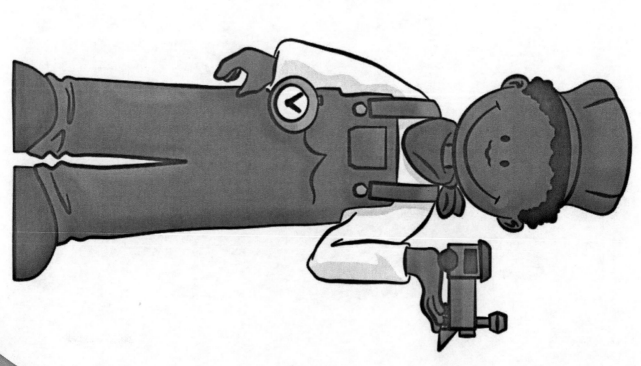

Wally
Word Choice Detective

What words will paint a picture for my reader?

✔ Did I use some amazing words?

✔ Did I use sensory words?

✔ Did I use action words?

✔ Did I use a variety of words?

Val and Van
Voice

What is the purpose of my writing?

✎ Did I write to an audience?

✎ Did I share my feelings?

✎ Did I make my reader smile, cry, think?

✎ Does my writing sound like me?

(Gentry, McNeel, and Wallace-Nesler 2012b)

Callie
Super Conventions Checker

How do I edit my paper?

✔ Did I check my capitalization?

✔ Did I check my punctuation?

✔ Did I check my spelling?

✔ Did I use good spacing?

✔ Did I read over my story?

(Gentry, McNeel, and Wallace-Nesler 2012b)

Ida

Idea Creator

What is my writing about?

❧ Did I narrow and focus my topic?

❧ Did I gather background knowledge for my topic?

❧ Did I provide rich details, examples, reasons, and facts?

❧ Are details specific and related?

❧ Did I present ideas in an interesting/original way?

(Gentry, McNeel, and Wallace-Nesler 2012b)

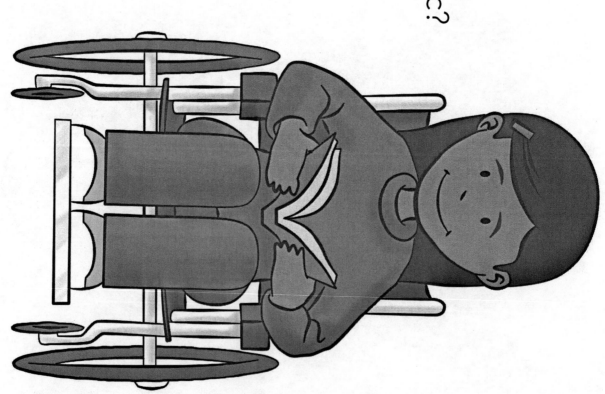

Simon
Sentence Builder

What kinds of sentences will I use?

❧ Did I use a variety of sentence patterns (simple, compound, complex)?

❧ Did I use a variety of sentence beginnings?

❧ Did I use a variety of sentence lengths?

❧ Did I include a variety of sentence lengths?

❧ Are my sentences musical and rhythmic?

(Gentry, McNeel, and Wallace-Nesler 2012b)

Owen

Organization Conductor

How do I plan my writing?

- Did I organize and prioritize my thinking?

- Did I include an inviting beginning?

- Did I organize my thoughts in a logical sequence?

- Did I use appropriate transition words and phrases to make connections?

- Did I provide an adequate conclusion statement?

(Gentry, McNeel, and Wallace-Nesler 2012b)

Wally
Word Choice Detective

What words will paint a picture for my reader?

❮ Did I use purposeful words?

❮ Did I use interesting yet appropriate word selections?

❮ Did I use precise nouns, verbs, and adjectives that evoke images?

❮ Did I use figurative language when necessary?

(Gentry, McNeel, and Wallace-Nesler 2012b)

Val and Van
Voice

What is the purpose of my writing?

❯ Did I express myself with my own originality?

❯ Did I convey the purpose of my writing?

❯ Did I recognize and connect with my audience?

❯ Did I sound honest and confident in my position?

(Gentry, McNeel, and Wallace-Nesler 2012b)

Callie
Super Conventions Checker

How do I edit my paper?

✔ Did I check for capitalization and punctuation?

✔ Did I use the correct grammar?

✔ Did I spell words conventionally?

✔ Did I reread for accuracy?

✔ Is my draft ready for publishing?

(Gentry, McNeel, and Wallace-Nesler 2012b)

Name: _____ Date: _____

Cornell Notes Template

Name		Date

Topic		Class/Subject

Sequencing

1	→	2	→	3
4	→	5	→	6
7	→	8	→	9

Venn Diagram

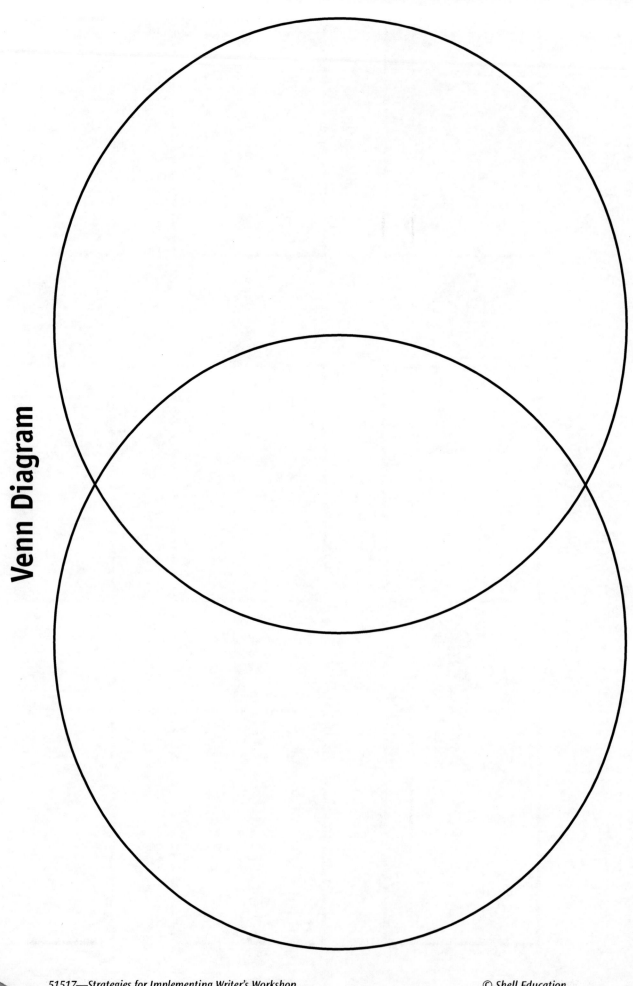

Name: _____   Date: _____

Cause and Effect 1

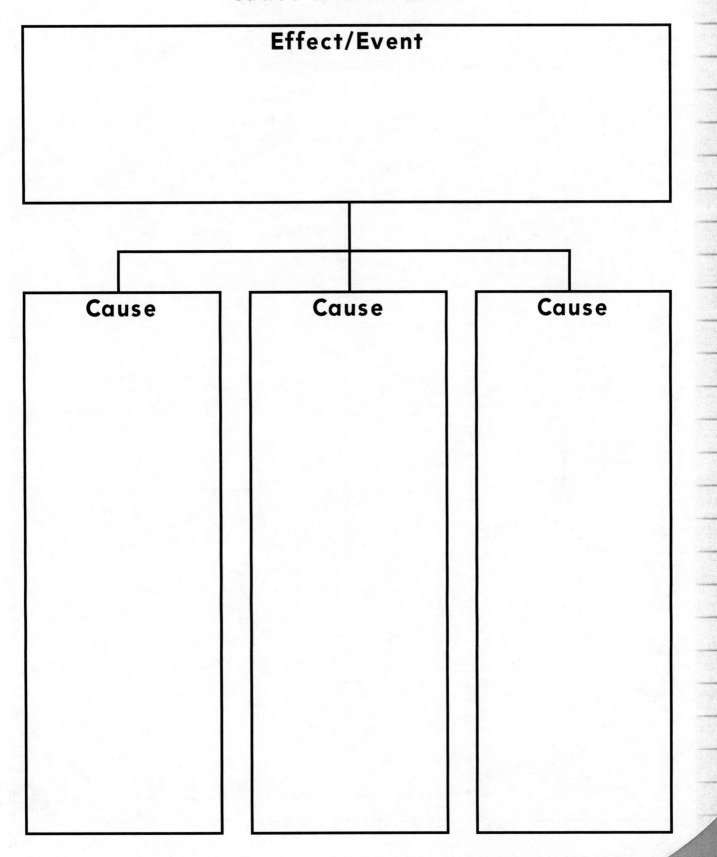

Effect/Event

Cause	Cause	Cause

Name: _____ Date: _____

Cause and Effect T-Chart

Cause	Effect

Name: _____ Date: _____

Problem and Solution

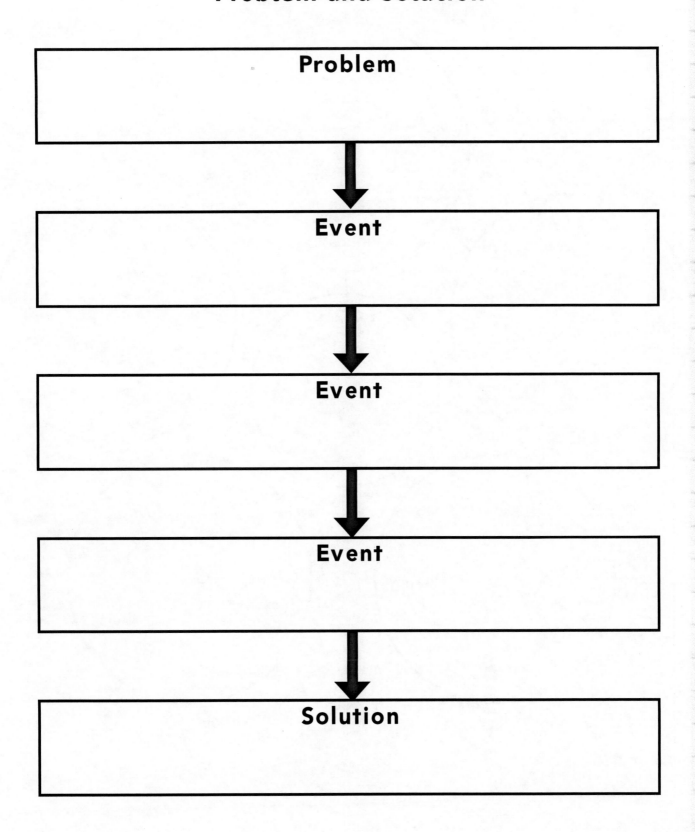

Problem

Event

Event

Event

Solution

Descriptions

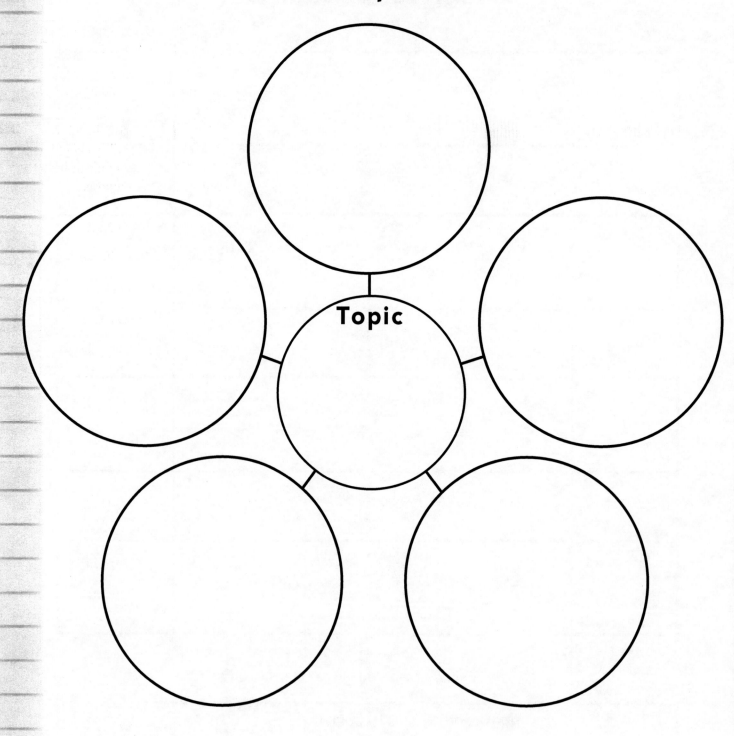

Topic

Name: _____   Date: _____

R-F-A-P-A Chart

Role	Format	Audience	Purpose	Approach
Choose one or possibly two. Most assignments will have one.	Choose only one. Only in rare cases would combining formats make sense.	Choose one or more. If more than one, designate a primary audience.	Choose one or more. If more than one, designate a primary purpose.	Choose several. Longer pieces will require more varied approaches.
The student takes on a role and writes from this perspective.	The final version must be published in exactly this format.	This is the student's intended audience. This is to whom the piece is being written.	This is why the piece is being written. The writer works toward achieving this goal.	This is how the writer will go about achieving his or her purpose.
Advertiser	Magazine Article	Friends	Change Thinking	Analyze
Newscaster	Editorial	Parent	Inform	Challenge
Tour Guide	Brochure	Self	Explain	Classify
Curator	Short Story	Teacher	Change Action	Compare
Panelist	Play	Young Students	Entertain	Conclude
Reporter	Fairy Tale	Public Figures	Initiate Thinking	Contrast
Product Designer	Myth	Persons of Authority	Tell a Story	Defend
Artist	Poem	Supervisor	Instruct	Define
Biographer	Novel	General Public	Initiate Action	Demonstrate
Political Candidate	Report	People from Other Cultures		Describe
Biologist	Diary			Evaluate
Engineer	Journal	People from other Time Periods		Explain
Historian	Biography			Interpret
Expert in…	Autobiography	Professional in same discipline		Investigate
Parent	Newspaper Article	Investor		Justify
Teacher	Letter	Judge or Jury		Persuade
Self	Booklet	School Board		Predict
Detective	Interview			Propose
Editor	Textbook			Question
				Reflect

Project Due Dates Template

❑ Generate Ideas—Create the vision

Due date for preliminary topic: _____

❑ Read across texts to collect information.

List-of-readings due date: _____

❑ Decide on text features for the type of writing being planned.

❑ Choose key words and text features that fit the text structure.

❑ Describe the genre. Explain it in detail and why you chose it.

Due date for your plan for the project: _____

❑ Begin a first draft.

Create the following:

   ❑ Table of Contents

   ❑ Introduction

   ❑ Main body

   ❑ Conclusion

   ❑ Glossary (if appropriate)

First draft due date: _____

Revision/Editing checklist due date: _____

Publication due date: _____

Mini-Lesson Log

Date	Mini-Lesson Title/Topic	Resources

Class Conference Frequency Record

Student Name														

 51517—*Strategies for Implementing Writer's Workshop*

Class Conferring Log

Instructional Focus/Goal: _____   Week(s) of: _____

P: Praise—What strategies is the writer using independently?

TP: Teaching Point—What TP will move this child forward in his/her development as a writer?

Name: **Date:** P: TP:	**Name:** **Date:** P: TP:	**Name:** **Date:** P: TP:	**Name:** **Date:** P: TP:	**Name:** **Date:** P: TP:
Name: **Date:** P: TP:	**Name:** **Date:** P: TP:	**Name:** **Date:** P: TP:	**Name:** **Date:** P: TP:	**Name:** **Date:** P: TP:
Name: **Date:** P: TP:	**Name:** **Date:** P: TP:	**Name:** **Date:** P: TP:	**Name:** **Date:** P: TP:	**Name:** **Date:** P: TP:
Name: **Date:** P: TP:	**Name:** **Date:** P: TP:	**Name:** **Date:** P: TP:	**Name:** **Date:** P: TP:	**Name:** **Date:** P: TP:
Name: **Date:** P: TP:	**Name:** **Date:** P: TP:	**Name:** **Date:** P: TP:	**Name:** **Date:** P: TP:	**Name:** **Date:** P: TP:

Conferring Log

Instructional Focus:			
Student Name/Date:	**Observe/Praise:** What strategies is the writer using independently?	**Guide:** What can I teach today to help this writer tomorrow?	**Next Steps:** What other needs surfaced during conversations? (Note any follow-up dates.)

Individual Student Conferring Log

Name: _____ Goal(s):	Target Skills:

	Observe/Praise (P): What do I notice the writer doing well? Guide (TP): What strategy, skill, or craft does this writer need?	Next Steps (NS): What is the writer going to continue to work on? What other ways can I help this writer meet his/her writing goals?
Date: P: TP: NS:		
Date: P: TP: NS:		
Date: P: TP: NS:		
Date: P: TP: NS:		

Small-Group Conferring Log

Instructional Focus:

Date:	Praise/Compliments:	Micro-Lesson:	Observations:
Writers:			
	Focus Strategy/Skill:		

Date:	Praise/Compliments:	Micro-Lesson:	Observations:
Writers:			
	Focus Strategy/Skill:		

Date:	Praise/Compliments:	Micro-Lesson:	Observations:
Writers:			
	Focus Strategy/Skill:		

Contents of the Digital Resource CD

Page Number(s)	Title	Filename
59–60	Mini-Lesson Template	minilesson.pdf
63–64	Sentence Trees Examples	trees.pdf
67	S.T.O.R.Y. Graphic Organizer	organizer.pdf organizer.docx
70	I Know My Audience	audience.pdf
75	Conflict Themes for Famous Literature and Film	themes.pdf
80	The Writing Process (K–2)	writingK2.pdf writingk2.docx
81	The Writing Process (3–5)	writing35.pdf writing35.docx
82	The Writing Process (6–8)	writing68.pdf writing68.docx
83	The Traits of Quality Writing	traits.pdf
101	Movin' to Edit	edit.pdf
104	Be a Word Wizard Notebook Entry	wizard.pdf
107	Boot Camp Caps Chant Notebook Entry	capschant.pdf
126	How-To/Procedural Checklist	howto.pdf howto.docx
127	Emergent Writer Narrative Checklist	emergentchecklist.pdf emergentchecklist.docx
128	Early Writer Narrative Checklist	earlychecklist.pdf earlychecklist.docx
129	Opinion Essay Checklist	opinionchecklist.pdf opinionchecklist.docx
130	Informative/Explanatory Essay Checklist	informativechecklist.pdf informativechecklist.docx
131	Narrative Writing (Real/Imaginary) Checklist	narrativechecklist.pdf narrativechecklist.docx
132	Argument Writing Checklist	argumentchecklist.pdf argumentchecklist.docx
150	Beginning, Middle, and End	beginning.pdf beginning.docx
151	My Story Mountain	storymountain.pdf storymountain.docx
152	Telling a Story	story.pdf story.docx

Page Number(s)	Title	Filename
153	Steps to Success	success.pdf success.docx
154	The Story Coaster	coaster.pdf
156	Hand Plan	handplan.pdf
157	Researching from A to D	researching.pdf researching.docx
158	123 Paragraphs: Informing	informing.pdf informing.docx
159	Triple-Decker Sandwich	tripledecker.pdf tripledecker.docx
161	In My Opinion…	myopinion.pdf myopinion.docx
162	My Point of View	pointofview.pdf pointofview.docx
163	Opinion Writing Tree	writingtree.pdf writingtree.docx
164	TREES Graphic Organizer	treegraph.pdf treegraph.docx
165	It's Newsworthy	newsworthy.pdf newsworthy.docx
166	Organizing Thinking for Expository Writing	organizing.pdf organizing.docx
167	My Argument Planning Frame	argumentframe.pdf
181	My Publishing Checklist (K–2)	checklistk2.pdf checklistk2.docx
182	My Publishing Checklist (3–5)	checklist35.pdf checklist35.docx
183	My Publishing Checklist (6–8)	checklist68.pdf checklist68.docx
219	Personal Word Wall	wordwall.pdf wordwall.docx
220	Topic Ideas for ABC Book Projects	abcbook.pdf
221	Amazing Animal Facts A–Z	animalfacts.pdf animalfacts.docx
222	Ida Idea Creator (K–2)	idak2.pdf
223	Simon Sentence Builder (K–2)	simonk2.pdf
224	Owen Organization Conductor (K–2)	owenk2.pdf

Appendix C

Page Number(s)	Title	Filename
225	Wally Word Choice Detective (K–2)	wallyk2.pdf
226	Val and Van Voice (K–2)	valk2.pdf
227	Callie Super Conventions Checker (K–2)	calliek2.pdf
228	Ida Idea Creator (3–5)	ida35.pdf
229	Simon Sentence Builder (3–5)	simon35.pdf
230	Owen Organization Conductor (3–5)	owen35.pdf
231	Wally Word Choice Detective (3–5)	wally35.pdf
232	Val and Van Voice (3–5)	val35.pdf
233	Callie Super Conventions Checker (3–5)	callie35.pdf
234	Ida Idea Creator (6–8)	ida68.pdf
235	Simon Sentence Builder (6–8)	simon68.pdf
236	Owen Organization Conductor (6–8)	owen68.pdf
237	Wally Word Choice Detective (6–8)	wally68.pdf
238	Val and Van Voice (6–8)	val68.pdf
239	Callie Super Conventions Checker (6–8)	callie68.pdf
240	Cornell Notes Template	cornell.pdf cornell.docx
241	Sequencing	sequencing.pdf sequencing.docx
242	Venn Diagram	venn.pdf venn.docx
243	Cause and Effect 1	causeeffect.pdf causeeffect.docx
244	Cause and Effect T-Chart	tchart.pdf tchart.docx
245	Problem and Solution	problemsolution.pdf problemsolution.docx
246	Descriptions	descriptions.pdf descriptions.docx
247	R.F.A.P.A. Chart	rfapa.pdf rfapa.docx

Page Number(s)	Title	Filename
248	Project Due Dates Template	duedates.pdf duedates.docx
249	Mini-Lesson Log	minilog.pdf minilog.docx
250	Class Conference Frequency Record	conffreq.pdf conffreq.docx
251	Class Conferring Log	classlog.pdf classlog.docx
252	Conferring Log	conferring.pdf conferring.docx
253	Individual Student Conferring Log	studentlog.pdf studentlog.docx
254	Small-Group Conferring Log	grouplog.pdf grouplog.docx